Quod scriptura, non iubet vetat

The Latin translates, "What is not commanded in scripture, is forbidden:'

On the Cover: Baptists rejoice to hold in common with other evangelicals the main principles of the orthodox Christian faith. However, there are points of difference and these differences are significant. In fact, because these differences arise out of God's revealed will, they are of vital importance. Hence, the barriers of separation between Baptists and others can hardly be considered a trifling matter. To suppose that Baptists are kept apart solely by their views on Baptism or the Lord's Supper is a regrettable misunderstanding. Baptists hold views which distinguish them from Catholics, Congregationalists, Episcopalians, Lutherans, Methodists, Pentecostals, and Presbyterians, and the differences are so great as not only to justify, but to demand, the separate denominational existence of Baptists. Some people think Baptists ought not teach and emphasize their differences but as E.J. Forrester stated in 1893, "Any denomination that has views which justify its separate existence, is bound to promulgate those views. If those views are of sufficient importance to justify a separate existence, they are important enough to create a duty for their promulgation ... the very same reasons which justify the separate existence of any denomination make it the duty of that denomination to teach the distinctive doctrines upon which its separate existence rests." If Baptists have a right to a separate denominational life, it is their duty to propagate their distinctive principles, without which their separate life cannot be justified or maintained.

Many among today's professing Baptists have an agenda to revise the Baptist distinctives and redefine what it means to be a Baptist. Others don't understand why it even matters. The books being reproduced in the *Baptist Distinctives Series* are republished in order that Baptists from the past may state, explain and defend the primary Baptist distinctives as they understood them. It is hoped that this Series will provide a more thorough historical perspective on what it means to be distinctively Baptist.

The Lord Jesus Christ asked, *"And why call ye me, Lord, Lord, and do not the things which I say?"* (Luke 6:46). The immediate context surrounding this question explains what it means to be a true disciple of Christ. Addressing the same issue, Christ's question is meant to show that a confession of discipleship to the Lord Jesus Christ is inconsistent and untrue if it is not accompanied with a corresponding submission to His authoritative commands. Christ's question teaches us that a true recognition of His authority as Lord inevitably includes a submission to the authority of His Word. Hence, with this question Christ has made it forever impossible to separate His authority as King from the authority of His Word. These two principles—the authority of Christ as King and the authority of His Word—are the two most fundamental Baptist distinctives. The first gives rise to the second and out of these two all the other Baptist distinctives emanate. As F.M. Iams wrote in 1894, "Loyalty to Christ as King, manifesting itself in a constant and unswerving obedience to His will as revealed in His written Word, is the real source of all the Baptist distinctives:' In the search for the *primary* Baptist distinctive many have settled on the Lordship of Christ as the most basic distinctive. Strangely, in doing this, some have attempted to separate Christ's Lordship from the authority of Scripture, as if you could embrace Christ's authority without submitting to what He commanded. However, while Christ's Lordship and Kingly authority can be isolated and considered essentially for discussion's sake, we see from Christ's own words in Luke 6:46 that His Lordship is really inseparable from His Word and, with regard to real Christian discipleship, there can be no practical submission to the one without a practical submission to the other.

In the symbol above the Kingly Crown and the Open Bible represent the inseparable truths of Christ's Kingly and Biblical authority. The Crown and Bible graphics are supplemented by three Bible verses (Ecclesiastes 8:4, Matthew 28:18-20, and Luke 6:46) that reiterate and reinforce the inextricable connection between the authority of Christ as King and the authority of His Word. The truths symbolized by these components are further emphasized by the Latin quotation - *quod scriptura, non iubet vetat*— i.e., "What is not commanded in scripture, is forbidden:' This Latin quote has been considered historically as a summary statement of the regulative principle of Scripture. Together these various symbolic components converge to exhibit the two most foundational Baptist Distinctives out of which all the other Baptist Distinctives arise. Consequently, we have chosen this composite symbol as a logo to represent the primary truths set forth in the *Baptist Distinctives Series*.

Church Communion,

as practiced by the baptists,

Explained and Defended

CHURCH COMMUNION,

AS PRACTICED BY THE BAPTISTS,

EXPLAINED AND DEFENDED

BY W. W. GARDNER,

PROFESSOR OF THEOLOGY IN BETHEL COLLEGE, RUSSELVILLE, KY.

With a Biographical Sketch of the Author by John Franklin Jones

"And they continued steadfastly in the Apostles' doctrine and fellowship, and in breaking of bread, and in prayers." —ACTS ii : 42.

"Now I praise you, brethren, that ye . . . keep the ordinances as I delivered them to you.—For I have received of the Lord that which also I delivered unto you," &c.—PAUL.

CINCINNATI:
GEORGE BLANCHARD & CO.,
BOSTON: GOULD & LINCOLN.   NEW YORK: SHELDON & CO.
LOUISVILLE: SHERRILL & SON.   ATLANTA, GA.: J.J. TOON.
MEMPHIS: SOUTHWESTERN PUBLISHING COMPANY.
1869

he Baptist Standard Bearer, Inc.
NUMBER ONE IRON OAKS DRIVE • PARIS, ARKANSAS 72855

Thou hast given a *standard* to them that fear thee;
that it may be displayed because of the truth.
-- *Psalm 60:4*

Reprinted 2006

by

THE BAPTIST STANDARD BEARER, INC.
No. 1 Iron Oaks Drive
Paris, Arkansas 72855
(479) 963-3831

THE WALDENSIAN EMBLEM
lux lucet in tenebris
"The Light Shineth in the Darkness"

ISBN# 157978500X

CONTENTS.

INTRODUCTORY REMARKS.

1. CHRIST, the only Head and Lawgiver to his churches. 2. The powers of a church judicial and executive only. 3. Baptism and the Lord's Supper the only positive rites. 4. Baptism briefly defined. 5. Communion and fellowship distinguished. 6. The communion of saints on earth is of three kinds only—*Christian, Church,* and *Denominational.* 7. The Lord's Supper the appointed *token,* not of Christian nor of denominational, but of *church* fellowship. 8. Summary statement of the threefold communion of saints on earth............ 11–23.

CHAPTER I.
POINTS OF AGREEMENT.

I. As to the NATURE of the Lord's Supper. All agree, 1. That it is an ordinance of the New Testament, instituted by Jesus Christ. 2. That it is a positive ordinance established by positive law. 3. That it is a *church* ordinance, and, as such, involves and expresses *church* fellowship. 4. That it is a commemorative ordinance. 5. That it is an ordinance of frequent recurrence. 6. That it is a perpetual ordinance.

II. As to the DESIGN of the Lord's Supper. All agree that it is designed, 1. As a sacred memorial or remembrance of Christ. 2. As an emblematic exhibition of Christ's death. 3. As a symbolic declaration of our spiritual union and communion with Christ by faith.

III. As to the QUALIFICATIONS for communion at the Lord's Table. All agree, 1. That the new birth is a scriptural qualification. 2. That valid baptism is a scriptural qualification. 3. That regular church membership is a scriptural qualification.. 24–53.

CHAPTER II.
BAPTIST PRACTICE EXPLAINED AND DEFENDED.

1. The Baptists practice *Church* Communion on principles *held in common* with mixed communionists. 2. The question, then, arises: "*Why do they differ in practice, since they agree in principle?*" 3. The Baptists can not remove the *barriers* to intercommunion without the sacrifice of admitted principles, while others can do it without any such sacrifice. 4. The Baptists hence are *unjustly* blamed for their practice of *Church* Communion at the Lord's Table. 5. It is both *inconsistent* and *unkind* in others either to ask or invite intercommunion with the Baptists. 6. Scriptural views of the Lord's Supper would entirely relieve the minds of Baptists and others in regard to *Church* Communion.. 54–96.

CHAPTER III.
OBJECTIONS TO CHURCH COMMUNION ANSWERED.

OBJECTION 1st. "It is the *Lord's Table*, and therefore all the Lord's children have *a right* to it." 2d. "We have no scriptural right *to judge of the fitness* of communicants for the Lord's Table." 3d. "*Church* Communion, as practiced by the Baptists, *unchristianizes* all other denominations." 4th. "It not only unchristianizes, but also *unchurches* all others." 5th. "It *debars* many pious persons from the Lord's Table who have been *immersed*." 6th. "It *divides* God's people, and *prevents* love and union among them." 7th. "It is '*exclusive, illiberal*, and *selfish*' in the Baptists." 8th. "All Christians will commune together in heaven, and *therefore* all should commune together on earth".........97–172.

CHAPTER IV.
EVILS OF MIXED COMMUNION EXPOSED.

1. MIXED COMMUNION is *unscriptural*, and, as such, not binding upon the churches. 2. It perverts the design of the Lord's Supper, and hence *invalidates* the ordinance. 3. It tends to destroy the *effect* of church discipline, and compels a church to commune with its own excluded members. 4. It is *glaringly inconsistent* in the present divided state of the Christian world. 5. It compels its advocates to *indorse* and *fellowship* what they believe to be *error*. 6. It violates the *declared principles* of those who practice it. 7. It is not only bad policy, but *suicidal* to the Baptists..173–243.

CHAPTER V.
FACTS DEDUCED FROM THE SUBJECT.

1. Church Communion, as practiced by the Baptists, is both consistent and scriptural. 2. Mixed communion is not only unscriptural and inconsistent, but *a great evil*. 3. It is not "close communion" in fact, but *close baptism* that separates the Baptists and others at the Lord's Table. 4. Mixed Communicants, by their unholy opposition to *Church* Communion, do great injustice to the Baptists, and great injury to the cause of Christ and the souls of men. 5. Free Communion Baptists are very inconsistent, and *practically* surrender their denominational principles. 6. The Campbellites are the most inconsistent of all others in their professions of mixed communion. 7. There is not, in fact, any such thing as "*open communion*" in existence. 8. The duty of all Christians, and especially of the Baptists, in regard to the Lord's Supper...................244–281.

CONCLUDING REMARKS.

1. Recapitulation. 2. The duty of Mixed Communionists. 3. The duty and interest of Baptists. 4. The special duty of Baptist ministers. 5. All boasting and severity disclaimed. 6. Desire and prayer of the Author.........................282–294.

PREFACE.

The substance of the following treatise on CHURCH COMMUNION was preached, by special appointment, before the "Bracken Baptist Association," of Northern Kentucky, in the fall of 1853; and in the fall of 1856, the author was requested by that body to condense the sermon into a circular letter for the churches composing the body. Several thousand copies were printed and circulated with profit to the members. This accounts for the fact that the present book retains somewhat the form of the original discourse.

A copy of the minutes containing the circular was sent to the "*Southern Baptist Publication Society*," then located in Charleston, S. C., and, in 1858, that society requested permission to republish the letter in a permanent form, as "*A Tract for the People.*" The request was granted, the author reserving the right to revise and use it at pleasure. With all its defects, the little "missile" was highly commended by many of our editors and ministers in the South and West, and several thousand copies were sold the first year. During the war, however, the plates were lost, and the tract is now out of print.

Not long before our late war commenced, the author was urged by judicious brethren to revise and expand the tract into a small book. Accordingly, he did so, and sent the manuscript to the Southern Baptist Publication Society for examination. It was examined, approved, and ordered to be printed. The corresponding secretary of said society wrote the author several letters commendatory of the work. But the unsettled state of our country and other causes induced the author to recall the manuscript, and its publication was indefinitely postponed.

Recently, however, a number of brethren renewed the request for its publication, believing that a small practical work of the kind was needed by our churches. In compliance with this oft-repeated request, the author has employed his *scraps* of time for a few months past in correcting, improving, and enlarging the treatise, which has grown into a small book. The **revision** has been hastily made, under a press of other duties, and hence the work is by no means satisfactory to the author. Still, it embodies many important facts, and claims to be a work of *authority*, so far as the numerous quotations and statements are concerned; while the positions assumed and the views advanced are believed to be both *denominational* and *scriptural*. The book contains some *new* matter, and possesses a *character of its own*. The author has labored extensively, both as evangelist and pastor, in Middle, Northern, and Southern Kentucky, and hence has been compelled to grapple with mixed communion in its various forms, as held by Campbellites, Pedobaptists, and uninstructed Baptists, and he here gives but the *results* of twenty-five years' experience and preaching on the subject.

The following treatise has been written, not for critics, but FOR THE PEOPLE, and hence its style is designedly plain and simple. The Communion question has been so complicated that repetition was unavoidable. With more leisure, the work might have been condensed with advantage, but the author's engagements prevented it. His sole design in writing at all was to *do good*, and if he fail in this, his object will be defeated. The subject to many is distasteful, and he can expect to reap no laurels from its discussion. The argument is somewhat *ad hominem*, but it is presented in *all kindness*, and with a sincere desire to promote truth and righteousness, and to suppress error and prejudice among God's people.

It is confidently believed that the better Christians of different denominations understand each other's views and practice on all religious subjects, the more charity will they feel one for another, and the sooner they will come to the unity of the faith. It is a melancholy fact, however, that the views and practice of the Baptists, in regard to the Lord's Supper, are generally misunderstood, and hence every-where misrepresented; and even some Baptists, owing to mistaken views of the nature and design of the ordinance, are disposed rather to *excuse* than to defend our practice. *These things ought not so to be.* The only proper means of correcting such evils is to instruct the people generally, and the Baptists in particular, on this subject. Owing to the false teachings of mixed communionists, many young converts, holding Baptist sentiments, and even some of our young members, are troubled in regard to our *Church* Communion. The author himself was greatly troubled on this subject when he first made a profession of religion. All such

PREFACE. ix

persons ought to be supplied with suitable BOOKS and TRACTS on Communion, and pastors ought to *preach frequently* on the subject. There is really nothing offensive in our practice of *Church* Communion when rightly understood; and if our views are explained and defended *in a Christian spirit*, no one will take offense, but all will see their reasonableness.

The chapter on the "*Evils of Mixed Communion*" contains the substance of an *essay* which was written by appointment, and read before the "*Bethel Baptist Minister and Deacon's Meeting*" of Southern Kentucky in 1864; and after free criticism, was unanimously requested for publication in tract form; but the limited means of the author prevented compliance with the request. The positions *assumed* in the treatise on Church Communion, respecting the ADMINISTRATOR of baptism, seem to require something more on that subject than could be given in the body of the work. Hence, the author has prepared a "MISSILE" on the subject, to accompany the book, showing *Who is a Scriptural Administrator of Baptism*; it being the substance of a sermon recently preached to his own congregation, and requested for publication by his brethren who heard it. The subject, though overlooked in our works on baptism generally, is a *vital* one, and demands special consideration. It is a point in the baptismal controversy on which Baptist ministers and churches ought, if possible, to harmonize in their views and practice. On this, as on all other points of faith and practice, THE NEW TESTAMENT, and not expediency, must be our sole guide. What our inspired CREED requires, all true Baptists will obey.

Free use has been made of the best works, in the author's possession, on the subject treated, and his indebtedness to Drs. Curtis, Howell, Hibbard, and others is hereby gratefully acknowledged. The author holds himself responsible for the *correctness* of every quotation made, and, as far as possible, has quoted directly from the original works, giving book, chapter, and page. If any mistake has been made, it was unintentional, and will be corrected, as far as possible.

With these prefatory remarks, the little book is commended to all sincere inquirers after truth, with the fervent hope and prayer that God will bless it to the good of his churches and the glory of his name.

W. W. GARDNER.

RUSSELLVILLE, KY., *February* 10, 1869.

CHURCH COMMUNION.

INTRODUCTORY REMARKS.

1. CHRIST, the only Head and Lawgiver to his churches. 2. The powers of a church judicial and executive only. 3. Baptism and the Lord's Supper the only positive rites. 4. Baptism briefly defined. 5. Communion and fellowship distinguished. 6. The communion of saints on earth is of three kinds only—*Christian*, *Church*, and *Denominational*. 7. The Lord's Supper the appointed *token*, not of Christian nor of denominational, but of *church* fellowship. 8. Summary statement of the threefold communion of saints on earth.

1. The Lord Jesus Christ is the only Head of the Church, and the only Lawgiver in Zion. His laws, therefore, as recorded in the New Testament, and as interpreted by his inspired apostles, and illustrated in the practice of the churches established by them, furnish the *only divine and authorized rule* for the constitution and government of Christian churches to the end of the world. These laws, like their author, are *perfect* and *unchangeable;* and no church, convention, general assembly, or general conference has any divine

right to alter, amend, add to, or to take *one iota* from them. Accordingly, our Lord most emphatically declares, that "*If any man shall add unto these things, God shall add unto him the plagues that are written in this book: and if any man shall take away from the words of the book of this prophecy, God shall take away his part out of the book of life.*" (Rev. xxii: 18, 19.)

2. No *legislative* power, therefore, is granted by Jesus Christ to any church or association of churches, to any minister or body of ministers whatever. It is *his* prerogative alone to *enact laws* and *institute ordinances,* and it is our bounden duty to obey those laws and keep those ordinances *as* they were first delivered to the churches by the Savior and his inspired apostles. The powers of a church, then, are *judicial* and *executive* only, and not legislative; while that of associations, conventions, councils, etc., is merely *advisory.* Hence, the BIBLE, faithfully translated from the inspired originals, and the Bible *alone* is the only *rule* of the faith and practice of Christians and Christian churches, and the *supreme standard* by which all human conduct, *creeds*, and opinions must be tried.

3. Christ abolished the cumbrous rites of the Jewish ritual, and instituted two and but two *positive ordinances* for the perpetual observance of his people, viz.: BAPTISM and THE LORD'S SUPPER; the one an *individual*, and the other a *church* ordinance. He erected but two monumental pil-

lars in his kingdom—one *without* and the other *within* his churches; on the first of these—that which fronts the world—he inscribed the name of the TRIUNE GOD; on the other—that which is within his churches—he inscribed the MEMORIALS of his death. Baptism, therefore, is the *initiatory* ordinance into his visible kingdom, and the *vestibule* to his churches in that kingdom; and none have a divine right to cross the threshold and enter these sacred inclosures until they have received the print of the sacred Name in the appointed way by a properly authorized administrator.

4. In the following treatise we shall confine our attention to the latter of these two ordinances, viz.: THE LORD'S SUPPER; and shall take it for granted that *valid* baptism is the *immersion in water into the name of the Trinity*, of a professed *penitent believer*, not in order to, but *in declaration of* the remission of sins *previously obtained* through faith in Christ, by a *scripturally-qualified* administrator; *i. e.*, by a minister of the Gospel who has been thus *baptized* on a credible profession of his faith, and duly *authorized* to administer the ordinance by the authority of his church, through the conjoint agency of a presbytery of regularly ordained ministers.

5. Now, the term COMMUNION, as used in the New Testament, has both a literal and a figurative signification. It is used, *literally*, to denote that *spiritual union and fellowship* which exists

between Christians *as such*. The word is, probably, derived from the Latin *communis*, common, and corresponds with the Greek term *koinonia*, which is generally rendered *fellowship* in the New Testament; as, for instance, in 1 John i: 3–7. Primarily, the term expresses, not a particular *act*, but the *state* of the mind and heart. And this, no doubt, is the reason why the word was translated *fellowship*, rather than *communion*, in the passage referred to above.

The word communion is used once, *figuratively*, to denote the *joint participation* of the Lord's Supper by the members of a church, as in 1 Cor. x: 16, 17; where, by a figure of speech, the bread and wine are denominated "the *communion* of the body and blood of Christ." Here, the word evidently denotes an *act* or *exercise*, rather than a *state* of the mind and heart. This is the sense in which the term *communion* is generally used by Christians at the present day, though not strictly proper.

Hence, we see that the literal meaning of *koinonia* is *fellowship*, and its figurative meaning is *communion;* the latter denoting an *act*, the former a *state*. Communion, therefore, is the more *intense*, fellowship the more *enduring*. Thus we *commune* with God in prayer, and have *fellowship* with our brethren. With this explanation we shall employ the terms almost interchangeably in the following pages as the connection may require.

6. The communion of saints on earth is of three and only three kinds, viz.: 1. *Christian fellowship;* 2. *Church fellowship;* and 3. *Denominational fellowship;* each of which has its appropriate *acts* and *exercises* by and in which it is enjoyed and expressed. Whatever act or exercise is designed to indicate our fellowship with an individual, church, or society, is a *token* of that fellowship. All those acts and exercises, therefore, by and in which we express and enjoy communion with *Christians* as such, with a *church* as such, or with a *denomination* as such, are properly *tokens* of our fellowship with them. Let us, then, briefly consider and compare these three kinds of communion, with their respective tokens.

I. CHRISTIAN FELLOWSHIP, WITH ITS TOKENS.

Christian fellowship is based upon mutual Christian confidence, and embraces that spiritual union and communion which we have with each other *as Christians*, independent of outward ordinances and visible church relations. It grows out of similarity of moral character and oneness of spirit, and involuntarily springs up in the heart the moment we have evidence to believe that an individual is converted. *For instance*, let a young convert relate his Christian experience, and instantly we have Christian fellowship for him, and can hold Christian communion with him. And this, indeed, is the *basis* of all true Christian union, without which there can be no union of hearts.

Now, Christian Communion, based as it is upon Christian fellowship, is fully enjoyed in religious conversation, social prayer and praise, mutual efforts for the salvation of sinners, and in all those spiritual acts and exercises by which we express our mutual Christian confidence and love for each other as brethren in Christ, independent of positive ordinances and visible church connections. In fact, Christian fellowship, based upon real or supposed piety, always exists *prior* to baptism and church membership. Hence we can and do enjoy full and perfect *Christian* Communion with our *candidates* for baptism, though we do not and can not hold *Sacramental* Communion with them until they have been baptized and admitted to church membership. Precisely so do we regard and treat our brethren of other denominations, whom we believe to be pious. In proportion to their piety, we cherish Christian fellowship for them, and hold *Christian* Communion with them, irrespective of external ordinances and visible church relations; notwithstanding we can not commune with them at the Lord's Table—which, indeed, is not a *token* of Christian fellowship, but merely of *church* fellowship.

Such, then, is *Christian* fellowship, with its *tokens*, embracing all those spiritual acts and exercises which involve and express our mutual Christian confidence and love as brethren in the Lord

II. CHURCH FELLOWSHIP, WITH ITS TOKENS.

Church fellowship presupposes Christian fellowship, but does not necessarily include it, and it is based upon *mutual church relations*. Hence it is more *limited* and more *specific* than Christian fellowship, being restricted to the particular church of which we are members. When properly formed, it is not only more specific and restricted, but more *ardent* and *intense* than Christian fellowship; just as the affection which we have for the members of our own particular family is more ardent and intense than that which we have for our friends and fellow-men in general. Indeed, it would be any thing else than a virtue for a man to love the wife and children of another man with the same ardor and intensity that he does his own. The affection due to a wife and family is peculiar, and differs vastly from that regard due to friends and fellow-citizens. It is both reasonable and scriptural, therefore, that we should feel a more ardent and intense affection for the member of our own particular church or family than for those of any other church, even of the same faith and order; while we should cherish an ardent affection for all who love our Lord Jesus Christ in sincerity, irrespective of all ordinances and visible church connections.

Now, as church fellowship grows out of mutual church relations, and hence is restricted to the members of each particular church, so *Church*

Communion grows out of church fellowship, and is necessarily *limited* to those *church acts and privileges* which belong to the members of the same particular church. Such communion is fully enjoyed in choosing a pastor, electing deacons, providing for the poor, receiving and dismissing members, *celebrating the Lord's Supper*, and in all those church acts and exercises which pertain exclusively to church members. In all these *church acts and exercises*, the members of no other church, not even of the same denomination, have any scriptural right to participate, any more than the members of one family have a right to control the domestic affairs of another family. *For illustration:* A member of one Baptist church has no more right to claim the privilege of *voting* in another Baptist church than has a Campbellite, Methodist, or Presbyterian.

The same is equally true of *communion* at the Lord's Table, which is a *church act*, and the appointed TOKEN, not of the Christian nor denominational, but of the *church fellowship* subsisting between communicants at the same table. Hence it follows that a member of one Baptist church has no more right, *as a right*, to claim communion in another Baptist church than he has to claim the right of *voting*, for both are equally *church acts and church privileges.* The Lord's Supper being a *church* ordinance, as all admit, and every church being required to exercise *discipline* over all its communicants, it necessarily follows that no church can scripturally extend its Communion *beyond the limits* of its discipline. And this, in fact, settles the question of CHURCH COMMUNION, and restricts the Lord's Supper to the members of each particular church *as such*. Such, then, is *church* fellowship, growing out of church relations; and such are its *tokens*, among which is the *joint participation* of the Lord's Supper by the members of the same particular church.

III. DENOMINATIONAL FELLOWSHIP, WITH ITS TOKENS.

As Christian fellowship is based upon mutual Christian confidence, and church fellowship upon mutual church relations, so *denominational fellowship* presupposes both, and is based upon *mutual agreement* in the doctrines, ordinances, and polity of the Gospel. In the days of the Apostles, denominational fellowship was unrestricted, because there was perfect *unity* of faith and practice among all the churches. There was "*one Lord, one faith, one baptism*" (Eph. 4: 5), and all the churches were *similarly* constituted, governed, and officered. Hence, wherever the Apostles and Evangelists found "disciples" or churches, they were recognized as members of the same Christian denomination, and cordially coöperated in every good word and work. They voluntarily united their efforts and means to spread the Gospel and save sinners at home and abroad. It was on this very ground that Paul urged the Gentile churches to aid the poor saints in Judea. Accordingly, they not only contributed "beyond their ability" to this charitable object, but earnestly engaged in the work of home and foreign missions; thus obeying the apostolic injunction, to "do good unto all men, especially unto the household of faith."

But while the first Christians thus recognized each other as members and ministers of the same denomination, and extended to each other the appropriate *tokens* of denominational fellowship, still they exercised great caution, and required satisfactory evidence of correct faith and practice. *For instance*, when Saul of Tarsus first went up to Jerusalem, three years after his conversion, he attempted to join himself to the "disciples;" but they would not believe that he was a disciple, until Barnabas took him and brought him to the Apostles, and declared that he had seen the Lord in the way, and had boldly preached the Gospel at Damascus in the name of Jesus. (See Acts ix: 26-28; Gal. i: 15-18.) And John not only exhorted Christians to receive and help all true brethren in their labors of love and works of faith, "*that they might thus be fellow-helpers to the truth*" (3 John 5-8), but he also warned them against receiving and encouraging "any" who might come to them and bring not the doctrine of Christ, adding: "*For he that biddeth him God-speed, is partaker of his evil deeds.*" (2 John 9-11.)

The same is equally true of the Baptists as a denomination. Being of the same faith and order, and all our churches being similarly constituted and governed, we can consistently and safely coöperate together as churches and ministers, and extend to each other the *tokens* of denominational fellowship. And while it is our duty to oppose all error and to reject all errorists, still we may and should unite our efforts and means as a denomination in promoting home and foreign missions, establishing Sunday-schools, distributing Bibles, and other denominational books, endowing and sustaining our colleges and theological seminaries, and in advancing all those grand and comprehensive schemes of Christian benevolence which contemplate the salvation of our lost world and the universal triumphs of Messiah's kingdom. Such cordial coöperation and united effort among Baptists is essential to the accomplishment of our great mission on earth.

It is on the *basis* of denominational fellowship, growing out of unity of faith and practice among our churches, that our associations, conventions, and missionary unions are formed; and on the same basis the whole denomination might and ought to unite in one common effort to build up the cause of Christ at home and abroad. Such associated and coöperative bodies are purely voluntary, and can in no way interfere with church independence and church sovereignty. "*Union is strength;*" and it gives each the combined strength of the whole body.

Of course, our denominational fellowship for others can extend only so far as we agree in faith and practice. With some of them, as the Congregationalists, Methodists, and Presbyterians, we agree substantially in what is essential to salvation, however much we may differ as to baptism, communion, and church polity; and hence we can consistently coöperate with them *as Christians* in the great work of conversion, and in whatever else we agree, though we can not extend to them the *tokens* of church fellowship.

Summary Statement.

Such, then, is the threefold communion of saints on earth, with its peculiar tokens, viz.:

1st. *Christian Communion based upon christian fellowship.* Christian Communion extends to all Christians, *as such*, irrespective of positive ordinances and visible church relations, and it embraces all those *spiritual acts and exercises* by and in which mutual Christian fellowship is expressed and enjoyed. Such communion is enjoyed fully in heaven.

2d. *Church Communion, based upon church fellowship, growing out of mutual church relations.* Church Communion is necessarily *limited* to the members of the *same particular church,* for such only sustain mutual church relations. It embraces all those *church acts and privileges* by which church fellowship is expressed and enjoyed, and in which none but members of the same church have a right to participate. *For instance,* the Lord's Supper being a *church ordinance,* as all agree, and as such, expressive of *church fellowship,* none but those who sustain mutual church relations can properly participate together.

3d. *Denominational communion, based upon denominational fellowship, arising from unity of faith and practice.* Denominational communion properly extends to all the churches and ministers of the same denomination, but it is necessarily *restricted* with others to those points of faith and practice in which they mutually agree. Among Baptists, for example, there is unity of faith and practice; and hence, we can and do extend to each other all those *tokens* of denominational fellowship which properly belong to such communion. As we have shown, the *joint participation* of the Lord's Supper is a *token,* not of Christian nor of denominational, but of *church* fellowship; and when we intercommune by invitation, we regard each other as members of the same particular church for the time being, and treat each other as such in that act. It is still *Church Communion.*

CHURCH COMMUNION.

CHAPTER I.

POINTS OF AGREEMENT.

I. As to the NATURE of the Lord's Supper. All agree, 1. That it is an ordinance of the New Testament, instituted by Jesus Christ. 2. That it is a positive ordinance established by positive law. 3. That it is a *church* ordinance, and, as such, involves and expresses *church* fellowship. 4. That it is a commemorative ordinance. 5. That it is an ordinance of frequent recurrence. 6. That it is a perpetual ordinance.

II. As to the DESIGN of the Lord's Supper. All agree that it is designed, 1. As a sacred memorial or remembrance of Christ. 2. As an emblematic exhibition of Christ's death. 3. As a symbolic declaration of our spiritual union and communion with Christ by faith.

III. As to the QUALIFICATIONS for communion at the Lord's Table. All agree, 1. That the new birth is a scriptural qualification. 2. That valid baptism is a scriptural qualification. 3. That regular church membership is a scriptural qualification.

Now the Baptists and Protestant denominations generally agree in theory on the following points, viz. :

I. As to the NATURE of the Lord's Supper.

1. All agree that it is *an ordinance of the New Testament, instituted by Jesus Christ.*

For instance, the EPISCOPALIANS declare, that "There are two sacraments *ordained by Jesus Christ in the Gospel,* namely, baptism and *the supper of the Lord.*" (See *Book of Common Prayer,* Art. 25.) The METHODISTS declare the same thing in the same words. (See *Discipline* for 1868, Art. of Relig. 16.)

And the PRESBYTERIANS declare, that "*Our Lord Jesus,* in the night wherein he was betrayed, *instituted* the sacrament of his body and blood, called *the Lord's Supper,*" etc. (See *Confession of Faith,* chap. 29, sec. 1.) The CONGREGATIONALISTS hold and teach the same on this point. (See *Platforms,* Confession of Faith, chap. 30, sec. 1.) So the Campbellites, Lutherans, and all others believe and teach.

2. The Baptists and others agree that the Lord's Supper is a *positive ordinance, established by positive law.*

The supper, like baptism, is established by *positive law,* as all agree, and hence the obligation to observe it differs essentially from that of a *moral* requirement. For example, duties imposed by moral law are *right in themselves;* they are founded in the nature of things; and grow out of the immutable principles of truth and justice. But duties imposed by *positive* law are right simply *because* a righteous God has commanded them, and for no other reason. They are based solely upon the *authority* of the lawgiver, and are designed to evince the love and test the loyalty of his subjects. In short, a *moral* duty is commanded because it is *right;* a *positive* duty is right because it is *commanded.* A moral requirement may be obeyed acceptably in any way that comports with the *spirit* of the law; as, for instance, the duty of love to God and our neighbor, which may be discharged in various ways. But a positive requirement must be obeyed according to the *very letter* of the law, and in the *exact manner,* and for the *specific design* prescribed by the lawgiver; as, for instance, the Jewish passover, Christian baptism, or *the Lord's Supper.* To alter or change a positive institution in any respect whatever, is to destroy its *validity,* and to insult the King in Zion.

Happily, on this important point all Christian denominations agree in *theory,* if not in practice. For example, BISHOP BUTLER, of the Church of England, in showing the *distinction* between what is *moral* and what is *positive* in religion, says: "Moral *precepts* are precepts, the reason of which we see; positive *precepts* are precepts, the reason of which we do not see. Moral *duties* arise out of the *nature* of the case, *prior* to external command. Positive *duties* do not arise out of the nature of the case, but from *external command;* nor would they be duties *at all,* were it not for such command received from Him, whose creatures and subjects we are." Yet he adds, "That commands merely positive, admitted to be from Him, lay us under *a moral obligation* to obey them; an obligation moral in the strictest and most proper sense." (*Analogy of Religion*, part 2, chap. 1, pp. 225, 229.)

And BISHOP HOADLEY, a distinguished Episcopalian, remarks on this point, that "The partaking of the Lord's Supper is not a duty of itself, or a duty apparent to us from the nature of things, but a duty made such to Christians by the *positive institution of Jesus Christ*. All *positive* duties, or duties made such by institution alone, depend entirely on the *will* and *declaration* of the person who institutes or ordains them with respect to the *real design* and *end* of them, and consequently to the *due manner* of performing them. . . . . . It is plain, therefore, that the *nature*, the *design*, and the *due manner* of the Lord's Supper, must of necessity depend on what Jesus Christ, who instituted it, has said about it." (*Hoadley's Works*, vol. 3, pp. 845, *et seq.*)

3. The Baptists and others agree that the Lord's Supper is a *church ordinance, and as such, involves and expresses church fellowship.*

In proof of this all appeal to the facts, that Jesus Christ *instituted* the Holy Supper as a *church ordinance*, and that the Apostles and first Christian churches observed it *as such*. For example, the "*model church*" at Jerusalem observed the Lord's Supper as a *church ordinance,* and none but the *members* of that church participated together in the "*breaking of bread.*" Accordingly, Luke says: "Then they that gladly received his word (*i. e.,* rejoiced in the pardon of their sins through *faith* in Jesus Christ) were baptized; and the same day there were added unto them (*i. e.,* to the *church,* Acts 1: 15; 2: 47) about three thousand souls. And they (the members of that particular church) continued steadfastly in the Apostle's doctrine and fellowship, and *in breaking of bread and in prayers.*" (Acts 2: 41, 42.) Such was the *practice* of the first gospel church established by Christ himself, acting under the immediate instructions of His inspired Apostles.

Again: "*The disciples,*" or church at Troas, observed the Lord's Supper as a *church* ordinance when assembled in *church* capacity. (Acts 20: 7.) "And upon the first day of the week, when the disciples *came together to break bread,* Paul preached unto them, ready to depart on the morrow." Here we are expressly told that these disciples *came together for the very purpose of celebrating the Lord's Supper,* and that they observed the ordinance according to the Apostle's directions.

And again: the church at Corinth was instructed to observe the Lord's Supper as a *church* ordinance, and was sharply rebuked for celebrating it otherwise. Says Paul: "When ye come together into one place (*i. e.*, in the *manner* ye do), this is not to eat the Lord's Supper;" *i. e., acceptably* to God. "For in eating every one taketh before others his own supper; and one is hungry and another is drunken." That is, some feasted to excess on their own bread and wine, while others had nothing, instead of all partaking of the sacred elements together, *as a church*, in remembrance of Christ. They had thus mistaken the nature and perverted the design of the ordinance, so that it was not in fact the Lord's Supper. Hence the Apostle charged them with having vitiated the ordinance, despised the Church of God, and incurred great guilt. (1 Cor. 11: 20-30.)

Other examples might be given, but these are sufficient. The Lord's Supper was unquestionably regarded by Christ and his Apostles as a *church* ordinance, and all the primitive churches were taught to observe it *as such*. No instance to the contrary is recorded in the New Testament. Nor have we any certain evidence that the members of one Apostolic church ever partook of the ordinance with any other church, even by invitation.

So all believe and teach on this point. How much soever the Baptists and others may differ as to baptism and church polity, still they agree that the Lord's Supper is a *church* ordinance. For instance, Dr. Hibbard, a standard Methodist writer on this subject, says: "The eucharist, from its very nature, is a *church ordinance*, and as such can be properly participated in only by *church members*. As a church ordinance, it never can be carried *out of the church*. This is so evident that no words can make it more plain or add to its force. (See *Hibbard on Baptism*, part 2, p. 185.)

And the Presbyterian *Confession of Faith*, chap. 29, sec. 1, declares that "Our Lord Jesus, in the night wherein he was betrayed, instituted the sacrament of his body and blood, called the Lord's Supper, to be observed *in his Church* unto the end of the world," etc. Thus the CONGREGATIONALISTS hold and teach. (See *Platforms*, Conf. of Faith, chap. 30.) So all believe and teach.

4. The Baptists and others agree that the Lord's Supper is *a commemorative ordinance*.

This is plain from the language of our Savior and his Apostles. Luke says: "He took bread, and gave thanks, and brake it, and gave unto them, saying: This is my body, which is given for you; *this do in remembrance of me*." (Luke 22: 19.) And Paul says: "The Lord Jesus, the same night in which he was betrayed, took bread; and when he had given thanks, he brake it, and said: Take, eat; this is my body, which is broken for you; *this do in remembrance of me*." (1 Cor. 11: 23-26.)

On this point also there is perfect agreement between all denominations. For example, the PRESBYTERIANS declare that "The Lord's Supper is to be observed in his Church unto the end of the world; *for the perpetual remembrance* of the sacrifice of himself in his death." (See *Confession of Faith*, chap. 29, sec. 1.)

Dr. Whitby, of the Church of England, in his Commentary on Matthew 26: 26, remarks: "Our Lord saith, '*Do this in remembrance of me;*' i. e., eat this bread broken *in remembrance* of my body broken on the cross."

And the eloquent and pious Melvill observes: "Inasmuch as the bread and the wine represent the body and blood of the Savior, the administration of this ordinance is *so commemorative* of Christ's having been offered as a sacrifice, that we seem to have before us the awful and mysterious transaction, as though again were the cross reared, and the words 'It is finished' pronounced in our hearing. (See *Melvill's Thoughts*, p. 240.)

5. The Baptists and others agree that the Lord's Supper is an ordinance of *frequent recurrence*.

As there is no positive command nor specific directions given in the New Testament as to the *frequency* of celebrating the Lord's Supper, the practice of *weekly* communion can not be enjoined upon the churches as an *imperative duty*. It is simply said: "This *do* in remembrance of me;" and "as *often* as ye eat this bread and drink this cup, ye do show the Lord's death till he come." But as there seems to be Scripture evidence (Acts 20: 7, and 1 Cor. 11: 20) that some, at least, of the apostolic churches were accustomed to "break bread" every Lord's day, and as the records of church history teach that the practice was general for some two centuries after Christ, and as the design of the ordinance, as well as the language used, implies *frequency* in its observance, there can be no reasonable objection to *weekly communion*. Certain it is that no objection can be urged against the practice on the ground that such frequency would diminish its solemnity, that might not with equal force be urged against weekly prayer, praise, and preaching in our churches. Many Baptist churches in Great Britain, and some in the United States, have celebrated the Lord's Supper every Lord's day, from the time of their constitution, with increasing interest and solemnity. For example, Dr. Carson's Church, at Tubbermore, Ireland, has celebrated the ordinance weekly for more than sixty years. And the Tabernacle Baptist Church (formerly Mulberry Street), New York, which was gathered by the late Dr. Maclay, in 1809, and over which he presided as pastor for some thirty years, practiced weekly communion during the whole of his pastorate. This practice is still common among the Baptists and others in Scotland and Ireland; and it is to be regretted that it is not more common in this country. (See Memoir attached to *Carson on Baptism*, p. 40; and also Benedict's History of the Baptists.)

On this point all agree in *theory*, though they differ widely in practice. For instance, JOHN CALVIN, in complaining of the infrequency of celebrating the Lord's Supper, remarks: "*Every week*, at least, the Table of the Lord should be spread for Christian assemblies; and the promises declared, by which, in partaking of it, we might be spiritually fed." (As quoted by ORM, ON THE LORD'S SUPPER, p. 219.)

JOHN WESLEY, in his "*Advisory Letter*" to America, in 1784, says: "I also advise the elders to administer the Supper of the Lord *every Lord's day*."

DR. THOMAS SCOTT, of the Church of England, in his Commentary on Acts 20: 7, observes: "*Breaking of bread*, or commemorating the death of Christ in the eucharist, was one of the *chief ends* of their assembling; this ordinance seems to have been *constantly administered every Lord's day*."

ALBERT BARNES, in his Notes on 1 Cor. 11 : 20, remarks: "The Apostle here particularly refers to their assembling *to observe the ordinance of the Lord's Supper.* At that early period it is probable that this was done *every Lord's day*."

ALEXANDER CAMPBELL and his followers, as is well known, enjoin *weekly* communion as a duty, and practice accordingly in their churches generally.

DR. J. B. JETER, in his "*Campbellism Examined*," p. 288, observes: "There is no objection to *weekly* communion, provided it is not imposed on the churches as a *term* of communion. The practice is not binding on the churches. But it is admitted that among the *early Christians*, it is highly probable, that it *did generally*, if not *universally* prevail. I do not perceive any *solid objection* against returning to the practice. It may be well for our churches *seriously* and *candidly* to inquire, whether a *more frequent* celebration of the Lord's Supper—a rite so pregnant with instruction, and so eminently expressive—would not contribute *to increase their piety and usefulness."*

And PROFESSOR CURTIS adds: "Baptism is appointed for each individual once, and but once. The Lord's Supper '*often.*' 1 Cor. 11: 26. *The first Christians made it a part of their regular worship."* (*Curtis on Communion,* p. 73.)

6. The Baptists and others agree that the Lord's Supper is a *perpetual ordinance.*

This is expressly declared in 1 Cor. 11: 26: "For as often as ye eat this bread and drink this cup, ye do show the Lord's death *till he come;*" *i. e.*, to judge the world. "An explicit declaration," says Melvill, "that there is in the Lord's Supper such a manifestation of the crucifixion of Jesús as will serve to set forth that event *until his second appearing."* (*Melvill's Thoughts,* p. 240.)

Accordingly BURKITT, of the Church of England, in his Notes on this passage, says: "The sacrament of the Lord's Supper was instituted as a *standing memorial* of Christ's death and suffering for us."

The Presbyterian Confession of Faith, chap. 29, sec. 1, declares: "The Lord's Supper is to be observed in his Church *unto the end of the world.*"

And ALBERT BARNES, in his Notes on 1 Cor. xi: 26, remarks: "*Till he come;* till he return to judge the world. This demonstrates that it was designed that this ordinance should be perpetuated and observed *to the end of time.* In every generation, therefore, and in every place where there are Christians, it is to be observed *until the Son of God shall return;* and the necessity of its observance shall cease only when the whole body of the redeemed shall be permitted to see their Lord, and there shall be no need of those *emblems* to remind them of him, for all shall *see him as he is.*"

Hence, we see that the Baptists and others agree as to the NATURE of the Lord's Supper; all agree, 1. That it is an ordinance of *the New Testament instituted by Jesus Christ;* 2. That it is *a positive ordinance* established by *positive law;* 3. That it is a *church* ordinance, and, as such, involves and expresses *church fellowship;* 4. That it is a *commemorative* ordinance; 5. That it is an ordinance of *frequent* recurrence; and 6. That it is a *perpetual* ordinance.

II. The Baptists and others agree on the following points as to the DESIGN of the Lord's Supper:

1. All agree that the ordinance is designed *as a sacred memorial or remembrancer of Christ.*

In proof of this fact they appeal to the express declarations of the Savior and his Apostles. For instance, when our Lord instituted the holy supper, he took bread, and gave thanks, and brake it, and gave to his disciples, saying: "This is my body, which is given for you; this do *in remembrance of me*. Likewise, also, the cup," etc., Luke xxii: 19, 20. And Paul declares, "That the Lord Jesus, the same night in which he was betrayed, took bread; and when he had given thanks, he brake it, and said, Take, eat; this is my body, which is broken for you; this do *in remembrance of me*. After the same manner, also, he took the cup, when he had supped, saying, This cup is the New Testament in my blood; this do ye, as oft as ye drink it, *in remembrance of me*." (1 Cor. xi: 23–25.)

Accordingly, the *Episcopal Prayer-Book*, in the exercise for *confirmation*, contains the following question and answer:

"*Q.* Why was the Sacrament of the Lord's Supper ordained?

"*A.* For the *continual remembrance* of the sacrifice of the death of Christ," etc.

Dr. Adam Clark (Methodist) says: "Do this *in remembrance of me* is a command by which our blessed Lord has put both the affection and piety of his disciples to the test. If they love him, they will keep his commandments; for to them that love him, *his commandments are not grievous*." (*Discourse on the Eucharist*, p. 31.)

POINTS OF AGREEMENT. 37

The PRESBYTERIANS declare that our Lord Jesus instituted the Lord's Supper "*for a perpetual remembrance of himself in his death,*" etc. (*Confession of Faith,* chap. 29, sec. 1.) The CONGREGATIONALISTS declare the same. (See *Platforms,* chap. 30, p. 125.)

And ALBERT BARNES, in his Notes on 1 Cor. xi : 25, remarks : " *In remembrance of me.* This expresses the whole design of the ordinance. It is a simple *memorial* or *remembrancer;* designed to recall in a striking and impressive manner the *memory* of the Redeemer. It does this by a tender appeal to the senses—by an exhibition of the broken bread and the wine."

So all believe and teach on this point. The Lord's Supper, then, is a sacred *memorial* or *remembrancer* of Christ, designed to keep in remembrance our absent Lord. It is a holy *keepsake*— a precious *memento* of him who loved us and gave himself for us. And as often as we partake of the sacred symbols, we declare the fact that he still lives in our *memory,* though absent in person.

2. The Baptists and others agree that the Lord's Supper is designed as *an emblematic exhibition of Christ's death.*

" And as they were eating (the *paschal* supper), Jesus took bread, and blessed it, and brake it, and gave it to the disciples, and said, Take, eat ; this is (*i. e., represents*) my body. And he took the cup, and gave thanks, and gave it to them, saying, Drink ye all of it ; for this is (*i. e., repre-*

sents) my blood of the New Testament, which is shed for many for the remission of sins." (Matt. xxvi: 26–28.) "For," adds Paul, "as often as ye eat this bread and drink this cup, ye do *show the Lord's death* till he come." (1 Cor. xi: 26.)

Hence we see that the broken bread and the wine are the divinely appointed *emblems* of the broken body and shed blood of the Savior; and as often as we eat this bread and drink this wine in a proper manner and with a scriptural design, "Jesus Christ is evidently set forth"—*in emblem*—"crucified among us." (Gal. iii: 1.) In the language of Dr. Howell, "The Supper of the Lord was intended to teach the most wonderful of all truths, and to exhibit the most wonderful of all transactions. It is a *memorial* of God's love to us, and of *Immanuel's death* for us, in memory of whom it is received." (*Howell on Com.*, p. 105.)

Accordingly, the Presbyterian Confession of Faith, Larger Catechism, *Ans.* to *Question* 168, declares: "The Lord's Supper is a sacrament of the New Testament, *wherein* by giving and receiving bread and wine according to the appointment of Christ, *his death is shown forth*," etc. (See p. 344.)

Dr. Adam Clark, in his Commentary on 1 Cor. xi: 26, says: "*Ye do show the Lord's death.* As in the Passover they showed forth the bondage they had been in, and the redemption they had received from it: so, in the Eucharist we *show forth the sacrificial death of Christ*, and the redemption from sin derived from it."

ALBERT BARNES, in his Notes on 1 Cor. xi: 29, observes: "*Not discerning the Lord's body.* The humblest and obscurest follower of the Savior, with the weakest faith and love, may regard it (the Supper) as *designed to set forth the death of his Redeemer;* and observing it thus will meet with the divine approbation."

And the learned and pious MELVILL, in speaking of the Lord's Supper, says: "It is like a pillar, erected in the waste of centuries, indelibly inscribed with the *memorials* of our faith, or rather, it is as the *cross itself*, presenting to all ages the *immolation* of that innocent victim who put away sin by the *sacrifice of himself.*"—(Melvill's Thoughts, p. 241.) Thus the Lord's Supper is, as all agree, designed to be *an emblematic exhibition* of Christ's death.

3. The Baptists and others agree that the Lord's Supper is designed as *a symbolic declaration of our spiritual union and communion with Christ by faith.*

As in Baptism, we publicly "*put on Christ,*" and declare once for all our *faith* in a crucified, buried and risen Savior, with the *effects* of that faith in our death to sin, burial from it, and resurrection to a new life: so, in the Lord's Supper, we symbolically declare from time to time our *spiritual union and communion with Christ by faith.* "And as in Baptism we *profess* to have received spiritual life; so, in communicating at the Lord's Table, we have the *emblems* of that heavenly food by which we *live*, by which we *grow*, and in virtue of which we hope to live forever." (See *Booth's Vindication*, p. 29.)

Accordingly, Dr. Charles Hodge, speaking of Baptism and the Supper, remarks: "They are both divinely appointed *symbols* of our *union* with Christ, and of our *participation* of the benefits which flow from his mediation and death." (*Way of Life*, p. 261.)

And Prof. T. F. Curtis, speaking of the Lord's Supper, observes: "It is on our part a ratification and re-affirmation of the baptismal profession and pledge. It is a profession of our *constant communion* with Christ, of our feeding by *faith* upon him." (*Curtis on Com.*, p. 76.)

The Scriptures fully sustain these views. For instance, Paul in writing the Church at Corinth on this subject, said: "The cup of blessing which we bless, is it not the *communion* of the blood of Christ? The bread which we break, is it not the *communion* of the body of Christ? For we being many are one bread, and one body; for we are all partakers of that one bread." (1 Cor. x: 16, 17.) That is, the bread which we break, and the wine upon which we ask the Divine blessing, are the appointed *symbols* of Christ's broken body and shed blood, and represent our *spiritual union and communion* with Him by *faith;* while the "*joint participation*" of the ordinance symbolizes both the *Christian and Church oneness* of those who rightly partake together, as in the case of the Corinthian Church.

The Apostle is here exhorting the Corinthians not to partake with idolaters of meats offered to idols in their temples, for by such participation they would be regarded as professing union and communion with idols. So when he speaks of the bread being " the *communion of the body* of Christ," and the wine "the *communion of the blood* of Christ," he evidently means that the *joint participation* of the Lord's Supper by the members of a church, is a *symbolic declaration* of their spiritual union and communion with the Savior by *faith;* just as partaking with idolaters of meats offered to idols was a symbolic acknowledgment of union and communion with idols, although he affirms that "an idol is nothing, neither that which is offered in sacrifice to idols." (1 Cor. x : 14–22.)

Accordingly, NEANDER remarks : " These sacrifices bore the same relation to the heathen worship—as the Lord's Supper to the social acts of Christian worship. And in accordance with this fact Paul says : 'The cup of blessing which we bless, is it not the communion of the blood of Christ? The bread which we break, is it not the communion of the body of Christ?' This can only mean that it *marks*, it *represents* this communion," etc. (*Neander's Planting and Training*, p. 277.)

Indeed, it is manifest from the very nature of the Lord's Supper, that no person can partake of it acceptably without both *faith* and a *personal interest* in Christ. For an unbeliever to partake of the ordinance—"*not discerning the Lord's body*"—would be a monstrous falsehood and a flagrant sin. (See 1 Cor. 11: 29.) It is evident, therefore, that the Lord's Supper is designed as a *symbolic declaration* of the spiritual union and communion of believers with Christ. So all believe and teach.

Hence we see that the Baptists and others agree as to the DESIGN of the Lord's Supper on the following points: 1. That it is designed as a *sacred memorial*, or *remembrancer* of Christ; 2. As an *emblematic exhibition* of Christ's death; and 3. As a *symbolic declaration* of the spiritual union and communion of believers with Christ.

III. The Baptists and others agree as to the QUALIFICATIONS for communion at the Lord's Table.

1. All agree that the *new birth* is a scriptural qualification for communion.

The new birth, or regeneration, embraces three things: (1.) *A change of heart*, or "the renewing of the Holy Ghost;" (2.) *A change of state*, or justification, including pardon; (3.) *A change of relations*, or adoption into the divine family. It is effected by our Heavenly Father through the agency of the Holy Spirit and the instrumentality of the truth, in immediate and inseparable connection with repentance toward God and faith in our

Lord Jesus Christ. The subjects of this spiritual birth, therefore, are said to be "*born of God—born of the Spirit—born again, not of corruptible seed, but of incorruptible, by the word of God—created in Christ Jesus unto good works—passed from death unto life—quickened—washed, sanctified, and justified in the name of the Lord Jesus, and by the Spirit of our God,*" etc. Hence they are said to be "*accepted in the beloved;*" to be "*complete in Him;*"—to be "*the children of God by faith in Christ Jesus;*" to be "*saved by grace through faith;*" to be "*heirs of God, and joint-heirs with Christ;*" to be "*new creatures* in Christ, old things having passed away, and all things become new," etc.

The *necessity* of this spiritual birth arises from the total depravity and desperate wickedness of man, and from the holiness and justice of God and the spirituality of his kingdom and worship. *As it is written:* "The heart is deceitful above all things and desperately wicked. All have sinned and come short of the glory of God. Be ye holy, for I am holy. Without holiness no man shall see (or enjoy) the Lord. Except a man be born again, he can not see (or enjoy) the kingdom of God. For the kingdom of God is not meat and drink, but righteousness, and peace, and joy in the Holy Ghost. Ye must be born again. Except ye repent, ye shall all likewise perish. He that believeth not, shall be damned," etc.

The *evidences* of the new birth are of two kinds, *internal* and *external*, or those which we *feel* and those which we *profess*. He who is "born of God," is *conscious* of feeling a change of heart; and being justified by faith, he enjoys peace with God through our Lord Jesus Christ. He hates sin and loves holiness; he loves God and his people; he loves Christ and desires to obey him in all things; he delights in prayer, praise, and preaching, and desires the salvation of sinners. All who *feel* these evidences, should *profess* the fact as God directs.

Now, from the beginning to the end of the apostolic age, we have no account of any person being baptized and admitted to church membership and communion at the Lord's Table, who did not *profess* to be a subject of regenerating grace. Accordingly, the "Hudson River Association," in its Circular Letter, written in 1824, by the late Dr. S. H. Cone, states: "The children of God are bound to give thanks always to their Heavenly Father, because he hath from the beginning chosen them to salvation, through *sanctification of the Spirit and belief of the truth*, whereunto they are called by the Gospel; and THEN as lively stones, are built up a spiritual house, a holy priesthood, to offer up spiritual sacrifices, acceptable to God by Jesus Christ; and to manifest their attachment to the *laws, doctrines,* and *ordinances* once delivered unto the saints. . . . . . To the first Gospel Church in Jerusalem, it is said, '*The Lord added daily such as should be saved; and they continued steadfastly in the Apostles' doctrine and fellowship, and in breaking of bread, and in prayers.'* The church at Corinth consisted of those who were *sanctified in Christ Jesus, called to be saints, and who called upon the name of Jesus Christ our Lord.* The members of the church at Colosse, had *put off the old man with his deeds, and put on the new man, which is renewed in knowledge after the image of Him that created him;* and the brethren at Rome were *the called of Jesus Christ, beloved of God, called to be saints.* Now if the apostolic churches received only such as *professed* to be 'born of God,' and gave *evidence* that they were 'begotten again to a lively hope by the resurrection of Jesus Christ from the dead,' *we* should imitate their example; and if there come unto us any, and bring not this doctrine, we are commanded not to receive them into our houses, neither to bid them God-speed; for he that biddeth them God-speed is partaker of their evil deeds: and how can we more fully do this than to receive them to our *communion* and give them the appointed *tokens* of church fellowship? All candidates for church membership and communion, therefore, must give satisfactory evidence that they are *born of God.* This is the *first scriptural qualification* for communion at the Lord's Table." (See *Terms of Com.*, pp. 3, 4.)

On this point all Protestant denominations agree with the Baptists in theory, however much they may differ in practice. It is for this reason that Pedobaptist churches debar their *infant members* from their communion tables—they do not, in fact, regard them regenerated.

2. The Baptists and others agree that *valid baptism* is a scriptural qualification for communion.

As to what constitutes *valid* baptism, we must, for the present, refer the reader to THE NEW TESTAMENT. But however much the Baptists and others may differ as to the action, subjects, design, and administrator of baptism, still they all agree that *valid* baptism is an *indispensable* prerequisite to church membership, and consequently to *communion at the Lord's Table.* In support of this position, they appeal to the *teachings* of the Savior and his Apostles, and to the *practice* of the churches established by them.

(1.) All maintain that the *order* of Christ's commission to his disciples, establishes the *priority* of baptism to the Lord's Supper: "And Jesus came and spake unto them, saying, All power is given unto me in heaven and on earth. *Go ye therefore, and teach (or disciple) all nations; baptizing them in the name of the Father, and of the Son, and of the Holy Ghost: teaching them to observe all things whatsoever I have commanded you.* And lo, I am with you alway, even unto the end of the world." (Matt. 28: 18–20. Compare Mark 16: 15, 16; and Luke 24: 45–48.) This commission, as recorded by Matthew, Mark, and Luke, is admitted by all to be the great LAW of baptism for all ages and nations to the end of time. It expressly requires three things, viz.: (1.) To *preach* the Gospel to every creature. (2.) To *baptize* those who repent and believe; and (3.) To *teach* them to observe "*all things whatsoever*" Christ has commanded. Among these things is the command—"*This do in remembrance of me.*"

Accordingly, Dr. F. G. Hibbard,* of the Genesee Conference, a standard Methodist writer on "Christian Baptism," remarks: "It is certain that baptism is enjoined as the *first public duty* after discipleship. . . . . The *very position*, therefore, that baptism is made to occupy in relation to a course of Christian duty, namely, *at the commencement*, sufficiently establishes the conclusion that *the ordinance of the Supper*, and all other observances which have an exclusive reference to the Christian profession, must come in as *subsequent duties*. . . . . And thus we hold that Christ enjoined the *order*, as well as the duties themselves; and in this order of Christ, baptism *precedes* communion at the Lord's table." (*Hibbard on Baptism*, part 2, p. 177.)

(2.) All maintain that the *teachings* of the Apostles, and the *practice* of the churches planted by them, establishes the *priority* of baptism to the Lord's Supper.

---

* Dr. Hibbard's book on "Christian Baptism" is recognized by the General Conference of the M. E. Church as a standard work, and used as a *text-book* for their theological students in the "third year" of their "course of study." (See *Discipline*, p. 217, under the head "*Systematic Divinity*." Ed. of 1852.)

On this point Dr. Hibbard may be allowed to speak for all denominations. He says: "It will be more satisfactory to inquire, *How* the Apostles understood the commission with respect to the *relative order* of the Christian institutes? The argument from *apostolic precedent* is undeniably important. They were commissioned to *teach* the converted nations 'to observe *all things* whatsoever' Christ had *commanded*. This was the extent, and this the limit of their authority. . . What, then, did the Apostles teach and practice with respect to the *time* and *relative order* of baptism? On the day of Pentecost, when the people inquired of the Apostles: 'Men and brethren, what shall we do? Peter answered, *Repent and be baptized every one of you in the name of Jesus Christ,*' etc. (Acts ii: 38.) Luke sums up the glorious *results* of that memorable day thus: 'Then they that *gladly received* his word were *baptized;* and the same day there were added unto them about three thousand souls. And they continued steadfastly in the Apostles' doctrine and fellowship, and *in breaking of bread,* and in prayers.' (Acts ii: 41, 42.) This was the first occasion on which the Apostles had been called upon to exercise their high commission. And here, indeed, we are called upon to notice particularly the *order* in which they enforced the divine precepts. Upon their anxious hearers they enjoined, *first,* repentance; *then* baptism; *then* the duty of church membership; and *then* 'breaking of bread,' or the Lord's Supper. Comparing the *order* here observed with the *order* of the words of the commission, we are struck with admiration at the prompt fidelity of the Apostles." (*Hibbard on Baptism*, part 2, pp. 176–179.)

And after quoting Acts viii: 12; ix: 18; x: 47, 48; xiii: 36–38; xvi: 14, 15–33; and xviii: 8, on pages 179 and 180, "*to illustrate the uniform practice of the Apostles,*" Dr. Hibbard adds: "The above quotations need no comment to make them plainer in their teaching respecting the *relative order* of baptism. They bear unequivocal testimony to the point that baptism was commanded and observed as the *first act* of religious duty *after* conversion. *This was apostolic practice.* . . . . It will not be doubted that what the Apostles enjoined upon *their* converts, is *equally binding upon the disciples of Jesus in all ages.* . . . Is not baptism binding upon *us* as the *next* duty after conversion, as much as it *was* upon *Cornelius* or the *converts* on the day of Pentecost?" (*Hibbard on Bap.* as above.)

Such was the *teaching* of Christ and his inspired Apostles, and such the *practice* of the churches established by them. And the records of ecclesiastical history clearly prove that for *sixteen hundred years* after Christ baptism was regarded by all churches as an *indispensable* prerequisite to the Lord's Supper.

In the truthful language of the late ABRAHAM BOOTH, of London: "If we appeal to the persuasion and practice of Christians in all ages and nations, it will clearly appear, that *baptism* was universally considered, by all the churches of Christ, as a *divinely appointed prerequisite* to the Lord's Supper, till about the middle of the last (18th) century, when some *few of the Baptists* in England began *practically* to deny it, by defending and practicing mixed communion. . . . . . The ingenious author of the '*Pilgrim's Progress*' was one of the first who dared to assert that the want of baptism is '*no bar to communion*,' and acted accordingly." (*Booth's Vindication*, pp. 20, 21.)

Accordingly, LORD CHANCELLOR KING, a distinguished Episcopalian, in his "*Inquiry*," part 2, p. 44, says: "Baptism was *always precedent* to the Lord's Supper; and none were ever admitted to receive the eucharist till they were *baptized*. This is so obvious to every man that it needs no proof." So all denominations believe and teach at the present day. Hence it is that no church of any denomination, except a few Free Communion Baptists, will admit any person, however pious, to its communion table, *unless* he has been *baptized* in some way. This is the great reason why the advocates of "open communion" withhold the elements from their *own candidates* for baptism, and from the *pious Quakers*, who deny all water baptism.

3. The Baptists and others agree that *regular church membership* is a scriptural qualification for communion.

This is evident from the very nature of the Lord's Supper. It is, as all admit, a *church ordinance*, and hence none but *church members* have a right to partake of it. The New Testament records no instance of any person's being admitted to the Lord's Table, who was not a regular church member. As we have shown, none but the members of the church in Jerusalem united together "*in breaking of bread,*" or celebrating the Lord's Supper. The same was true of the church at Corinth, and of all the apostolic churches, so far as we have any record.

On this point there is perfect agreement among all denominations. For example, Dr. Hibbard remarks: "The eucharist, from its very nature, is a *church ordinance*, and as such, can be properly participated in by *church members only*. As a church ordinance, it never can be carried *out of the church*. This is so evident that no words can make it more plain, or add to its force." (*Hibbard on Baptism*, part. 2, p. 185.)

The Presbyterians declare, that "The Lord's Supper (is) to be observed *in his church* unto the end of the world." (*Confession of Faith*, chap. 29, sec. 1.) And the Congregationalists declare that "The Lord's Supper (is) to be observed *in his churches* to the end of the world," etc. (*Platforms, Conf. of Faith*, chap. 30, sec. 1.) The Campbellites and all others believe and teach the same.

Hence it is that no church or denomination, except the Methodists, who occasionally invite their "*seekers,*" will admit any person, however pious, to its communion table, who is not a regular church member in good standing. This indeed is the *great reason* why all churches concur in *denying* the communion to their own *candidates* for baptism, for none regard such persons as regular church members until they have been *baptized* in some way. Thus, by universal consent, *the terms of church membership are terms of communion* in all churches. It is true indeed of all organizations, that their terms of membership are terms requisite to the enjoyment of their immunities; as, for example, the *Odd-Fellows, Masons, Good Templars*, etc.

Now, we have rights as *citizens* of this government. But no man can legally enjoy any *peculiar right* of citizenship—such, for instance, as the right of *suffrage*—without himself first being a qualified citizen. The terms of citizenship are necessarily terms of suffrage. And the same is equally true of the churches of Christ. The Lord's Supper is, as all admit, a *church ordinance*, and hence communion at the Lord's Table is a *church privilege*. None, therefore, have a divine right to this privilege but regular church members, who have complied with the scriptural terms of church membership. So all hold and teach.

For example, Dr. Hibbard (Methodist) says: "*The concurrent voice of the Christian world excludes an unbaptized person from fellowship in the visible Church of God.*" (See *Hibbard on Baptism* as above.)

POINTS OF AGREEMENT.

Dr. EDWARD D. GRIFFIN (Presbyterian), late President of Williams College, in his celebrated "LETTER on Communion at the Lord's Table, addressed to a member of a Baptist Church," in 1829, remarks: "*That we ought not to commune with those who are not baptized, and of course are not church members, even if we regard them as Christians.*" (See *Fuller on Communion*, p. 270.)

And DR. NATHANIEL EMMONS (Congregationalist) observes: "As to the Gospel Church, it is plain that it was composed of none but *visible saints*. No other but *baptized persons* were admitted to communion; and no adult persons but such as professed *repentance and faith*, were admitted to baptism, which shows that they were visible saints." (See *Platforms*, p. 2.)

Hence, we see that the Baptists and others agree as to the QUALIFICATIONS for communion. All agree, (1.) That the *new birth* is a scriptural qualification; (2.) That *valid baptism* is a scriptural qualification; and (3.) That *regular church membership* is a scriptural qualification.

Such, then, are the POINTS OF AGREEMENTS between the Baptists and others: (1.) As to the *nature;* (2.) As to the *design;* and (3.) As to the *qualifications,* for the Lord's Supper.

CHAPTER II.

BAPTIST PRACTICE EXPLAINED AND DEFENDED.

1. THE Baptists practice *Church* Communion on principles *held in common* with mixed communionists. 2. The question, then, arises: "*Why do they differ in practice, since they agree in principle?* 3. The Baptists can not remove the *barriers* to intercommunion without the sacrifice of admitted principles, while others can do it without any such sacrifice. 4. The Baptists hence are *unjustly* blamed for their practice of *Church* Communion at the Lord's Table. 5. It is both *inconsistent* and *unkind* in others either to ask or invite intercommunion with the Baptists. 6. Scriptural views of the Lord's Supper would entirely relieve the minds of Baptists and others in regard to *Church* Communion.

In explaining and defending Baptist practice, we observe,

1st. *The Baptists practice Church Communion on principles held in common with mixed communionists.*

As we have shown, all denominations, except the Quakers and Free Communion Baptists, agree in theory as to the *scriptural qualification* for communion at the Lord's Table. They all maintain that the new birth or regeneration, valid baptism, and regular church membership, are *indispensable* prerequisites to the Lord's Supper; in other words, that *the terms of church membership are terms of communion in all churches.* Accordingly, Mixed Communion Pedobaptists not only debar their *candidates* for baptism from the Lord's Table, but also withhold the elements from their *infant members*, until they give evidence of *conversion*, notwithstanding they regard them *baptized*. And the creeds, disciplines, and standard writers of all denominations teach, that no person, however pious, has a Divine right to partake of the ordinance, who is destitute of *any one* of these scriptural qualifications. In proof of this, we need quote but a few of the many authorities, as no intelligent minister or member of any church will pretend to deny the fact. For example,

Dr. Wall (Vicar of Shoreham, in Kent, and author of the celebrated " *History of Infant Baptism*," for which he received the thanks of the whole Pedobaptist clergy) says: "No church ever gave the communion to any persons before they were *baptized;* among all the absurdities that ever were held, none ever maintained *that*, that any person should partake of the communion *before* he was baptized." (*History of Inft. Bap.*, part 2, chap. 9, pp. 484 and 493.)

Dr. Doddridge, a learned and pious Independent Pedobaptist, remarks: "It is certain that as far as our knowledge of primitive antiquity extends, no *unbaptized* person ever received the Lord's Supper. How excellent soever any man's character is, he must be *baptized* before he can be looked upon as completely a member of the Church of Christ." (*Doddridge's Miscellaneous Works*, p. 510.)

Dr. Timothy Dwight (Congregationalist), late president of "Yale College," affirms: "It is an *indispensable* qualification for this ordinance that the candidate for communion be a member of the visible Church of Christ *in full standing*. By this I intend that he should be a person of *piety;* that he should have made a *public profession* of religion; and that he should have been *baptized.*" (*Dwight's Theology*, vol. 4, p. 365.)

Dr. John Dick (Presbyterian), in maintaining that "baptism is *requisite* to entitle a person to a seat at the table of the Lord," says: "I do not know that this was ever called in question till *lately*, that a controversy has arisen among the English Baptists, whether persons of other Christian denominations may not be *occasionally* admitted to the holy communion with them; and it became necessary for those who adopted the affirmative to maintain that baptism is *not* a previous condition. This assertion arose out of their peculiar system, which denies the *validity* of infant baptism. But to every man who contents himself with a plain view of the subject, and has no purpose to serve by subtleties and refinements, it will appear that baptism is as much the *initiating ordinance* of the Christian as circumcision was of the Jewish dispensation. An *uncircumcised* man was not permitted to eat the Passover, and an *unbaptized* man should not be permitted to partake of the Eucharist." (*Dick's Theology*, Lect. 92, p. 494.)

Dr. Adam Clark (Methodist), in his "Discourse on the Eucharist," remarks: "As no person could partake of the Paschal lamb before he was *circumcised* (Exod. xii: 43-48), so, among the early followers of God, no person was permitted to come to the Eucharist till he had been *baptized*." (See *Eucharist*, p. 46.)

Dr. Hibbard, a standard Methodist writer, states: "It is but just to remark, that in *one principle* the Baptist and Pedobaptist churches agree. They both agree in *rejecting* from communion at the table of the Lord, and in *denying* the rights of church fellowship to *all who have not been baptized*. Valid baptism they (the Baptists) consider as *essential* to constitute visible church membership. *This we* (Pedobaptists) *also hold*. The only question, then, that here divides us is: "What is essential to valid baptism?" (*Hibbard on Bap.*, part 2, p. 174.)

Robert Hall, the celebrated leader of Free Communion Baptists in England, says: "Let it be admitted," as it unquestionably is by all other mixed communionists, "that baptism is, under all circumstances, a *necessary* condition of church fellowship, and it is impossible for the Baptists to act otherwise;" *i. e.*, than to *restrict* their communion at the Lord's Table to their *own churches*. "The recollection of this may suffice to rebut the *ridicule* and silence the *clamor* of those who so loudly condemn the Baptists for a proceeding which, were they (Mixed Communionists) but to change their opinion on the subject of baptism, their *own principles* would compel them to adopt. They both concur in a *common principle* (namely, that baptism is *prerequisite* to the Lord's Supper), from which the practice (of *restricted* communion), deemed so offensive, is the *necessary* result." (*Hall's Works*, vol. 2, p. 213.)

And ALEXANDER CAMPBELL, the distinguished founder of the "current reformation," remarks: "The converts made to Jesus Christ by the Apostles were taught to consider themselves, and were addressed, as *pardoned, justified, sanctified, reconciled, adopted,* and *saved* persons by all who first preached the Gospel of Christ." (*Christianity Restored*, p. 191.) Of course, in Mr. Campbell's judgment, they had been *baptized*, for he boldly affirms that all these spiritual blessings are "CONSEQUENTS" of baptism. (See *Campbell on Bap.*, pp. 275, etc.)

Such is but a *specimen* of the teachings of all denominations on this point. Many other authorities might be quoted, but these are sufficient to prove that the Baptists practice *Church* Communion on precisely the *same principles* on which others practice *Mixed* Communion. The question, then, naturally arises here—

2. "*Why do they differ in practice, since they agree in principle?*"

This is confessedly an important question, and it necessarily involves other questions equally important, which our limits will not permit us to answer fully at present. Among the questions here involved are the following: (1.) What is essential to valid baptism? (2.) Is such baptism essential to visible church membership? and (3.) Is such church membership essential to communion at the Lord's Table? Let us, then, briefly inquire,

(1.) What is *essential* to valid baptism? The answer to this question properly belongs to the baptismal controversy, and can be but partially given here. Suffice it to state, that baptism, to be *valid*, must include at least four things, viz.: A scriptural *action*; a scriptural *subject*; a scriptural *design*; and a scriptural *administrator*. If any *one* of these four things be wanting, the baptism is *invalid*, even though it may be *immersion*; just as was the baptism of "*certain disciples*" at Ephesus, whom Paul *re-immersed*, on finding their baptism defective in its *administrator* and *design*. (See Acts 19: 1-7.) Baptism, like the Lord's Supper, is a *positive ordinance*, established by *positive law*, and must therefore be *right* in its action, subject, design, and administrator, or it is not scriptural and valid baptism. (See *Missile* No. 2.)

Now, there is but "ONE LORD, ONE FAITH, ONE BAPTISM" (Eph. 4: 5); and we believe that this "ONE BAPTISM" is the *immersion* in water into the name of the TRINITY of a *penitent believer*, not in order to, but *in declaration of*, the remission of sins, *previously* obtained through *faith* in Christ, by a *scripturally-qualified* administrator; that is, one who has been thus baptized on a profession of his faith and regularly authorized by a gospel church to administer the ordinance through the agency of a presbytery. In proof of the *validity* of such baptism, we confidently appeal to the *primary meaning* of the original word *baptize;* to the *circumstances* and *places* where baptism was administered; to the *figurative representations* of the ordinance; to the *general practice* of the Christian world for THIRTEEN HUNDRED YEARS after Christ; to the *uniform practice* of the Greek Church down to the present day; to the *numerous admissions* of standard Pedobaptist writers; and to the *total want* of Scripture proof for any other baptism. This "*one baptism,*" like gold, is current every-where and in all churches. All denominations *practically admit* its validity by receiving it *as such*, even where they refuse to immerse themselves. But if this is *valid* baptism, nothing else is, for there is but the "ONE BAPTISM" ordained by Jesus Christ. Hence we see what is *essential* to valid baptism.

(2.) Is such baptism *essential* to visible church membership? The scriptural *order*, as we have shown, is: First *faith*, next *baptism*, and then *church membership*. The New Testament furnishes neither precept nor example to the contrary. Accordingly, all denominations regard *valid* baptism as *necessary* to visible church membership.

For instance, the PRESBYTERIANS declare that "Baptism is a sacrament of the New Testament, ordained by Jesus Christ, not only *for the solemn admission of the party baptized into the visible church*," etc. (*Confession of Faith*, chap. 28, sec. 1.) "*And whereby the parties baptized are solemnly admitted into the visible church*, and enter into an open and professed engagement to be wholly and only the Lord's." (*Larger Catechism*, Ans. to Ques. 165.)

Accordingly, DR. JOHN DICK (Presbyterian), speaking of "The two sacraments of the Christian Church," remarks: "I begin with *baptism, by which we are initiated into the fellowship of the church*, and which, in the order of dispensation, *precedes* the Lord's Supper," etc. (*Dick's Theology*, Lect. 88.)

And DR. GRIFFIN (Presbyterian), in his able "*Letter against Close Communion*," observes: "I agree with the advocates for close communion in two points:* 1. That baptism is the *initiating ordinance which introduces us into the visible church*. Of

---

* The Baptists regard *valid* baptism as a necessary *qualification* for church membership, and hence an *indispensable* prerequisite to communion at the Lord's Table, but they deny that it is the "*initiating*" ordinance which "*introduces*" us into any visible church. Baptism introduces the penitent believer into the *visible kingdom* of Christ, and thus *qualifies* him for membership in a visible church in that kingdom, but baptism does not *confer* membership in any church. The *voice of a church*, expressed or implied, *confers* membership in its body, and the same voice alone can dismiss or exclude from its membership. For example, the *converts* on the day of Pentecost were first *baptized*, and then *added to* the "model church" at Jerusalem. (See Acts ii: 41-47.)

course, *where there is no baptism there are no visible churches;* 2. That we ought not to commune with those who are *not baptized,* and of course, are *not church members,* even if we regard them as CHRISTIANS." (See *Fuller on Com.,* p. 270.)

"*I admit,*" says DR. N. L. RICE, "*That we can not get into the visible church without baptism;* but I will not agree that we can not be pardoned before baptism." (See *Campbell and Rice Debate,* p. 488.)

The EPISCOPALIANS hold and teach the same doctrine. (See *Book of Common Prayer,* Art of Relig. 19.) They not only require baptism, but also *confirmation* by a diocesan bishop, in order to *full* church membership, and to *communion* at the Lord's Table.

Accordingly, DR. MANTON, a distinguished Episcopalian, says: "None but *baptized persons* have a right to the Lord's Supper." (See *Supplement to Morning Exercises,* p. 199.)

The METHODISTS hold and teach the same doctrine as the Episcopalians on this subject, omitting confirmation. (See *Discipline,* Art. of Religion 13.) They recognize no person as *a church member* who has not been *baptized* in some way.

Accordingly, DR. J. L. DAGG remarks: "Baptism has been placed by Christ, at the *beginning* of all outward duties which he requires of his followers. It is, therefore, an *initiatory* service. But all agree that, as in the case of the ETHIOPIAN EUNUCH, baptism does not *introduce* to membership in a particular church; and it is clear that an individual must be a member of *Christ's spiritual body by faith*, before *baptism* or any other duty can be acceptably performed. . . . . . Baptism is, therefore, a *qualification* for admission into a church of external organization; but it does not *confer* membership." (As quoted in " *Church Polity*," by Dr. J. L. Reynolds, pp. 47, 48.)

Accordingly, DR. HIBBARD, who has been styled the " CARSON of Methodism on baptism," says: "Baptism, from its very nature, stands at the *opening* of the visible career. It is a *badge* of the Christian profession—the seal of the Gospel covenant—*the ordinance of admission into the visible Church of Christ.* Previously to baptism, the individual has no rights in the visible Church. . . . No society of Christians would receive an *unbaptized* person into their community, and tender to him the privileges of their body. So far as proper church rights and privileges are concerned, he is regarded in the same light as any unconverted man. The converts on the day of Pentecost were first *baptized*, and then *added to the church. The concurrent voice of the Christian world excludes an unbaptized person from fellowship in the visible Church of God.*" (*Hibbard on Baptism*, part 2, pp. 184, 185.)

Even the late ROBERT HALL, of England, whose peculiar views of communion compelled him to *deny* that baptism is, under all circumstances, a *necessary* prerequisite to the Lord's Supper, says:

"The APOSTLES, it is acknowledged, admitted *none* to the Lord's Supper but such as were *previously baptized.*" (See *Hall's Works*, vol. 1, p. 360.' If this was the practice of the *inspired Apostles*—the founders and instructors of Christ's churches to the end of the world—what right have we to practice otherwise?

And BAPTIST W. NOEL, who adopted Mr. Hall's views of communion, in giving his "REASONS" for leaving the Pedobaptists and uniting with the Baptists, states: "In the first place, there is *no instance* in the New Testament of an *unbaptized* person, after the institution of Christian baptism by our Lord, *coming to the Lord's Table;* and, therefore, if we should continue to attend the Lord's Table *without being baptized,* knowing that PEDOBAPTISM is not the baptism appointed by Christ, we should be acting *contrary* to all the *precedents* of the New Testament." (As quoted by *Curtis on Communion,* p. 247.)

As to the late ALEXANDER CAMPBELL and his *followers,* it is scarcely necessary to remark, that they regard valid baptism as not only *prerequisite* to church membership and to communion at the Lord's Table, but also as an *indispensable condition* of pardon, like faith and repentance. Indeed, their peculiar views of the design of baptism *force* them to the conclusion that a penitent believer is "*unpardoned, unjustified, unsanctified, unreconciled, unadopted,* and *lost* to all Christian life and enjoyment," until "the *very instant*" he is put under the water (see *Christianity Restored*, p. 196); and hence, consistency compels them to regard all persons who have not been immersed for the *actual* remission of their sins, as *disqualified* for church membership and for communion at the Lord's Table. And yet they intercommune with Pedobaptists!

Many other authorities might be adduced, but these are sufficient to show conclusively that all denominations regard valid baptism as *essential* to visible church membership, and to communion at the Lord's Table. Then let every believer go to THE NEW TESTAMENT for himself, and, with a meek and lowly heart, there learn what *valid* baptism is. As there is but "*one* Lord and *one* faith," so there is but "*one* baptism." If it is immersion, then it is not sprinkling or pouring; and *vice versa*. The BIBLE must settle this question.

(3.) Is visible church membership *essential* to communion at the Lord's Table? After what has been said on this point it is unnecessary to dwell here. As was proved both from the New Testament and standard authorities, *regular church membership* is a scriptural *qualification* for communion at the Table of the Lord. On this point there is perfect agreement among all denominations.

Accordingly, DR. HIBBARD, having proved conclusively that baptism is *essential* to visible church membership, adds: "On the contrary, the EUCHARIST, from its very nature, is a *church* ordinance, and as such can be properly participated in *only by church members.* As a church ordinance, it never can be carried *out of the church.* This is so evident that no words can make it more plain, or add to its force. And here lies the *relative* dependence of the ordinances. Baptism is the ordinance of *initiation* into the church; it is therefore applied, not to church members, but to persons *without,* in order to bring them *within* the pale and fellowship of visible Christianity. But the Eucharist is not an initiatory ordinance; it belongs to those who have been brought into the church by *baptism;* to recognized and acknowledged members. Hence it has a *retrospective* relation to baptism." (*Hibbard on Baptism,* part 2, p. 185.)

And Dr. Griffin, after admitting that "Where there is no baptism there are no visible churches," and that "we ought not to commune with those who are not baptized," and hence "not church members, even if we regard them as *Christians,*" adds: "Should a *pious Quaker* so far depart from his principles as to wish to commune with me at the Lord's Table, *while he yet refused to be baptized, I could not receive him;* because there is such a relationship established between the two ordinances that I have *no right* to separate them; in other words, I have no right to send the sacred elements *out of the church.*" (See *Fuller on Com.,* p. 270.)

So all denominations believe and teach on this point. It is the "*concurrent voice of the Christian world"*, that valid baptism is *essential* to visible church membership, and that **visible** church membership is *essential* to communion at the Lord's Table. It is plain, then, that the *great question* which separates the Baptists and others at the communion table, is: WHAT IS VALID BAPTISM? Nothing can be *valid* baptism but what Christ has *commanded* and *obeyed* himself. And until all Christians are willing to take THE NEW TESTAMENT as their sole guide on this subject, and to submit to "*one baptism*," on a profession of "*one faith*" in "ONE LORD," we must continue to differ in *practice*, notwithstanding we agree in *principle*.

But while it is true that baptism is the *principal* barrier to intercommunion between the Baptists and others, still it is not the *only* barrier. There are others, which we can but mention here; such as *apostolic succession, church government, infant baptism and church membership, baptismal-remission, sacramental salvation*, etc. For instance, we can not hold communion at the Lord's Table with the CAMPBELLITES, who practice exclusive immersion, and whose church government was borrowed from ours, because they make baptism a *necessary condition* of pardon, and virtually discard the fundamental doctrine of salvation by grace through faith. We can not hold intercommunion with PROTESTANT PEDOBAPTISTS, because they have substituted adult and infant *sprinkling* and *pouring* for believer's immersion, and have changed the *constitution* and *government* of Christ's churches, by admitting *infants* to membership, and by exalting the ministry *above* the churches in power. Nor can we intercommune with the ROMAN CATHOLIC CHURCH in any way, because she is the *embodiment* and *source* of all the above errors, and many others; and hence is not now, and never was a true Church of Christ, but has ever been "ANTICHRIST"—"THE MOTHER OF HARLOTS AND ABOMINATIONS." (Rev. 17: 5.) In short, we can not consistently and innocently intercommune at the Lord's Table with any of the above-named denominations, for two reasons especially: (1.) Because they all hold and propagate *fundamental errors*—errors for which we would *exclude* our own members and ministers; and (2.) Because by such intercommunion we would necessarily indorse their errors, and thus become *partakers* of their sins.

But, aside from all these barriers, we never can commune with others at the Lord's Table, so long as they remain separate and distinct denominations. The Lord's Supper being a *church ordinance*, as all admit, there can be no scriptural communion at the Lord's Table without *church-fellowship;* there can be no church-fellowship without *church relations;* and there can be no church relations without *valid baptism*. No such relations do exist nor can exist between the Baptists and other denominations. Therefore it would be *false in symbol* either to give or receive the divinely appointed *tokens* of church-fellowship, where no church relations do nor can exist.

Accordingly, Dr. Hibbard, after showing that the Lord's Supper is a *church ordinance*, and as such involves *church fellowship*, remarks: "If the celebration of the Lord's Supper be a recognition and acknowledgment of *church fellowship* among the communicants, I know not *how* it is to be extended to those who hold *no such fellowship* with Christians." (*Hibbard on Bap.*, part 2, p. 185.)

And Prof. Curtis appropriately adds: "The Lord's Supper being then a *church ordinance*, indicates *church relations* as subsisting between the parties who unite together in its celebration. It is much more than a recognition of the *Christian* character; it indicates a *visible church fellowship* as existing between them. Not to extend an invitation to the Lord's Supper, therefore, merely shows the absence of *church*, and not of Christian relations. A Jew, merely because he was a Jew, had no right to go into any Jewish house he pleased to celebrate the Passover, with any other family than his *own*, except by mutual consent and invitation; nor was he obliged to invite every Jew, or any person out of his own family, to partake with him. Not to invite any one out of his family to the Passover, therefore, was no indication that he was not regarded as a *true* and *pious* Israelite; because that was a *family*, as this is a *church* ordinance. The Lord's Supper was instituted by our Savior at one of those Paschal feasts with the "*twelve*," his more especial family of disciples. Each Christian church is a family of such disciples now; and the Lord's Supper was so constituted as to *express*, not merely the Christian, but the *church fellowship* of those who unite at the same table." (See *Curtis on Communion*, pp. 136, 137.)

Now, if the Lord's Supper be a church ordinance, as all admit, and as such involves church relations and expresses church fellowship as subsisting between communicants at the same table, of course none can consistently and scripturally unite together in its celebration, except those between whom such relations and fellowship either do exist or might exist, without any change of faith and practice, as between members of the same church or denomination. But no such relations and fellowship do exist or can exist between persons belonging to churches of different denominations, and therefore they can not consistently and scripturally participate together at the same table. For such persons to unite together in the celebration of the Lord's Supper, is not only false in symbol, but it is to *express* more than they would be willing to realize in action. Hence we see why it is that the Baptists and others differ so widely in *practice*, though they agree in *principle*.

3. *The Baptists can not remove the barriers to intercommunion without the sacrifice of admitted principles, while others can do it without any such sacrifice.*

The advocates of mixed communion, without

an exception, admit that Baptist churches are *true Gospel churches*, and that regular Baptists possess *all* the scriptural qualifications for communion at the Lord's Table. This is evident both from their practice and teachings. For instance, while the Pedobaptists and Campbellites generally claim to practice *open* communion, they *deny* each other's qualifications for the Lord's Supper; and, hence, do not invite each other, *as such*, to their respective communion tables; still, they all admit the *fitness* of Baptists for the ordinance, and cordially invite them to partake with them. This is also true of the Old and New School Presbyterians, and many others. They debar each other from their communion, but welcome the Baptists, and complain bitterly because we refuse to accept the invitation. Thus, while Mixed Communionists generally deny each other's fitness for the Lord's Supper, they all *practically* admit that the *Baptists* are scripturally qualified, and "keep the ordinances" *as* they were delivered unto the first churches by Christ and his inspired Apostles.

But it is certain that we, as Baptists, can never reciprocate the courtesy, without thereby surrendering our *admitted principles*, and indorsing *grave errors*, which we regard as subversive of the very constitution and government of Christ's churches. As we have shown, the advocates of mixed communion all maintain that *valid* baptism is essential to visible church membership, and that *visible church membership* is essential to communion at the Lord's Table. And each charges the other with holding *errors so fundamental*, that they can not consistently and safely unite together in permanent church relations; hence the continued existence of distinct and separate denominations; and hence, also, the ceaseless strife and warfare between them, notwithstanding their boasted "*open communion.*"

Now, we fully agree with Mixed Communionists as to these fundamental principles and errors; and, while we cheerfully grant that many of them are *Christians*, and, as such, we can and do hold *Christian Communion* with them in prayer, praise, and all those acts and exercises which Christ has enjoined as expressive of such communion; still we can not hold communion at the Lord's Table with any of them, without thereby sacrificing our *admitted principles*, and sanctioning their *acknowledged errors*. While, therefore, we most gladly recognize their piety in all proper ways and on all proper occasions, we never can admit the *validity* of their baptisms, or acknowledge them to be *Gospel churches*, which we would do by such intercommunion with them; for if valid baptism be *essential* to visible church membership, and visible church membership *essential* to communion at the Lord's Table, as all admit; and if they be *destitute* of such baptism, as we verily believe, then it follows, as a necessary consequence, and by their own consent, that they are not Gospel churches. In the truthful language of DR. GRIFFIN, we say: " Where there is *no baptism* there are no *visible churches;*" and, therefore, " we *ought not* to commune with those who are *not baptized,* and, of course, are *not church members,* even if we regard them as CHRISTIANS" (see *Fuller on Communion,* p. 270); for, adds DR. HIBBARD, " The *concurrent voice* of the Christian world *excludes an unbaptized* person from fellowship in the visible Church of God;" and " if the celebration of the Lord's Supper be a *recognition and acknowledgment* of church fellowship among the communicants, I know not *how* it is to be extended to those who hold *no such fellowship* with Christians" (see *Hibbard on Bap.,* part 2, p. 185); as most unquestionably is the case with Baptists and Mixed Communionists. The Lord's Supper, then, being a *church ordinance,* and, as such, expressive of *church fellowship,* as all admit; and *valid baptism* being by universal consent *essential* to visible church fellowship and to communion at the Lord's Supper, we can not consistently and scripturally either *give* or *receive* the appointed *tokens* of such fellowship from those whom we believe to be *destitute* of such baptism, " even if we regard them as *Christians.*"

Hence, we see that Baptists can not remove the *barriers* to intercommunion at the Lord's Table without the sacrifice of *admitted principles* and the indorsement of *acknowledged errors,* while others can do it without any such sacrifice or indorsement; for, as before shown, they can and do *practically* admit that we possess *all* the scriptural qualifications for communion at the Lord's Table, and that we are *true* Gospel churches.

But how much soever the advocates of mixed communion may differ with the Baptists as to the action, subjects, design, and administrator of baptism, still they all admit that OUR baptism is *valid*, and habitually receive it *as such;* while, on the other hand, we do not and can not conscientiously admit that adult and infant *sprinkling* or *pouring*, or immersion for the *actual remission of sins*, is scriptural and valid baptism at all, and, therefore, we can neither admit the *validity* of such baptism nor give up our *own* baptism, without the sacrifice of admitted principles and the indorsement of acknowledged errors. But, as before remarked, *others* can dispense with adult and infant *sprinkling* or *pouring*, and immersion for the *actual* remission of sins, and still have a baptism which they all *practically acknowledge* to be both scriptural and valid; for OUR BAPTISM, like pure gold, is *current every-where and in all churches*. For instance, a Baptist in good and regular standing in his own church, can join any church of any denomination in Christendom *on his baptism*, without the slightest change of faith or practice, which is not true of a member of any other church or denomination in the world. This is notoriously true and can not be successfully denied. It would, indeed, be a *new thing* under the sun for a regular and worthy Baptist to be denied admission into any church on account of his baptism.

It is evident, therefore, that so far as *baptism* is concerned, the advocates of mixed communion can remove this insuperable *barrier* to intercommunion without the sacrifice of a single admitted principle, or the indorsement of a single admitted error; for Baptists have an *undisputed baptism*, and no one blames them for what they *do believe and practice* in regard to the ordinances, but merely for what they *do not* believe and practice. That others can remove the barriers to intercommunion at the Lord's Table without any sacrifice of admitted principles or indorsement of acknowledged errors, will appear, not only from their *uniform practice* on this subject, but also from their *declared principles*. For example:

The EPISCOPALIANS can adopt *our* baptism without sacrifice. Their *Book of Common Prayer* directs: "Then shall the minister take each person to be baptized by the right hand; and placing him conveniently by the font, *shall dip him in the water*, or pour water upon him, saying: 'I baptize thee in the name,'" etc. (See *Ministration of Baptism*, p. 133.)

Accordingly, DR. WALL, the champion of Pedobaptism, speaking of the first century, says: "Their general and ordinary way was by *immersion*, or *dipping* the person," etc. And he adds: "This is so plain and clear by an infinite number of passages, that, as one can not but pity the weak endeavors of such Pedobaptists as would maintain the negative of it; so also we ought to disown and show dislike of the *profane scoffs* which some people give to the English *Anti-Pedobaptists* (or Baptists) merely for their using *dipping.*" (See *History of Infant Bap.*, part 2, chap. 9, sec. 2, p. 384.)

And Dr. Whitby, a learned Episcopalian, in his Commentary on Rom. 6: 4, remarks: " It being so expressly declared here and Col. 2: 12, that '*we are buried with Christ in baptism,*' by being buried under the water; and the argument to oblige us to a conformity to his death, by dying to sin, being taken hence, and this *immersion* being religiously observed by ALL CHRISTIANS FOR THIRTEEN CENTURIES, and approved by *our church*, and the change of it into *sprinkling*, even without any allowance from the AUTHOR of this institution, or any license from any *council* of the church—it were to be wished that this custom (of *immersion*) might be again of *general use*, and *aspersion* only permitted, as of old, in case of the *clinici* (*i. e.*, the *sick*), or in present danger of death."

The LUTHERANS can adopt our baptism without sacrifice. For instance, MARTIN LUTHER, their distinguished founder, asserts: "For to *baptize* in Greek is to *dip*, and *baptizing* is *dipping*. Being moved by this reason, I would have those who are to be baptized to be *altogether dipped into the water*, as the word doth express, and as the mystery doth signify." (See *Luther's Works*, Wittemb., Ed., vol. 2, p. 79.)

Accordingly, Dr. MOSHEIM, a standard Lutheran writer, speaking of the first century, states: "The sacrament of *baptism* was administered in this century, without the public assemblies, in places appointed and prepared for that purpose, and was performed by *an immersion of the whole body in the baptismal font.*" (*Eccl. Hist.*, vol. 1, p. 46.)

And Dr. NEANDER, a learned Lutheran, remarks: "Baptism was originally administered by *immersion*, and many of the comparisons of St. Paul allude to this form of its administration. The immersion is a symbol of *death*, of being buried with Christ; the coming forth from the water is a symbol of a *resurrection* with Christ, and both taken together represent the *second birth*, the death of the old man, and a resurrection to a new life." (See *Church History* of 1843, p. 197.)

The PRESBYTERIANS can adopt our baptism without sacrifice. Though they rarely administer immersion of late years, still they *practically* admit its *validity* by receiving Baptists on their immersion. Their CONFESSION OF FAITH, chap. 28, sec. 3, declares: "*Dipping* of the person into the water is not *necessary;* but baptism is *rightly* administered by *pouring* or *sprinkling* water upon the person." That is, dipping is not indispensable, but pouring or sprinkling will answer. The very language implies that *dipping* is valid baptism, while it assumes that pouring or sprinkling will do.

For illustration, if I assert that sending a son to college is not necessary; but that he may obtain an education in a private school, my language implies that sending him to college is *right* and *proper*, but that some other means will answer the purpose. If *dipping* is not valid baptism, why declare that it is not *necessary*, but that baptism is *rightly* administered by pouring or sprinkling?

Now the Calvinistic reformers all admit that immersion is scriptural and valid baptism, and that it was the practice of the apostolic churches. For example, JOHN CALVIN, the illustrious founder of Presbyterianism, says: "But whether the person who is baptized be wholly immersed, and whether once or thrice, or whether water be only poured or sprinkled upon him, is of no importance; churches ought to be left at liberty in this respect, to act according to the difference of countries. The very word *baptize*, however, signifies to *immerse;* and it is certain that immersion was the *practice* of the ancient church." (*Institutes of Religion*, vol. 2, bk. 4, chap. 15, sec. 19, p. 491, by Allen.)

DR. GEORGE CAMPBELL, a distinguished Scotch Presbyterian, in his "Notes" on Matt. 3: 2, says: "The word *baptizein* (infinitive mode, present tense, of *baptizo*), both in sacred authors and in classical, signifies *to dip, to plunge, to immerse,* and was rendered by Tertullian, the oldest of the Latin Fathers, *tingere*, the term used for dyeing cloth, which was by *immersion*. It is always construed suitably to this meaning."

And Dr. CHALMERS, the great light of the Presbyterian Church, in his Lectures on Romans (Lec. 30 on chap. 6: 3–7), says: "The original meaning of the word baptism, is *immersion*, and though we regard it as a point of indifferency, whether the ordinance so named be performed in this way or by sprinkling, yet we doubt not that the prevalent style of the administration in the Apostles' days, was by an *actual submerging of the whole body under water*. We advert to this for the purpose of throwing light on the analogy that is instituted in these verses."

SIR DAVID BREWSTER, editor of the Edinburgh Encyclopedia, *Art. Baptism*, says: "The word *baptize* means to *immerse*, or Paul would never have said, that we are '*buried*' with Christ by baptism. IMMERSION WAS PRACTICED BY ALL CHRISTIANS UNTIL THE BEGINNING OF THE FOURTEENTH CENTURY. The Council of Revenna, held in 1311, *first sanctioned sprinkling;* but corrupt as was the Church of Rome, whose council this was, it did not *enjoin* sprinkling, but merely said, that it was *admissible*."

Accordingly JOHN CALVIN, in his Commentary on John 3: 23, remarks: "From these words we perceive *how* baptism was administered by the *ancients*, for they *immersed the whole body in water*." And he adds: "The *Church* (*i. e.*, the Church of Rome) did grant *liberty* to herself, *since* the beginning, to *change* the rites (*i. e.*, of baptism and the Lord's Supper) somewhat, excepting the substance."

And Dr. Hodge, a learned Presbyterian, and professor in the Princeton Theological Seminary, in his "Way of Life," says: "Believers are said to be '*buried with Christ in baptism*,' that as he arose from the dead they also should walk in newness of life." (See *Way of Life*, p. 264.)

The Methodists can adopt our baptism without sacrifice. They not only admit that immersion is scriptural and valid baptism, but their Discipline recognizes it as such, and requires their elders and ministers to administer it both to *adults* and *infants*, if preferred by the parties. In chap. 3, sec. 4, the Discipline directs: 1. "Let every *adult* person, and the *parents* of every child to be baptized, have the *choice* either of *immersion*, sprinkling, or pouring. 2. We will not on any account whatever make a change for administering *baptism*,"* etc.

Accordingly, John Wesley, the acknowledged founder of Methodism, *immersed both adults and*

---

* Since 1850, the Methodist bishops have reversed the above order, placing immersion *after* sprinkling and pouring; and in the baptismal service, immersion is included in a *parenthesis*. Next we may expect its *exclusion* from the Discipline. Indeed, Pedobaptists are evidently endeavoring to prepare public sentiment for a revision of the New Testament, in which all allusion to immersion shall be excluded. But God has intrenched believer's immersion in the original Scriptures, and history bears testimony to the practice through all the past; and the Baptists will be on hand to defend Christ's ordinance.

infants, and refused to sprinkle or pour, except in case of *sickness*. In his "*Journal*," of February 21st, 1736, he writes: "Mary Welch, aged *eleven days*, was baptized according to the *custom* of the first church, and the *rule* of the Church of England—by *immersion*." And in his "Notes" on Rom. vi: 4, he says: "*Buried with him*—alluding to the ancient manner of baptizing by *immersion*." Hence, in his "*Journal*," of May 5th, 1736, vol. 3, p. 24, (published by J. Emory and B. Waugh, for the M. E. Church, New York, 1831,) Mr. Wesley adds: "I was asked to baptize *a child* of Parker's, second bailiff of Savannah (Geo.); but Mrs. Parker told me, 'Neither Mr. Parker nor I will consent to its being *dipped*.'" I answered, "If you certify that the child is *weak*, it will suffice (the rubric says) to pour water upon it." She replied, "Nay, the child is not weak, but I am resolved it shall not be dipped." This argument I could not confute, so I went home, and the child was baptized by another person."

And GEORGE WHITEFIELD, the worthy colleague of John Wesley, in his 18th Sermon, p. 297, remarks: "It is *certain* that in the words of our text, Rom. vi: 3, 4, there is an illusion to the *manner* of baptizing, which was by *immersion*, which is what *our* church allows," etc.

The CONGREGATIONALISTS can adopt our baptism without sacrifice. On this point, they perfectly agree with the Presbyterians, and use the same language. (See PLATFORMS, *Conf. of Faith*, chap.

29, p. 124.) They not only receive our immersion as *valid* baptism, but their *standard writers* admit that it is scriptural. For example,

The late Moses Stuart, long a distinguished Professor in the "Andover Theological Seminary," (in the "*Biblical Repository*" for April, 1833, p. 298,) says: "*Bapto* and *baptizo* mean to *dip, plunge, or immerge* into any thing liquid. *All lexicographers and critics of any note are agreed in this.* My proof of this position, then, need not necessarily be protracted; but for the sake of *ample confirmation*, I must beg the reader's patience, while I lay before him, as briefly as may be, the *results* of an investigation, which seems to leave no room for doubt. Take the following examples from the *classics*," etc. (See *Stuart on Baptism*, pp. 51, 52; published by *Graves, Marks & Co.*) "Prof. Stuart does not pretend, that in practicing *immersion*, we deviate either from the *command* of Christ or the *example* of the Apostles; but he thinks we are pharisaically rigid, and superstitiously attached to rights and forms, in that we will allow of *no alteration* of the original form of the institution." (See *Stuart on Bap.*, p. 229.) So Congregationalists generally believe and teach.

The Campbellites, of course, can adopt our baptism without sacrifice. Alexander Campbell, their great founder and leader, and many of their *ablest* and *best* ministers, together with the most *pious* portion of their ruling elders and private members, were regularly immersed on a profession of their faith *before* they left our churches; and if *our baptism* answered for them, *why* would it not answer for all? It is a well-known fact, that from the very birth of the "current reformation," they have made almost superhuman efforts to proselyte Baptists to their new faith, and we have yet to learn that any Baptist was ever rejected on account of his baptism.

It is evident, then, both from the practice and teachings of Mixed Communionists that they can adopt *our baptism* without the sacrifice of principle or the indorsement of error, and thus remove the *greatest barrier* to intercommunion at the Lord's Table.

Hence, we see that the Baptists can not remove the *barriers* to intercommunion without the sacrifice of *admitted principles*, while others can do it without any such sacrifice. In the language of the late Dr. Howell, we say, then: "All classes of Protestant Pedobaptists confess that we are *unquestionably baptized*. They can, therefore, if they think us orthodox and orderly, commune with us without the sacrifice of principle. We do not, we can not, believe that Pedobaptists are baptized. And as they teach us by their example to act, not upon their faith, but upon our *own*, they thus nullify all their arguments against us, for the *same reasons* that they decline communion with the Quakers." (See *Howell on Communion*, p. 109.) From all this we learn—

4. *That the Baptists are unjustly blamed for their practice of Church Communion at the Lord's Table.*

Now, if it be true, as we have shown, that the Baptists practice *Church* Communion on precisely the *same principles* upon which others practice *mixed* communion; and if the *great question* which separates the Baptists and others at the Lord's Table is, WHAT IS VALID BAPTISM? and if the Baptists can not remove the *barriers* to intercommunion without the sacrifice of *admitted principles*, while others can do it without any such sacrifice, THEN it is manifestly *unjust* and *unreasonable* in the advocates of mixed communion to abuse and blame us for our practice of *Church* Communion. Yet it is a melancholy fact that we are constantly abused and misrepresented on account of our *Church* Communion. On almost every sacramental occasion, and in almost every Mixed Communion church, as well as in the social circle and by the way-side, we are held up before the world as "*bigoted,*" "*exclusive,*" "*illiberal,*" "*uncharitable,*" and "*selfish,*" both by grave ministers and their misguided people; while our practice of *Church* Communion is denounced as an "*unchristian dogma,*" supported by "*the exclusive spirit of sectarian bigotry,*" etc.; and many simple-hearted persons believe the *slander*.

By this means the public mind is filled with prejudice against us as a denomination, and many pious persons, entertaining Baptist sentiments on every other subject, are thus turned away from the truth, and deluded into Mixed Communion churches—holding *radical errors,* which such persons do not, and never can believe and practice; as, for instance, apostolic succession and confirmation, adult sprinkling or pouring, infant baptism and church membership, clerical domination and rule, baptismal regeneration and remission, and numerous other errors; and all this through the *misrepresentation and slander* of those who profess to agree with us *in principle,* but differ with us in practice on this subject.

Now we solemnly protest against such unchristian treatment, and boldly denounce it as *unjust* and *uncharitable.* While Mixed Communionists admit the correctness of our principles *in theory,* they habitually violate them *in practice;* and then abuse and vilify us both privately and publicly because we carry out these admitted principles in our practice. Such a course of inconsistency and injustice may secure a temporary advantage, but it will ultimately recoil on the heads of those who are guilty of it. For our part, we have ever acted upon the principle that "honesty is the best policy" in religion as well as in every thing else; and "hitherto the Lord hath helped us." So that we may boldly say: "The Lord is our helper, and we will not fear what man shall do unto us." (Heb. 13:6.)

But the truth is, we cherish the most ardent affection for "all who love our Lord Jesus Christ in sincerity," so far as we know them, and we give the most substantial evidences of the sincerity of our love in all those acts of Christian worship which properly belongs to the "communion of saints," *as such.* In the language of Dr. Howell, we ask: "Who are more ready to acknowledge the Christian character of our brethren of other denominations than ourselves? Do we not feel as much fraternal regard for them; as ardently participate with them in social worship, and in efforts to save sinners; and give as unequivocal testimony of sincere sympathy and friendship *as any of them do toward each other?* In these particulars we are certainly not inferior to any of our opponents, and are, therefore, to say the least, *as free and liberal* in our communion. But in *sacramental* communion—in this we are told we do not unite with others. But even at the Lord's Table we are not the *only* close communionists; indeed, in this particular, we do not hesitate to say, that we are *still more liberal* than any of the sects around us," as we shall presently show. (See *Howell on Com.*, p. 229.) In short, we hold *spiritual* communion with all those with whom we spiritually agree and to whom we are spiritually united in Christ; but *ceremonial* communion with those *only* with whom we ceremonially agree and with whom we are united in visible *church* relations and fellowship. Nothing could be more consistent than this.

Accordingly, Prof. Curtis says: "If it be conceded, *as it must,* that the Lord's Supper is ever the *symbol* of particular *church* relations, then it is IMPOSSIBLE that Baptists should be rightly charged with *bigotry* or *want of charity*. There is *no unjust closeness* of communion in not inviting those who, as not having in our view a valid baptism, *could not*, according to our principles, be received into the membership of any of our churches, and whose *standards* would forbid them to enter into church relations with us. *Much more justly* might the charge be brought against those who refuse to admit *more than half* their own members to the Lord's Table; who, contrary to all the antiquity to which they appeal, first receive *infants* into their membership by baptism, and then withhold the *tokens* which belong to members. *The Baptists have no such close communion as this.*" (See *Curtis on Com.*, p. 138.)

Hence we see that it is manifestly *unjust* in Mixed Communionists to blame the Baptists for their practice of *Church* Communion at the Lord's Table. They are, in fact, the *only* consistent people upon earth in their practice of communion. They faithfully carry out in their practice the principles which they hold in common with others, while all others knowingly violate them. Hence we remark—

5. *That it is both inconsistent and unkind in others either to ask or invite intercommunion with the Baptists at the Lord's Table.*

As before proved, Mixed Communionists admit that our baptism is *valid*, and that we possess *all* the Scriptural qualifications requisite to communion at the Lord's Table; and hence they feel at liberty to invite us to partake with them. To the unthinking multitude, this might appear consistent and kind. But the very reverse is true. It is both inconsistent and unkind in them to *ask* or *invite* such intercommunion with us. *They know*, at the very time they invite us to their communion, that we can neither accept the invitation nor reciprocate the courtesy, without the abandonment of our admitted principles, and the indorsement of their acknowledged errors. For instance, the *Pedobaptists know* that we regard the *substitution* of pouring and sprinkling for baptism and of *infants* for believers as a flagrant violation of the positive laws of Christ, fraught with innumerable evils. And the *Campbellites know* that we consider baptism for the *actual* remission of sins as both unscriptural and dangerous. In a word, *they all know* that, with our views of the action, subjects, design, and administrator of baptism, we are bound to regard them as *unbaptized* persons, and, consequently as not *regular* church members; and as such, *disqualified* for the Lord's Supper. And *they know* that we practice *Church* Communion on precisely the *same principles* on which they practice mixed communion. This is admitted by their own standard writers. For example, Dr. Hibbard, in speaking of the Baptists, says: "Their views of baptism *force* them upon the ground of **strict** communion, and herein they act upon the *same principles* as other churches; *i. e.*, they admit *only* those whom they deem *baptized* persons to the Communion Table. Of course, they must be their *own judges* as to what baptism is." (See *Hibbard on Bap.*, part 2, p. 174.)

With a knowledge of these facts, how inconsistent and unkind is it in others to invite Baptists or to ask the privilege of communing with them, especially when *they know* that compliance on our part would involve the sacrifice of our conscientious principles, and compel us to fellowship what we believe to be unscriptural and of evil tendency. Nor is it any abatement to plead that others believe themselves qualified for the Lord's Supper; this we cheerfully grant. But we are responsible to God for *our own* faith and practice, and therefore must be governed in our action, not by what others believe, but by what *we ourselves* believe to be the requirements of Christ on this subject. In this we do unto others as we would have them do unto us, under similar circumstances.

At the same time, we should not regard Mixed Communionists as enemies, but faithfully admonish them as brethren in error. They have been mistaught on this subject, and are rather to be pitied than blamed. From their earliest recollection many of them have been accustomed to hear their parents and pastors abuse and denounce the Baptists as " bigoted, exclusive, illiberal, and selfish," and they have grown up with prejudice against our practice, without a knowledge of our principles. Often have they seen their loved parents and friends *contemptuously* leave the house of God while the Baptists were devoutly celebrating the Lord's Supper; and their prejudice against our *Church* Communion has thus grown with their growth and strengthened with their strength. Indeed, many of them are so prejudiced that they will neither hear nor read our views. We should, therefore, exercise great charity toward such deluded brethren and sisters, and endeavor to teach them the way of the Lord more perfectly. "*In meekness*," says Paul, "*instructing those that oppose themselves; if God peradventure will give them repentance to the acknowledging of the truth; and that they may be delivered from the snare of the devil, who are taken captive by him at his will.*" (2 Tim. ii: 25, 26.) Hence we remark,

6. *That scriptural views of the Lord's Supper would entirely relieve the minds of Baptists and others in regard to Church Communion.*

The celebrated ROBERT HALL eloquently depicts: "The uneasiness and anguish felt on sacramental occasions by good men seeing their most intimate friends and persons of exalted piety compelled to withdraw from the Lord's Table." (See *Hall's Works*, vol. 1, p. 243.) That "good men," including some uninstructed Baptists, feel such "uneasiness and anguish" on sacramental occasions, we readily admit. But the question arises, *Why is it so?* Evidently because they misapprehend the true *nature* and *design* of the Lord's

Supper. Such persons confound *Christian* fellowship with *church* fellowship, and hence they do not fully apprehend the *symbolic import* of the Lord's Supper as being not only the *emblem* of Christ's broken body and shed blood, but also the *appointed token*, not of the Christian, but of the *church* fellowship subsisting between communicants at the same table. If the Lord's Supper be a *church* ordinance, as all admit, and as such, *expressive*, not of the Christian, but of the *church* fellowship existing between those who celebrate together, then there can be no good reason for " uneasiness and anguish " on account of the " most intimate friends and persons of exalted piety " not partaking of the ordinance together, who do not and can not consistently sustain *visible church relations* with each other, as is the case with Christians of different denominations. While such persons may and should unite on all suitable occasions in all those Christian acts and exercises which properly belong to the " communion of saints," *as such*, irrespective of visible church relations; still they can not consistently and scripturally unite together in the celebration of the Lord's Supper, because it is confessedly a *church ordinance*, and, as such, says Dr. Hibbard, " a recognition and acknowledgment of *church fellowship* among the communicants," which does not, and can not, exist between persons belonging to churches of different denominations. And if " the most intimate friends and persons of exalted piety" can not conscientiously unite together in the same visible church, they can not consistently and scripturally unite together in the celebration of the Lord's Supper, which is universally admitted to be a church ordinance.

As we have shown, Christian communion and sacramental communion are entirely distinct, and either may be in full and perfect exercise in the *absence* of the other. We may, and often do, enjoy *Christian* Communion with those with whom we do not and can not hold sacramental communion, as in the case of our *candidates for baptism;* while, on the other hand, we may hold *sacramental* communion with those with whom we can not enjoy Christian Communion, as in the case of members of the same church with us in whose *piety* we have no confidence. The two things, therefore, are entirely distinct; so distinct, that the one may, and often does, exist where the other can not. Hence, we see that it is perfectly consistent and proper for Baptists to hold Christian communion with Christians of all denominations, just as we do with our candidates for baptism, and at the same time *restrict* sacramental communion to the members of their own churches; and, in so doing, we in no sense reflect on the Christian character of our brethren of other churches.

A correct understanding of this distinction between Christian and sacramental communion, together with the admitted fact that the Lord's Supper is a *church* ordinance, would entirely relieve the minds of Baptists and others of all "uneasiness and anguish" arising from "the most intimate friends and persons of exalted piety," who belong to churches of different denominations being separated at the Lord's Table. *For instance*, husbands and wives, parents and children, brothers and sisters, belonging to different denominations, may enjoy the most *unrestricted Christian* communion with each other *as Christians*, irrespective of visible church relations, just as they hope to enjoy it in heaven; and at the same time restrict their communion at the Lord's Table to their *own* churches with perfect consistency, and without, in any sense, reflecting upon each other's Christian character. In the one case, they commune with each other as *Christians* in prayer, praise, etc.; and, in the other, they commune merely as *church members* in showing forth the Lord's *death*, and not their love for one another as Christians; and such persons have no more reason to feel "uneasiness and anguish" on account of being debarred from the communion tables of each other's churches, than the pious Quaker or their own candidates for baptism have, on account of being denied the communion elements in all churches. The Lord's Supper, then, being a *church* ordinance, as all agree, and, as such, necessarily involving and expressing the *visible church relations and fellowship* subsisting between communicants at the same table, of course none can consistently participate together, except those between whom such relations and fellowship actually do exist, or might exist, as between members of the same denomination. And if the Lord's Supper be a church ordinance, communion at the Lord's Table is a *church act and a church privilege;* and, therefore, a member of one church has no more right to complain of another church, even of the same denomination, for not inviting him to her communion table, than he has to complain of her for not inviting him to vote for the reception or exclusion of a member; nor has he any more right, *as a right*, to claim the one than the other, for both are equally church acts and privileges.

This view of the Lord's Supper also relieves the Baptists of the charges of "bigotry" and "exclusivism," etc., so often preferred against them by Mixed Communionists. In the language of Prof. Curtis, we say: "The effect of a right understanding of this principle will be entirely to relieve Baptists from all possibility of being charged with *bigotry* on account of their views and practice in regard to the Lord's Supper. It is frequently urged that we refuse *Christian* communion with the members of different denominations, and thus commit the most flagrant of offenses against the law of charity. This is an error. On the contrary, we seek communion with them all in proportion to their piety. But we do not consider them, nor symbolize our communion with them, as belonging to the *same par-*

ticular church as ourselves; and, as we have shown, the Lord's Supper is a *church* ordinance. Wherever we find Christians, we commune with them *as such.* But the Lord's Supper, being a church ordinance, *none but the members of a particular church or Christian congregation can claim to partake of it.* Even members of another church of the same denomination only do so by *special request,* and not by right. There is nothing, therefore, in our views of the Lord's Supper to prevent our having the most perfect charity and fellowship *as Christians* with those who differ with us in many respects. We can and do commune with them *as such.* As, indeed, we never baptize any person until we believe him to be *a Christian already,* his baptism never can *introduce* him to our Christian fellowship. We never do regard, and never have regarded, the outward act of baptism as an *essential* to Christian character, and it is impossible we ever should." (*Curtis on Com.*, pp. 92, 93.)

"Proper views of the Lord's Supper," says Dr. Howell, "will also serve to *remove another perplexity* often found to exist in our churches. Not unfrequently does a member absent himself from the Lord's Table on account of the presence of some other member who has offended him. He will not take his seat there, because he imagines that by doing so he will *express* a fellowship that does not actually exist; and he chooses not to falsify by his *act* the true convictions of his heart." (See *Howell on Com.*, p. 115.) Such conduct is wrong. It proceeds upon the erroneous supposition that communion at the Lord's Table involves and expresses *Christian* fellowship. Now, our blessed Lord has given specific directions for the settlement of *personal* difficulties between brethren in Matthew, 18th chapter, and it is the immediate duty of the offended party to seek redress according to those directions. But so long as individuals remain members of the same church in good standing, they are sacredly bound to commune together at the Lord's Table, let their personal feelings toward each other be what they may, just as they are under obligations to perform all other church duties. The duty of a brother, under such circumstances, is to "examine *himself*, and so eat of the bread and drink of the wine," not in token of his love for his brethren, but to "show the Lord's *death* till he come." "*This do*," says Jesus, "*in remembrance of* ME." Nor is there any thing inconsistent or wrong in this, since the Lord's Supper is a *church* ordinance, and, as such, involves and expresses, not the Christian but the *church* fellowship subsisting between communicants at the same table.

Hence, we see that scriptural views of the Lord's Supper would relieve the minds of Baptists and others of all difficulty on the subject of *Church* Communion. It is evident, therefore, that Church Communion, as practiced by the Baptists, is both *consistent* and *scriptural*.

CHAPTER III.

OBJECTIONS TO CHURCH COMMUNION ANSWERED.

OBJECTION 1st. "It is the *Lord's Table*, and therefore all the Lord's children have *a right* to it." 2d. "We have no scriptural right *to judge of the fitness* of communicants for the Lord's Table." 3d. "*Church* Communion, as practiced by the Baptists, *unchristianizes* all other denominations." 4th. "It not only unchristianizes, but also *unchurches* all others." 5th. "It *debars* many pious persons from the Lord's Table who have been *immersed*." 6th. "It *divides* God's people, and *prevents* love and union among them." 7th. "It is '*exclusive, illiberal,* and *selfish*' in the Baptists." 8th. "All Christians will commune together in heaven, and *therefore* all should commune together on earth."

Among the many objections urged against the Baptist practice of *Church* Communion, the following are the most *plausible*, viz.:

1st OBJECTION: "*It is the Lord's Table, and therefore all the Lord's children have a right to it.*"

We grant that it *is* the Lord's Table, and therefore we are *compelled* to debar all those from it who have not complied with the Lord's acknowledged *terms* of communion. If it were *our* table, then we should feel at liberty to prescribe the terms of admission to it; and hence, would most cordially welcome all our brethren and friends to partake with us on these terms, just as we do in the hospitalities of social life. None could be

9

more free than the Baptists. But inasmuch as it is the LORD's Table, it must be governed by *His* laws. We have no right to make laws for its government, nor to prescribe the terms of admission to it; nor are we at liberty to invite any person to it who has not, in our judgment, complied with the *Lord's terms* of admission. The mere fact of being a *Christian* does not of itself entitle a person to communion at the Lord's Table in any church; there are other qualifications which the advocates of mixed communion, as well as the Baptists, regard as *indispensably necessary;* such as *valid* baptism, and *regular membership* in a visible church of Christ. As this point has already been established, we need add but a few *practical illustrations* of the fact.

For example, BISHOP WHITE, of Pennsylvania (Episcopalian), after inviting "all the Lord's children to His Table," some years since, felt conscientiously bound to "*refuse* the bread and wine to a *pious Quaker*," who desired to partake with him, because he had not, in the bishop's judgment, been *baptized*, although the honest Quaker considered himself baptized, and was known to be in good standing in his own church.

And BISHOP WILLIAMS, of Connecticut, recently declared that "No member of any religious society, *outside of the church*, can receive her holy communion without a violation of a *fundamental law* of the liturgy; and no clergyman can administer it to such a person without a violation of his *ordination vows*. The rubric commands that no persons shall be admitted to the holy communion until they have been, or are ready to be, CONFIRMED." (*Religious Herald*.)

Dr. Griffin (Presbyterian), as quoted for another purpose, says: "We *ought not* to commune with those who are *not baptized*, and of course are *not church members*, even if we regard them as Christians." He then instances a "*pious Quaker*," and adds: "Should he desire to commune with me, while he yet refused to be baptized, *I could not receive him;* because I have no right to send the sacred elements *out of the church.*" (See *Fuller on Com.*, p. 270. Also, Conf. of Faith, chap. 29, sec. 1.)

Dr. Hibbard (Methodist) says: "It is but just to remark, that in *one principle* the Baptist and Pedobaptist churches agree. They both agree in *rejecting* from communion at the Table of the Lord, and in *denying* the rights of church fellowship to *all who have not been baptized*." (*Hibbard on Bap.*, part 2, p. 174.)

Dr. Emmons (Congregationalist), in his "*Platforms* of Ecclesiastical Government," says: "And as to the *Gospel Church*, it is plain that it was composed of none but *visible saints*. No other but *baptized persons* were admitted to communion; and no adult persons but such as professed *repentance and faith*, were admitted to baptism, which shows that they were visible saints." (See *Platforms*, p. 2.)

And ALEXANDER CAMPBELL, in 1835, held a friendly correspondence with the REV. WILLIAM JONES, of London, a distinguished Baptist minister, who inquired: "*Do any of your churches admit unbaptized persons to communion,* a practice that is becoming very common in this country?" Mr. Campbell replied: "*Not one, so far as known to me.* I am at a loss to understand on what *principles*— by what *law, precedent,* or *license,* any congregation, founded upon the Apostles and prophets, Jesus Christ being the chief corner-stone, could dispense with the *practice* of the primitive church—with the *commandment* of the Lord, and the *authority* of the Apostles. Does not this look like making *void* the word or commandment of God by *human traditions?*" (See *Millennial Harb.,* vol. 6, p. 18.)

So all denominations hold and teach on this subject, notwithstanding the practice of some to the contrary. The mere fact, then, of being a child of God by faith in Christ Jesus, does not of itself entitle any one to communion at the Lord's Table in any church. Accordingly, no church of any denomination will admit its own candidates for baptism to its communion table, until they have been *baptized* in some way, notwithstanding it regards them as the Lord's children. The objection, therefore, that we have no right to debar any of the Lord's children from his table, rests as heavily against Mixed Communionists as it does against the Baptists, for they all claim and exercise this right. And surely we are not sinners above all others because we do what all others do.

2d OBJECTION: "*We have no scriptural right to judge of the fitness of communicants for the Lord's Table.*"

In support of this objection the advocates of Mixed Communion, with great confidence, quote the language of Paul in 1 Cor. 11: 28: "Let a man *examine himself*, and so let him eat of that bread and drink of that cup." From this passage it is contended that every communicant must judge of his *own* qualifications for the Lord's Supper, and that no church has a right to sit in judgment on his fitness for the ordinance. This objection is based upon a *misapplication* of the Apostle's language, as is evident from the context. Paul was not here addressing a mixed multitude of persons belonging to different churches, but the members of that particular church at Corinth who already possessed the scriptural qualifications for communion at the Lord's Table, but who had misconceived the nature and perverted the design of the Lord's Supper. (See verses 20-32.) Hence the Apostle first explains the nature and design of the ordinance, and then enjoins the *individual duty* of each communicant to examine himself *preparatory* to receiving the sacred elements, which in no sense conflicts with the *prior* duty of every church to judge of the *fitness* of applicants for membership and communion in its own body. That this is the true meaning of the passage, is admitted by those who deny the right to Baptists. For example—

BURKITT, an Episcopalian commentator, in his "Notes" on this verse, remarks: "We learn hence that it is the *special duty* of all those that desire safely and comfortably to approach the Table of the Lord, to *examine themselves before they come*," etc.

ALBERT BARNES, a popular Presbyterian commentator, in his "Notes" on this passage, says: "Let him examine himself, and see whether he have the *right feelings* of a communicant, and can approach the Lord's Table in a *proper manner.*"

And ADAM CLARK, a standard Methodist commentator, in his "Notes" on the same verse, says: "Let him try whether he has the *proper faith* in the Lord Jesus Christ; and whether he *discerns* the Lord's body; and whether he *duly considers* that the bread and wine point out the crucified body and spilt blood of Christ."

But while this passage refers exclusively to the individual duty of communicants, the same Apostle elsewhere enjoins upon all churches the duty of *judging of the fitness* of communicants at their respective tables. For instance, in 1 Cor. 5: 11–13, he says: "Now I have written unto you not to keep company, if any man that is called a brother be a fornicator, or covetous, or an idolater, or a railer, or a drunkard, or an extortioner; *with such a one no not to eat;*" *i. e.*, at the Lord's Table. And he adds: "*Do not ye judge them that are within?*" *i. e.*, within your own communion. Here the Apostle clearly teaches that it is both the duty and privilege of each church to judge of the *fitness* of those who come to its communion table. And this is as reasonable as it is scriptural. Indeed it is an inherent right of every church, and essential to the purity of its communion.

But if there is any force in this objection, it rests as heavily against Mixed Communionists as it does against the Baptists; for they all claim and exercise the right of judging of the qualifications of applicants for membership and communion in their respective churches, as is evident both from their teachings and practice. For instance, the PRESBYTERIANS (*Confession of Faith,* form of gov., bk. 1, chap. 1, sec. 1), declare: "That every Christian church, or union, or association of particular churches, is entitled to declare the TERMS of admission into its *communion,* etc., that, in the exercise of this right, they may, notwithstanding, *err* in making the terms of communion either too lax or too narrow; yet even in this case, they do not infringe upon the liberty or the rights of *others*, but only make an improper use of their *own*." Accordingly, *whole synods* have declared it inexpedient for Presbyterians to hold *intercommunion* with those denominations who entertain *Arminian sentiments;* such as the Episcopalians, Lutherans, Methodists, Campbellites, and others. For example, we quote the following extracts from "Synodical Records," published per *order* in the "*Union Evangelist and Presbyterian Advocate,*" in 1832, vol. 3, p. 240:

"The committee on a former resolution of synod on the subject of *intercommunion* reported. The report was adopted as follows, viz.: 'The committee are of opinion that for Presbyterians to hold communion in *sealing ordinances* with those who belong to churches holding doctrines *contrary to* OUR STANDARDS (as do Baptists, Methodists, and all others), is incompatible with the *purity* and *peace* of the (Presbyterian) Church, and *highly prejudicial* to the truth as it is in Jesus. Nor can such communion answer *any valuable* purpose to those who practice it, etc. In accordance with these views, your committee are of opinion *that the practice of inviting to the communion all who are in good standing in their own churches, is calculated to do much evil, and should not be continued;* while every *church session* is, however, left at liberty to admit to OCCASIONAL communion members of other denominations, *after having conversed with them, and received satisfaction as to their soundness in the faith and Christian practice.*'"

These "*Church rights,*" as declared in the Confession of Faith, and indorsed by whole synods, are fully sustained by the highest tribunal of the Presbyterian Church. The GENERAL ASSEMBLY, in 1839, declared unanimously that—"Every Christian church, or association of churches, is *entitled* to declare the TERMS of admission into its communion." (See "*Protestant and Herald,*" of Kentucky, as quoted by *Howell on Com.*, p. 240.) Hence we see that the Presbyterians claim the *right*, not only to judge of the *fitness* of communicants, but also to declare the *terms* of admission to their communion.

The METHODISTS, or rather their PREACHERS, are required to *judge of the fitness* of applicants for membership and communion in their church. In answer to the *question*, "How shall persons be received into the church?" the Discipline says: "1. When persons offer themselves for church membership, let the *preacher in charge inquire* into their spiritual condition, and see that they are acquainted with the moral discipline of the church, and *receive them into the church when they have given satisfactory assurances* of their desire to flee from the wrath to come, and to be saved from their sins; also of the genuineness of their faith and of their willingness to keep the rules of the church. 2. When *satisfied* on these points, let the preacher bring the candidates before the congregation, whenever practicable, and *baptize* them, if they have not been baptized," etc. (See *Discipline* for 1868, chap. 3, sec. 1, pp. 90, 91.)

Accordingly, BISHOP HEDDING, in his able "Discourse on the Administration of Discipline," pp. 72, 73 (delivered before the New York, New England, Providence, and Maine Conferences, and published by their request), asks: "Is it proper for a preacher to give out a *general invitation* in the congregation to members in good standing in other churches to come to the Lord's Supper?" To this the bishop gives the following emphatic answer: "NO; for the most unworthy persons are apt to think themselves in good standing, and sometimes persons who are not members of any church will take the liberty from such an invitation to come. And again, there are some communities called churches, which, from heretical doctrines or immoral practices, have no claim to the privileges of Christians, and ought not to be admitted to the communion of any Christian people. The RULE," says he, "in that case, is as follows: '2. Let no person be admitted to the communion without *examination*, and some *token* given by an elder or deacon. 3. *No person shall be admitted to the Lord's Supper among us who is guilty of any practice for which we would exclude a member of our church.*'" (See *Discipline* for 1868, chap. 5, sec. 1.)

Accordingly, DR. HIBBARD remarks: "In admitting persons to church fellowship, we do not act upon discretionary powers as to the *terms* to be dictated. Those terms are already settled by the great Head of the Church. All our discretion in the premises consists in *judging of the conformity* of the candidate to the terms already prescribed, whether he comes within the provisions of the charter, and may claim its rich and heavenly immunities." (*Hibbard on Bap.*, part 2, p. 187.)

The CONGREGATIONALISTS also claim and exercise

the same right. For instance, Dr. Emmons observes: "That every church has a right to admit members into their Christian communion according to the rules of the Gospel. It is essential to every voluntary society to admit whom they please into their number. They are the only proper and competent judges to determine who are worthy or unworthy to be admitted. It would be very irrational to suppose that any particular church is obliged to admit every one that offers to join their holy communion. They have an *undoubted right to judge of the qualifications* of proponents, and receive or reject them according to an impartial judgment of Christian charity. This right they never ought to give up." (See *Platforms*, pp. 6, 7.)

And the Campbellites claim the same right, whether they exercise it or not. Hence Alexander Campbell remarks: "As the government was upon the shoulders of the Great King, the church had not so much to do with it as we moderns imagine. Some things, it is true, are left to the brethren; such as the *reception of members*, the selection of officers," etc. (See *Christian Baptist*, vol. 6, pp. 236, 237.)

The same is true of the Episcopalians, Lutherans, and all other denominations. They *do judge* of the qualifications of applicants for membership and communion in their respective churches, and the New Testament makes it the duty of all to do it. The Lord Jesus Christ has established the *terms* of membership and communion in his churches, and every church is solemnly bound to debar all persons from her communion who have not, in her judgment, complied with those terms. The ordinances were committed to the churches (1 Cor. 10: 2), and Christ requires every church to guard his Table against unworthy persons, and to allow none to approach it except those who possess the *scriptural qualifications* for communion. If a church has no right to judge for itself of the fitness of its communicants, then it has no right to debar any person from the Lord's Table, and the holy ordinance is at once exposed to the unholy and profane. But the fact is, as we have shown, that all churches not only have the right thus to judge of the fitness of communicants, but they are solemnly bound to exercise that right; for the Lord's Supper is a *church* ordinance, and every church is responsible for its purity and safe keeping.

In conclusion we ask, What do Baptists more than others in regard to the Lord's Supper? We simply claim and exercise the right, in common with all Protestant churches, of interpreting the Scriptures for ourselves, and of judging accordingly of the fitness of applicants for membership and communion in our own churches. And if the objection urged against our practice had any force, it would rest as heavily against Mixed Communionists as against Baptists, for, as we have proved, they all claim the right to do themselves what they condemn in us. But the "legs of the lame are not equal."

3d OBJECTION: *"Church Communion, as held and practiced by the Baptists, unchristianizes all other Christians."*

This objection is based upon the false assumption that *Christian* fellowship and *church* fellowship are one and the same. They are not identical, however, but are essentially distinct, as we have already shown. Yet many honest Christians have fallen into this sad mistake through erroneous teaching and consequent prejudice. But our practice of Church Communion in no way whatever affects the Christian character of others. By our practice we simply declare our honest belief that they are *not baptized*, and consequently not *regular* church members; and, as such, we can not consistently and scripturally partake with them at the Lord's Table; for they, as well as we, hold that *valid* baptism and *regular* church membership are *indispensable prerequisites* to communion at the Lord's Table in any church. In the language of PROF. CURTIS, we say: "There is nothing in our views of the Lord's Supper to prevent our having the most perfect charity and fellowship, *as Christians*, with those who differ from us in many respects. We can and do commune with them *as such*. As indeed we never baptize any person until we believe him to be a *Christian already*, his baptism never can *introduce* him to our Christian fellowship. We never do regard, and never have regarded, the outward act of baptism as an *essential* to Christian character, and it is impossible we ever should. Nor do we any more refuse Christian communion with other denominations, than did the Savior with the seventy, or with his mother Mary, the blessed and highly favored among women." (*Curtis on Com.*, p. 93.)

Hence we see that the charge of "*unchristianizing*" others by our Church Communion is *false.* As before remarked, our practice simply declares that, in our judgment, they are *unbaptized*, and hence not *regular* church members; it does not in any sense reflect upon their Christian character. We regard all those who have heartily repented of their sins, and believed in Jesus Christ, as the children of God, and, as such, *fit subjects* for baptism; and we regard and treat all such persons of other denominations *precisely as we do our own candidates for baptism.* No Baptist church will receive any person as a candidate for baptism, unless he gives *scriptural evidence* of being "washed, justified, and sanctified in the name of the Lord Jesus, and by the Spirit of our God" (1 Cor. 6: 11); nor will any admit such a person to the Lord's Table, until he has been *baptized* on a profession of his faith, and *received* into regular church fellowship. There is nothing peculiar in our practice on this point. The advocates of Mixed Communion, as well as the Baptists, hold that Christ has placed valid baptism and regular Church membership *between* every believer and the Lord's Supper, and hence they all deny the bread and wine to their *candidates* for baptism. In the meantime, we regard our candidates for baptism as *brethren in Christ*, just as Ananias did Saul of Tarsus *previous* to his baptism (Acts 9 : 17); and we hold unrestricted *Christian* Communion with them, and love them, just as well *before* baptism as we do *after* they have submitted to the ordinance, notwithstanding we dare not admit them to the Lord's Table until they have complied with the *Lord's terms* of communion. Precisely so do we feel and act toward our brethren of other denominations. We love them as *Christians*, but can not consistently and scripturally extend to them the *tokens* of church fellowship, because we do not regard them baptized, and hence not regular church members. It is evident, therefore, that our practice of *Church* Communion in no way tends to *unchristianize* others, and it can not be so regarded by any, except those who consider baptism and the Lord's Supper as "*efficacious means of salvation.*"

In this particular, however, the Baptists act on principles *held in common* with Mixed Communionists. They treat their *candidates* for baptism, and all others whom they regard as *unbaptized*, precisely as we do; not one of them (except the *Methodists*, who violate their own declared principles by admitting "*seekers*" to the Lord's Table) will receive such persons to their communion *until* they have been baptized in some way and admitted to regular church membership, notwithstanding they may regard them *as Christians*. In this they are as *close* in their communion as we are, and act upon the very same principles. Yet no person ever supposed that they *unchristianized* their candidates for baptism and others by thus debarring them from the Lord's Table; they merely declare by the act that, in their judgment, such persons are *not baptized*, and of course *not church members*. Why, then, should the Baptists be charged with "*unchristianizing*" all others by doing only what all others do?

But even if it were as true, as it is false, that our practice of *Church* Communion does unchristianize others, it would be equally true of the practice of Mixed Communionists; for, while they charge us with "*close* communion," and vauntingly invite "*all Christians in good standing in their own churches*," still they actually debar from their communion *nineteen-twentieths* of those who profess to be Christians, all of whom are in *good standing* in their own churches, to say nothing of *infant members*, constituting *one-half* of Pedobaptist churches. For instance, there are about *one hundred and thirty* different denominations in Christendom, all claiming to be Christians, some *fifty* of whom reside in the United States; and not more than *eight* out of the whole number will admit each other's members to their communion tables. Of the seven different branches of the Presbyterian Church, there are *six* that hold the

Westminster Confession of Faith, and yet *no two* of them will commune together at the Lord's Table, although they subscribe to the *same creed*, and regard each other *as Christians*. Do they "*unchristianize*" each other by their *restricted* communion? Verily, Mixed Communionists should set their own houses in order before they stop to throw stones at the Baptists for doing the very thing which they themselves do.

Hence it is evident that our practice of *Church* Communion has no tendency whatever to "*unchristianize*" others, and even if it had, the same would be equally true of Mixed Communionists; for they all withhold their communion from many whom they admit to be Christians.

4th OBJECTION: "*Church Communion not only unchristianizes, but also unchurches all other denominations.*"

Well, if Mixed Communion churches are not *Gospel churches*, the sin rests upon *themselves*, and not upon the Baptists. If *valid* baptism be *essential* to visible membership in a church of Christ, as all admit, and if Campbellites and Pedobaptists be *destitute* of such baptism, as we verily believe, then it follows of necessity that they are not Gospel churches; and our practice of *Church* Communion merely *declares* an existing fact, for which we are in no way responsible. If Campbellite baptism be *defective* in its administrator, design, and subjects, as every intelligent Baptist must admit, then it is not scriptural and valid baptism; and, with such baptism, how can Campbellite churches be *Gospel* churches? And if Pedobaptist baptism be *defective* in its administrator, action, design, and subjects, as all Baptists must concede, then it can not be scriptural and valid baptism; and according to their own principles, Pedobaptist churches are not *Gospel* churches. But while this is unquestionably true, our practice of *Church* Communion is in no sense responsible for it; they have *unchurched themselves* by substituting immersion for the *actual* remission of sins, on the one hand, and adult and infant *sprinkling and pouring,* on the other hand, for believer's baptism. The remedy, however, for these evils is at hand, if they will employ it. We have A BAPTISM which they all *practically* admit to be both scriptural and valid, and our churches are, by universal consent, *Gospel churches;* all, therefore, can adopt *our baptism* and *our church polity* without sacrifice, and still they refuse to do it.

But this objection is founded upon the unscriptural idea of a "*universal visible church, of which all particular visible churches are branches.*" This error was the *root* of popery. Having imagined a "universal visible church," consistency required a "*visible head*" for the body, and the POPE, with his successors, was constituted that head. And all those Protestant churches, which either directly or indirectly came out of the Church of Rome, brought this error with them; hence arose "*Episcopal bishops,*" and *clerical denomination and rule* over the people, as well as *infant baptism and membership*, by which the very *constitution* and *government* of Christ's churches were radically changed.

Now, this erroneous assumption of a "universal visible church" is the very ground on which Mixed Communionists claim the *right* of all Christians in good standing in their own churches to partake of the Lord's Supper together. They say that "all who *profess* the true religion" (see *Presbyterian Confession of Faith*, chap. 25, sec. 2) are members of this "catholic" or "universal" church, and, therefore, have an *inalienable right* to partake of the Lord's Supper wherever they may find it. This no honest and intelligent advocate of mixed communion will deny. This, indeed, was the leading argument of the late ROBERT HALL (whose father brought this error with him from the Presbyterians) in support of his boasted "*Free* Communion;" and it is the only ground on which any can practice such communion.

But what is a *Gospel church* according to the Scriptures? In the New Testament the word *church* has *two*, and *only* two, significations, viz.: 1st. It is used *figuratively* to denote the *spiritual body of Christ*, embracing all the saved, living, and dead, in heaven and on earth (see Matt. 16: 18; Eph. 5: 25–27; Col. 1: 18; Heb. 12: 23, etc.); and 2d. It is used *literally* to denote *particular visible congregations of baptized believers*, each separate and independent, worshiping together statedly in one place; as *the church in Jerusalem*, Acts 11:

22; the church at Antioch, Acts 13: 1; the Church of God at Corinth, 1 Cor. 1: 2, etc.; and *churches of Judea*, Gal. 1: 22; churches of Galatia, 1 Cor. 16: 1; churches of Macedonia, 2 Cor. 8: 1, etc. The *spiritual* body or church of Christ has no ordinances, no visible organization, and never did and never will meet together on earth till the final judgment. To this body or church *all true believers* belong, of whatever name and order they may be, whether they have been baptized or not. Indeed, union with this spiritual body by faith is a *primary* qualification for baptism and membership in a visible church. But to *the visible churches of Christ*, as such, his laws and *ordinances* were committed (see 1 Cor. 11: 2), and they are the *executive bodies* in his visible kingdom; charged with discipline, formative and corrective, and the proper administration of baptism and the Lord's Supper.

In perfect accordance with these views, PROF. CURTIS remarks: "To the *visible churches* of Christ belong *ordinances* and *means of grace*, things temporary in their nature, and to be observed *only* 'till he come,' who is the Head of the Church. To the universal church, *as such*, which is a *spiritual*, and, therefore, *invisible* body, ordinances are impossible, since it *can not be convened;* and means of grace are unnecessary, since its members all drink from the fountain-head, and enjoy the *grace of the means.*" And he adds: "The records of church history plainly show that *originally* the Lord's Supper was every-where regarded as a *church ordinance.* For, even after centuries of gradual corruption had altered the forms of church government in many respects, and many separate congregations were united under the care of *one bishop*, and were considered as only *one church*, there was *ever one, and but one, altar* to each bishopric, at which alone the elements of the Eucharist were consecrated. To set up another altar or communion table was considered a violation of unity or a declaration of church independency." (*Curtis on Com.*, pp. 39 and 139.)

Such, then, are *Gospel churches*, and none others are Gospel churches. The New Testament knows nothing of a "*universal visible church*" with its numerous "*branches*," such as the Protestant Episcopal Church, the Presbyterian Church, the Methodist Episcopal Church, etc., embracing all the particular churches or societies belonging to those denominations. There is no such "*universal church*" with its "branches," and there never was any such Church of Christ. Hence the absurdity of representing the different denominations as "*branches* of the visible church," of which Mixed Communionists speak. If all these various denominations be the "branches," where is the *trunk?* There is no such trunk except the CHURCH OF ROME, and Baptists are not now, and never were, branches of that *rotten trunk;* for all history goes to show that we never had the remotest connection with that "MOTHER OF HARLOTS AND ABOMINATIONS." We are neither a daughter nor a granddaughter of such a mother.

But the *absolute independence* of all Baptist churches frees us from the charge of "*unchurching*" other denominations by our *Church* communion. For instance, one Baptist church is under no scriptural obligation to invite the members of other Baptist churches to partake with her at the Lord's Table, and yet the refusal to invite them on the part of one church would in no way interrupt the denominational relations and fellowship existing between all the churches, for each church is independent of all others, except so far as they may voluntarily associate themselves together as *advisory* and *coöperative* bodies for educational and missionary purposes. Hence, we see that Baptist *Church* Communion does not *unchurch* other denominations; they have unchurched themselves by their *unscriptural* baptism, in spite of our ceaseless protests against it.

5th Objection: "*Baptist Church Communion debars many pious persons from the Lord's Table who have been immersed.*"

In general, it would be a sufficient answer to this objection to state, that such persons belong to churches of other denominations, with whom we sustain no ecclesiastical connection whatever, and it would be *false in symbol* to extend to them the appointed *tokens* of visible church fellowship, when no such fellowship does nor can exist. Moreover, the Scriptures require every church to exercise a watchful and restraining *discipline* over all its communicants, and to debar unworthy persons from its communion table. In proof of this, see Rom. 16: 17; 1 Cor. 5: 4–12; 2 Thess. 3: 6, etc. Indeed, this duty grows out of the very nature of the Lord's Supper as a *church ordinance.* Now, since every church is required to discipline and restrain all its communicants, and since one church has no disciplinary power over the members of another church, it follows of necessity that we can not scripturally invite even the *immersed* members of other churches to partake with us at the Lord's Table. We have no right to extend our communion beyond *the limits* of our church discipline. And this of itself is a sufficient reason for our practice, were there no others.

But more particularly, those *immersed* persons in Pedobaptist churches are justly chargeable with "*walking disorderly,*" and we are "commanded" to "*withdraw ourselves*" (*i. e.,* our *church fellowship and communion*) from such (see 2 Thess. 3: 6); for, notwithstanding they have been immersed on a profession of their faith, still they are knowingly and willfully giving their influence and support to churches holding *fundamental errors,* which they do not and can not believe and practice; as, for instance, adult and infant *sprinkling and pouring* for believer's immersion, *sacramental salvation, clerical domination and rule,* and many others. Such persons are responsible to God and to men for their influence, and they are acting both *inconsist-*

ently and *wickedly* by thus continuing to give their influence and support to churches holding and propagating these grave errors. Nor will it excuse such immersed believers to plead, " *We do not believe and practice these errors.*" This is no doubt true; but no person thus holding Baptist sentiments, can belong to a Pedobaptist church without giving his or her influence to it, and virtually indorsing its errors, though he or she may not believe and practice them. In the language of PROF. CURTIS: " Such are their *terms* of membership, that a conscientious person, holding Baptist sentiments, could not join one of their churches. If he did, so are their *creeds, confessions of faith,* and *church covenants* framed, and that purposely, that he would be obliged to support INFANT BAPTISM. If he had children, he would be *pledged* to bring them forward for baptism. This a conscientious Baptist could not do. It is nothing to say that many, and an increasing number, do *practically* neglect it—neglect it because they have no faith in it. The STANDARDS of these churches are purposely so framed as to make it the *covenant obligation* of every member to conform to it." (*Curtis on Com.*, p. 98.)

Accordingly the PRESBYTERIAN CONFESSION OF FAITH, chap. 28, sec. 4, enjoins—" That *infants* of one or both believing parents *are to be baptized.*" The CONGREGATIONAL CONFESSION OF FAITH, chap. 29, sec. 4, enjoins the same duty upon parents. (See *Platforms*, p. 124.)

The METHODIST DISCIPLINE, Art. of Relig. 18, says: "*The baptism of young children is to be retained in the church;*" and in chap. 3, sec. 3, Ans. 5 to Question "What shall we do for the rising generation?" the Discipline says: "*Let the minister diligently instruct and exhort all parents to dedicate their children to the Lord in baptism as early as convenient; and—cause them to be faithfully instructed in the nature, design, privileges, and obligations of their baptism,*" etc.

And the EPISCOPALIAN BOOK OF COMMON PRAYER, Art. of Relig. 27, says: "*The baptism of young children is in anywise to be retained in the church,*" etc. So all Pedobaptist churches hold and teach. *Infant baptism* is a church doctrine and a church duty in all Pedobaptist bodies, and those members who do not believe and practice it, are guilty of willfully violating the *covenant vows* resting upon them.

Hence we see that it would not only be *inconsistent*, but *sinful* in Baptists to encourage immersed persons belonging to Pedobaptist churches, in such *disorder* and *wickedness*, by inviting them to the Lord's Table and giving them the *tokens* of regular church fellowship, and thereby become "*partakers* of their evil deeds." (See 2 John 9–11.) It is unkind and unreasonable to ask it.

But still more. Many of those pious persons have been immersed by *Pedobaptist ministers* who were never immersed themselves, and who are in the habit of denouncing immersion as "*unscrip-*

tural, indecent, and *dangerous;*" and of course they administered the ordinance reluctantly, not in obedience to Jesus Christ, but merely to gratify the "*whims*" of the candidates, and to prevent their joining the Baptists. While the Old School Presbyterians are very inconsistent in receiving Baptist immersions as baptism, they certainly deserve credit for ceasing to administer immersion to any one. Consistency and common honesty require all Pedobaptists either to abandon immersion or cease opposing it. Now we do not, and can not, regard such unauthorized and unwilling immersions as scriptural and valid baptism at all. Though the candidates may submit to it with proper intentions, yet the *administrators,* believing immersion to be "*unscriptural,* indecent, and dangerous," must administer the ordinance in *unbelief;* and "*whatsoever is not of faith is sin,*" says Paul, Rom. 14: 23. Now if they themselves regard immersion not only "indecent and dangerous," but "*unscriptural,*" as many of them say, how can they expect Baptists to recognize and regard it as scriptural baptism? And yet they do it; while some *modern* Baptist churches are *inconsistent enough* to receive it as baptism, though they would *exclude* their own ministers for holding and preaching the same errors. In our judgment there is *far less sin* in Pedobaptist sprinkling or pouring than there is in their immersions, though neither is scriptural and valid **baptism.** Such immersed persons, then, are deceived; they have *no baptism at all*, and therefore have no scriptural right to the Lord's Supper in any church.

And we would most affectionately address all such inconsistent and erring brethren and sisters in the language of Scripture: "*Wherefore come out from among them, and be ye separate, saith the Lord, and touch not the unclean thing; and I will receive you, and will be a Father unto you, and ye shall be my sons and daughters, saith the Lord Almighty.*" (2 Cor. 6: 17, 18.)

There are many pious persons among the CAMPBELLITES who were immersed on a profession of their faith by Baptist ministers *before* they entered the ranks of the "current reformation," with whom we do not and can not consistently and scripturally unite at the Lord's Table. They are not only members of other churches, and hence *beyond* the limits of our church discipline, but they were *excluded* from our churches on account of having embraced or fellowshiped the *errors* of ALEXANDER CAMPBELL; and while we still love many of them as brethren in Christ, yet we are bound to regard them as *excluded members in disorder and error*, and as such, we can neither invite them to our communion, nor accept an invitation to partake with them, without trampling upon our own church discipline and indorsing their *errors* and *irregularities*. And as the *causes* of their exclusion still exist, they have no more right to ask or expect intercommunion with us, than their own excluded members have to ask or expect it with them. Now, if they should ever renounce their errors and return to their former faith and practice, we would most cordially restore them to our church fellowship, and *then*, and not till then, can we consistently and scripturally extend to them the *tokens* of such fellowship. This, indeed, was the very ground on which the Old School Presbyterian General Assembly, in 1845, in the city of Philadelphia, refused the fraternal invitation of the New School General Assembly to unite with them in the joint celebration of the Lord's Supper; the former having excluded the latter from their church fellowship.

There are also pious persons among the Campbellites who never belonged to our churches, with whom we do not and can not commune at the Lord's Table. Some of them were converted under our own preaching, and others under that of Pedobaptists before they united with the Campbellites. They are fit subjects for baptism, and have been immersed by Campbellite preachers, but, like those immersed believers in Pedobaptist churches, they are "*walking disorderly*" by giving their influence and support to *radical errors;* and, as before shown, we are commanded to "*withdraw*" our church fellowship and communion from all such. (2 Thess. 3: 6.) Now, if these erring brethren and sisters have any confidence in their own conversion, they never can believe the peculiar doctrines of Campbellism : such as *baptismal remission*, etc., for they profess to have experienced pardon and peace through *faith* in Christ *previous* to baptism. All the religion they have they thus obtained *prior* to and *independent* of their baptism; and how can they believe that baptism is in order to *obtain* pardon? And yet they are giving their influence and support to a denomination whose distinguishing tenet is, that baptism is *equally necessary* with faith and repentance to forgiveness.

Now, such pious persons are not only living in *disorder* and *sin*, by thus giving their influence and support to this *soul destroying error*, but they are *destitute* of scriptural and valid baptism, although they have been immersed; and, as such, they are *disqualified* for communion at the Lord's Table in any church. Their baptism was radically defective both in its *administrator* and *design*, and hence is wanting in *two* of the four *essentials* to valid baptism. The authority of a *Gospel church* is necessary to qualify any man to administer the ordinances, as all admit, and, in our judgment, *Campbellite* ministers are not thus authorized; and even if they were, they administer baptism with an *unscriptural design*. Notwithstanding those pious persons professed to have obtained pardon and peace through *faith* in Jesus Christ *previous to* and *independent of* baptism, still those unauthorized preachers administered the ordinance to them in order to *obtain* the remission of their sins. The very act, therefore, involved a *contradiction*, and was *false in symbol.* No doubt the candidates submitted to the ordinance with the intention of obeying Jesus Christ, just as the believer may submit to Pedobaptist sprinkling or pouring, but the administrators performed the act with an *unscriptural design,* and hence the sin rests upon them, and not upon the candidates. Such immersion is far more *dangerous,* and no more valid than Pedobaptist sprinkling or pouring; the one is wrong in the administrator and action, while the other is wrong in the administrator and design; and both are equally unscriptural and invalid.

Nor can we, as Baptists, consistently and innocently indorse or recognize such unauthorized and unscriptural immersions as valid baptism, which we would do by intercommunion with such immersed persons. How is it possible for Baptists to indorse or receive such "*alien immersions*" as valid baptism without being guilty of the *grossest inconsistency,* not to say sin? *For illustration,* suppose a Baptist minister should embrace the *errors* of Campbellites and Pedobaptists on this subject, and, like their ministers, preach and practice those errors, would not his own church *exclude* him, and that *justly?* And should he continue to preach and practice the same errors while excluded, would any regular Baptist Church receive his immersions as valid baptism? But suppose he join either of said denominations holding and propagating those errors, and should immerse believers on a profession of their faith, would his immersions be any more valid? Surely not. How glaringly inconsistent, then, must it be in Baptist churches to indorse and receive the immersions of Campbellite and Pedobaptist ministers as *valid* baptism, when they deny the *validity* of their ordinations, and would *exclude* their own ministers for preaching and practicing the same errors that those ministers preach and practice!

Let *modern* Baptists, like the *apostles* and ancient *Anabaptists*, stand firm to God's truth, and *unitedly reject* all such unscriptural immersions, and we will not only have a conscience void of offense toward God and men, but we will receive *ten* of those deluded brethren and sisters to where we would receive *one* by admitting the validity of such immersions.

But in addition to these excluded Baptists and immersed converts in Campbellite churches, there is a large and growing number of *pure Campbellites*, who were immersed in order to *obtain* the remission of their sins, without professing a *previous* change of heart and pardon, with whom we do not and never can intercommune until they experience conversion and are scripturally baptized. No intelligent Baptist or Pedobaptist can regard such persons as either converted or baptized, and of course we can hold neither Christian nor sacramental communion with them, however highly we may esteem them as friends or relatives. Accordingly, no regular Baptist church will receive such immersed unbelievers as candidates for baptism, much less as church members, until they bring forth *"fruits meet"* for repentance, and give *scriptural evidence* of conversion. It is impossible that any person can be a Christian who depends upon baptism *in any sense* for pardon. A faith that does not secure pardon *before* baptism, will not secure it *in* baptism; and he who goes into the water unpardoned, will most certainly come out of the water unpardoned, though he may be satisfied with what he has done and indulge a *false* hope of heaven, just like the deluded Catholic. The fact is, baptismal remission changes the *whole ground* of salvation by grace through faith, and makes it of *works*. Hence the boastfulness of such persons.

It is evident, therefore, that either the Baptists or Campbellites are *destitute* of scriptural and valid baptism, for they differ as wide as the poles on the *design* of the ordinance. Both can not be right, and whichever party is wrong, has no valid baptism, and hence no scriptural right to the Lord's Supper in any church. This indeed is admitted by the *founder* of Campbellism himself. For instance, ALEXANDER CAMPBELL, in his " Christian Baptist," says: " When Paul was immersed, it was declared and understood by the parties that *all his previous sins were washed away in the act of immersion.*" (See *Christian Baptist*, vol. 5, Art. "*Ancient Gospel*," No. 3, p. 173.) And in his Lexington Debate with Dr. N. L. Rice, in 1843,

Mr. Campbell said: "If our baptism is for any other *end* or *purpose* than was that to which Paul submitted, it is *another* baptism, as much as bathing for health is different from a Jewish ablution for legal uncleannesss or impurity. The action has a *meaning* and a *design*; and it must be received in *that* meaning and for *that* design, else it is another baptism." (*Campbell and Rice Debate*, p. 439.)

Now, if this view of the *design* of baptism be correct, it necessarily *unbaptizes*, if not unchristianizes, the whole Baptist denomination, together with Mr. Campbell himself and all his ministers and people who left our churches, for not one of them was baptized in order to *obtain* the remission of sins, but all professed to have obtained forgiveness *previous* to baptism through *faith* in Christ. Hence it would seem that both they and we are destitute of valid baptism; and, as such, *unfit* for the Lord's Supper in any church. But while the whole Baptist family and every member of it *utterly repudiates* the doctrine of "baptismal remission," as held by Campbellites and others, still we admit the truth of Mr. Campbell's position, that an *error* in the design of baptism *invalidates* the ordinance and makes it "*another* baptism" than that to which Paul submitted; so that all those who have been immersed with a *wrong design*, are as really destitute of scriptural and valid baptism, as are those who have submitted to *sprinkling* or *pouring*. And such are all true Campbellites.

But a want of valid baptism is by no means the only reason why Baptists do not intercommune with Campbellites. We believe them to be *heterodox* in their views of repentance, faith, regeneration, justification, human depravity, spiritual influence, and other fundamental doctrines of the Gospel, as well as in their views of the design of baptism, and therefore we can not "*bid them Godspeed*" by receiving them to our communion, and thus giving them the appointed *tokens* of church fellowship, without becoming "*partakers*" of their evil deeds." (2 John 9–11.) These reasons are sufficient to justify the Baptists in refusing intercommunion at the Lord's Table with all Campbellites.

It is also true that there are a few small bodies of Baptists, including the Anti-Missionary, Free-Will, Seventh-Day, and others, who have seceded from the great Baptist body, with whom we do not and can not consistently intercommune, although we regard them as baptized Christians. They have no ecclesiastical connection with us, and hence are *beyond* the limits of our church discipline, and we have no scriptural right to extend our communion beyond the *limits* of our discipline. Besides, they are *factions*, and hold doctrines which we can not fellowship. Though baptized, they are destitute of some of the essential qualifications for communion at the Lord's Table. In short, the Lord's Supper, being a *church ordinance*, we can not consistently and safely commune with any except those with whom we sustain *church relations*.

6th OBJECTION: "*Baptist Church Communion divides God's people, and prevents Christian love and union.*"

Now we emphatically deny that the Baptists are in any proper sense responsible for the *divisions* which exist among God's people. There is nothing either in our principles or practices that legitimately tends to divide the Christian world. If others embrace error and oppose our scriptural principles and practices, and thus make them the *occasion* of division and strife, as our Lord foretold that they would do (see Matt. 10: 34-36), we are not accountable for their sins, any more than Christ was for the opposition to his teachings and practices. On the contrary, *Baptist principles* are the *only* principles upon which God's people ever can consistently and safely unite. Our views of doctrine, as all admit, are scriptural and sound, and will save all who heartily embrace them. We have an *undisputed* baptism and communion; all *practically* admit this fact. None blame us for what we *do believe and practice;* they only complain of what we *do not* believe and practice; while all can *adopt* our faith and practice without sacrifice.

Nor does Baptist Church Communion *prevent* Christian love and union. If it did, mixed communion would *promote* such love and union among those who practice it. That intercommunion at the Lord's Table has *no tendency* to promote Christian love and union among different denominations, is evident from the *fact* that there is quite as much, if not more, love and union between the Baptists and others, notwithstanding our *Church Communion,* than there is between the advocates of mixed communion themselves; and we oftener hold Christian communion together. Though a few denominations, and but a few, have professed to practice mixed communion for about sixty years past, still there is not at this moment any more brotherly love and union between these sects than there is between them and the Baptists. Is there now any more Christian love and union between the Episcopalians, Lutherans, Methodists, Presbyterians, Congregationalists, and Campbellites than there is between any or all of these sects and the Baptists? Let indisputable FACTS answer this question. *True*, these opposing sects come together *occasionally* in a kind of mass meeting, and, for the time being, suspend hostilities, while they professedly show their *love* one for another in a *joint celebration* of the Lord's Supper, and thus in fact unite in one common effort against *Baptist immersion*, under the odious name of "*close communion*"—just as "Herod and Pilate were made friends" on a certain day, in their common opposition to Jesus— but the volcanic fires of discord and strife burst forth again as soon as the baptismal controversy subsides, and the warfare continues until another communion season arrives, when the same solemn farce is repeated.

Accordingly, DR. T. G. JONES asks: "Are the intercommuning denominations more united than the non-intercommuning? Are Presbyterians and Methodists more affectionate toward each other than Presbyterians and Baptists? If so, is it brought about by free communion among them? We think not. The fact is that there is nothing in the nature of mere ceremonial communion peculiarly adapted to produce such union and coöperation. Practically, open communion is a nullity. It is a mere theory. Pedobaptists, while extolling it, rarely practice it." (See *The Baptist*, p. 159.) The same is true of the Campbellites and others. The practice has no tendency to unite Christians.

Hence we see that mixed communion has no tendency whatever to harmonize the views and feelings of different denominations, and to bring them together in love and union. The *causes* of separation between these different sects lie further back. They originate in an honest difference of sentiment in regard to the doctrines, ordinances, and requirements of the Gospel. Intercommunion can never remove these conscientious differences, nor has it any such tendency. They may now and then "strike a truce," and "vaunt their superior catholicity" by an *occasional* communion together, but still the Presbyterian remains a Presbyterian, the Methodist a Methodist, the Episcopalian an Episcopalian; and so of all the others.

Indeed, so far from mixed communion having a tendency to promote Christian love and union, it *needlessly exposes* our holy religion to the derision and scorn of the world. By the very act of intercommunion, the various sects profess, not only their mutual love as Christians, but also their *church fellowship*, when in fact no such fellowship does nor can exist between them. To-day they surround the communion table and professedly show their love one for another; tomorrow they engage in angry controversy and bitter denunciation. The world, seeing these things, holds religion accountable for such glaring inconsistencies and heartless professions of love and union; and thus Christ is wounded in the house of his professed friends.

Accordingly, Dr. Howell, speaking of the several Protestant denominations, justly remarks: " They all hold that manifest *corruption* in doctrine and worship is a *disqualification* for the reception of the Lord's Supper. Let that fact be remembered, and then how shall we answer the following interrogatories? Do not Methodists habitually and bitterly charge both these upon the Presbyterians, on the score of their *Calvinism?* Are the Presbyterians less ready and adroit in hurling back upon the Methodists the same imputations on the score of *Arminianism?* Each, too, has its own *internal* war, Old School, New School, Cumberland, Hopkinsian, and other Presbyterians; and Episcopal, Protestant, Whitefield, and other Methodists strive on the arena of ecclesiastical combat. Do they all commune together?

If they do, is it a feast of union, and the love of each other, for the truth's sake, which each *denies* is held by the other? If so, what means this clangor of arms, this shaking of shields, and the noise of their fierce combats which I hear? If they unite in love at the Lord's Table, why do they denounce each other in derision immediately after, in the conference, the session, and the pulpit?" Surely, if such tokens of brotherly love as these fail to unite the Christian world, then it will require *something more* than mixed communion to effect it! Hence it is manifest that *Church* Communion, as practiced by the Baptists, neither tends to divide God's people, nor to prevent Christian love and union on Christian principles.

7th OBJECTION: "*Baptist Church Communion is exclusive, illiberal, and selfish.*"

These and many similar charges are constantly being urged against our practice, not only by the ignorant and irresponsible, but also by such men as ALBERT BARNES, of Philadelphia, a Presbyterian writer of distinction. In his recent treatise on "EXCLUSIVISM," directed chiefly against the BAPTISTS, Dr. Barnes first classes us with "ROMAN CATHOLICS" on the score of "*exclusiveness*" (p. 3), and then prefers *specific charges* against us, among which are the following: (1.) He charges the Baptists with "deliberately, and on principle, *arrogating to themselves* whatever there is of sanctity and influence, in being in possession of a *true ministry* and *valid sacraments*" (p. 14). (2.) With *excluding* "all others from a public recognition as having any claim to the title of *Christians*," merely "on the ground of an *external rite* (p. 64). (3.) With *classing* "*all others but themselves*, so far as their act can go, and so far as they can have any influence, *with aliens and apostates, Saracens and skeptics, Brahminists and Buddhists*—shut out from any *covenanted* mercy, and any *promise* of heaven," simply "by *rebaptizing* all who enter their communion," and "by *excluding* from their *communion* all who have not been *subjected* to the rite of *immersion*" (p. 66); and (4.) As if to concentrate all these villainies into one, he charges the Baptists with uniting with the Church of Rome "in one of its *most offensive features*—in *claiming* to be the *only true church*, and in *denying* to every other church *all claim* to be regarded as *a part of the redeemed body of Christ*." (See *Exclusivism*, p. 21.) In conclusion, Dr. Barnes says: "We *claim* and *demand* of the Baptists, that they shall not merely recognize the *ministry* of other denominations, but their *membership also;* that while, if they prefer it, they may continue the practice of *immersion* in baptism as a part of their Christian liberty, they *shall* concede the same liberty to others, (*i. e.*, to practice adult and infant *sprinkling* or *pouring* for baptism;) and while they expect that *their* acts of baptism shall be recognized by others as valid, they *shall not* offer an affront to the Christian world by *rebaptizing* all who enter their communion, or by *excluding* from their *communion* all who have not been *subjected* to the rite of *immersion*. And we claim and demand of the Baptist churches that they shall recognize the members of other churches *as* members of the Church of Christ. We do not ask this as a boon, we claim it *as a right*." (See *Barnes on Exclusivism,* pp. 66 and 74.)

These are grave charges and high claims and demands. Are these charges true, and should these claims and demands be met by the Baptists? We must emphatically deny all these charges, and most positively refuse compliance with any of these claims and demands. We deny that our practice of Church Communion is *justly liable* to any such charges; and we also deny that Mixed Communionists have a *right* to make any such claims and demands upon us. But as Albert Barnes is a prominent minister of his denomination, and as he but utters the charges of all Mixed Communionists against our practice, and urges the claims and demands which all make upon us, we will briefly notice such as bear on the subject under consideration:

(1.) Then the Baptists are here charged with "*deliberately, and on principle, arrogating to themselves whatever there is of sanctity and influence in being in possession of a true ministry and of valid sacraments.*" (See *Barnes on Exclusivism,* p. 14.)

This is bold and strong language. To "*arrogate*" is "to make undue claims, from vanity or false pretensions to right or merit; as the Pope *arrogated* dominion over kings." (*Webster.*) Arrogance is a species of "moral usurpation; a compound of folly and insolence." (*Crabb.*) Now, are Baptists chargeable with such *arrogance* when they claim the sanctity and influence of a *true ministry?* Do not Mixed Communionists, including Dr. Barnes, admit that ours is a true ministry? Except the Episcopalians, who require Episcopal ordination, none will dispute this fact; and even Episcopalians admit the piety, the call, and the baptism of our ministry; they only deny the *validity* of our ordination. And the same is true, to the fullest extent, of the *sacraments* of baptism and the Lord's Supper as administered by Baptists. As has been shown, all denominations *practically* admit the *validity* of our baptism, and none object to our *communion*, except as to its restriction. Baptists have an *undisputed baptism and communion.* The charge of "arrogance," then, can be preferred against us *only* on the supposition that we set up an *exclusive* claim to a true ministry and valid sacraments.

Do we urge such a claim, in the sense here charged against us? That we do not, in relation to the *ministry*, all must admit who understand our views. We deny that preaching is an *official* act. Our *licentiates* as truly preach the Gospel as our *ordained* ministers; and we maintain that a call to preach lies *back* of ordinances and ordination, and imposes the duty upon every man who is divinely called, independent of ordination. Hence we encourage all in our churches to preach the Gospel, who give satisfactory evidence of personal piety and a divine call to the work, previous to ordination. Nor is there any thing in our views to prevent us from encouraging all *such men* of other denominations to preach the truth, though we may regard them in error on some points of faith and practice; and in doing this we by no means indorse their errors. There is no compromise of principle, or inconsistency, therefore, in our recognizing, as *ministers of Christ*, so far as preaching is concerned, those whom we can not receive as *communicants* at the Lord's Table; over whom we have no disciplinary control, and whom we believe to be destitute of some of the essential qualifications for communion.

But, while preaching is not an official act, the administration of the sacraments *is such;* and hence we maintain that no man, however pious and gifted he may be, has a scriptural right to administer baptism to others who has not only been baptized on a profession of his faith, but also *ordained* by the authority of a Gospel church. The ordinances were originally committed to the *churches* (see 1 Cor. 11 : 2), and the authority to administer them can be derived only *from* the churches, through regular ordination by a presbytery. This is unquestionably *Gospel order;* nor does the New Testament furnish either precept or example to the contrary. And in this view we are sustained by all Pedobaptists. The PRESBYTERIANS, to whom Dr. Barnes belongs, may speak for all on this point: "There be only two sacraments ordained by Christ our Lord in the Gospel, that is to say, baptism and the supper of the Lord; *neither of which may be dispensed by any but by a minister of the word, lawfully ordained."* (See *Confession of Faith*, chap. 27, sec. 4.) In this sense, then, and in no other, do we claim "whatever there is of sanctity and influence in being in possession of *a true ministry*," for none others have received *such ordination* by the authority of a Gospel church. And this is the reason why the Baptists not only baptize, but also *ordain*, all those ministers who come from other denominations, *before* they allow them to administer the ordinances. If we recognize the baptism of others as valid, we are bound to recognize their ordination as valid also; and the very fact that no Baptist church will receive their ordination, proves that we ought not to receive their baptisms.

Hence, while we can and do admit the right of all suitable men to preach the Gospel, though they may be irregular as to baptism and ordination, still we do not, and can not, recognize the *official right* of any to administer the ordinances, except our own *ordained* ministers; nor can we consistently and scripturally receive even the *immersions* of others as *valid* baptism, or welcome them to the Lord's Table. *True,* it is the duty of every man who is called to preach to be baptized on a profession of his faith, but the neglect of one duty can never release him from the obligation to exercise his gifts; and hence it is perfectly consistent in Baptists to encourage all such men to preach who hold truth enough to save souls, while they debar them from their communion and reject their baptisms. It is plain, therefore, that laying "an exclusive claim to the possession of a true ministry is one thing, and not inviting the ministers of other denominations to leave their own communion table and partake at ours is quite another thing." (See *Dr. Smith's Letter to Albert Barnes in answer to Exclusivism*, page 21.)

But do we lay *exclusive* claim to the possession of *valid sacraments?* In one sense we do, but in another we do not. The Baptists, as a body, do now, and always have claimed, that *immersion*, as held and practiced by them, is the *only* scriptural baptism; that of all others being *radically defective* in one or more of the *essentials* to valid baptism; and, as a *positive* ordinance, baptism must be *scriptural*, not only in its action, but also in its administrator, design, and subjects, or it is not valid baptism. The fact that some modern Baptist churches may occasionally receive "*alien immersions*" as baptism only evinces their own inconsistency; not so did the Apostles and ancient *Anabaptists*, as the New Testament and ecclesiastical history clearly prove. When Paul found "*certain disciples*" at Ephesus, whose baptism was *defective* in its administrator and design, he instructed them more perfectly and then baptized them on a profession of their faith, just as if they had not been immersed (Acts 19: 1–7); and the pages of church history are stained with the blood of martyred Baptists, whose only crime was, that they refused to recognize the *validity* of Pedobaptist *immersion,* especially that of *infants.* No considerations of *expediency* could induce those faithful and true witnesses of Christ to receive such unscriptural baptisms. They baptized *all* those who came into their churches from other denominations. Hence they were reproachfully styled *Anabaptists*; a name which they repudiated.*

Are we told that this theory involves "*an unbroken succession of authorized administrators of baptism from the Apostles till now?*" With the New Testament in our hands, we boldly claim such a succession, whether we can trace it through the labyrinths of uninspired history or not. We have the *infallible promise* of the Savior that "*the gates of hell should not prevail against his Church,*" built as is each of all his true churches by faith upon himself—the *foundation-stone* laid in Zion (see Matt.

---

* See *Mosheim's Church History,* vol. 2, chap. 5, sec. 2, p. 296. See my "MISSILES OF TRUTH," No. 2, on "A SCRIPTURAL ADMINISTRATOR OF BAPTISM," by Geo. S. Blanchard & Co. Price 25 cents single copy, postpaid, or five copies for $1.00.

16: 16–18; 1 Pet. 2: 4–6); and we believe that promise, though we might not be able to trace its fulfillment. Then we have the *special providence* of that God who has promised never to leave nor forsake his people. And we claim that *history*, recorded by our opponents, links the Baptists of to-day with the Baptists of apostolic times. It devolves upon those who deny this claim to disprove it; the burden of proof is upon them, and not upon the Baptists.

But we are told that "ROGER WILLIAMS, the reputed founder of American Baptists, was immersed by Ezekiel Holliman, an *unauthorized layman*, and thus the chain of our succession was broken." What if Roger Williams was baptized by an *unauthorized* man? Does that disprove the fact that baptism, to be *valid*, must be administered by an *authorized* administrator? By no means. It only proves that the great champion of civil and religious liberty was a Baptist, but destitute of scriptural and valid baptism. We deny, however, that any American Baptist living owes his baptism to Roger Williams, or to any one baptized by him. What are the *facts of history* on this point? Roger Williams was baptized by Ezekiel Holliman, March, 1639, and then he baptized Holliman and ten other persons. These formed a church or society, of which Williams became the pastor. In July following, *four months* after his baptism, Williams left the church, and never returned to it — being in doubt as to the validity of his baptism. The church thus formed "came to nothing," or dissolved soon after he left it. About ten years after this, another church was formed, under MR. THOMAS OLNEY as its pastor, the *only* minister ever baptized by Williams. Olney continued to serve the church until his death, in 1682, something over thirty years. The church gradually declined, and became extinct about the year 1718. No ministers are known to have gone out from Olney's church. Olney's baptism, therefore, whether valid or invalid, was not propagated. No other Baptist minister received his baptism from Roger Williams, or from any one whose baptism descended from his. The Baptist churches of America, then, did not, and could not, have descended from Roger Williams, or from the ephemeral society formed by him. Their true descent is from the Baptist churches of Piedmont and Wales, extending back to the days of the Apostles.

The slanderous charge, therefore, so often repeated by Mixed Communionists, that American Baptists *originated* with Roger Williams, and that his baptism being defective, *ours* must also be defective, is refuted by the established facts that Williams never baptized *any one* who became a minister, save *Thomas Olney;* and that Olney baptized *no one who baptized others;* and consequently their irregular baptisms perished with them and the few private persons whom they baptized.

With all due respect to that great and good

man, we acknowledge no ecclesiastical dependence upon him or any other man; we claim to be "built upon the *foundation* of the Apostles and prophets, JESUS CHRIST HIMSELF BEING THE CORNERSTONE" (Eph. 2: 20), and to keep *" the ordinances" as they were first delivered to the churches*. And though it may be difficult to trace back the stream of our ecclesiastical descent through the "*depths of antiquity*," still we maintain that it did exist, and that it finds its source in Christ and his Apostles.

But this *exclusive* claim to valid baptism by no means requires that we should be able to trace our apostolic succession back through the conflicting and erring records of ecclesiastical history, any more than we are required to trace our genealogy back to Adam in order to prove that we are his true descendants. We claim to be able to prove from the New Testament that, in every essential particular, the apostolic churches and Baptist churches are *identical;* and, in the truthful language of DR. T. G. JONES, president of Richmond College, Va., "We respectfully submit, that in view of this identity, the latter have a right to claim that they are the *true representatives* and *proper successors* of the former, without being under any *real necessity* of tracing a chain of succession, and showing that no single link is wanting in that chain. Many a link in the deep darkness of the long and dreary past, amid its revolutions and convulsions, may have been visible to the eye of GOD, nay, to the eyes of *men* then living, yet invisible to ours.

"For many centuries we have no connected and complete history of certain nations of marked peculiarities. Who doubts their continued existence throughout every hiatus in their history? For many centuries there was no *written* history of the human race. Yet who doubts the existence of the race? It existed as really and certainly during all the unrecorded centuries as during the historic ages. Its existence was in no manner dependent either upon the knowledge or the ignorance of men unborn. The first man, Adam, stood at one end of the line; another man, *just like him,* stood at the other. Is it difficult to believe, however wide and dark the interval which separated them, that the latter was the true and proper successor of the former? So the churches of the apostolic age stand at one end of the ecclesiastical line; the Baptists, *just like them,* stand at the other. Why doubt that the line has been continuous—though we may, in the darkness, or because of our own defective vision, be unable to see its *whole extent*—and that those who stand at this end, are the *true* descendants and successors of those who stand at that?" (See *The Baptists,* pp. 37, 38.)

Or, in the bold and strong language of DR. J. WHEATON SMITH to Albert Barnes, we say, that "Whatever is *found* in the New Testament is as worthy as if you traced it there. It is only a *doubtful* practice whose thread must be traced thus carefully through the labyrinth of history with painful uncertainty, lest you reach its end while yet a century or two from Christ. Why, sir, if between us and the apostolic age there yawned a *fathomless abyss*, into whose silent darkness intervening history had fallen, with a Baptist church on this side, and a New Testament on the other, we should boldly *bridge* the gulf and look for the record of our birth among the hills of Galilee. But our history is not thus lost. That work is now in progress which will link the Baptists of to-day with the Baptists of Jerusalem." (*Letter in answer to Exclusivism,* pp. 37, 38.) Although the Baptists " own no subjection, and acknowledge no dependence either on contemporary churches of their own country, or upon the churches of other lands or other times, except as those churches have held the same truth, clung to the same Head, and have exhibited the same spirit," but look directly and for themselves to the Savior, who pledged his presence to the end of the world, where two or three are gathered together in his name, still they claim a *real succession or continuity* of faith and practice from the Apostles; and this claim based upon the infallible record of God's word, is acknowledged and sustained by ecclesiastical history as written by their opponents, only a *specimen* of which can be admitted here. For example—

DR. MOSHEIM (Lutheran), speaking of the *Ana-*

baptists, says: "The origin of that sect, which acquired the denomination of *Anabaptists*, by their administering *anew* the rite of baptism to those who came over to their communion, and derived that of *Mennonites* from the famous man to whom they owe the greatest part of their present felicity, is *hidden in the depths of antiquity*, and is, of consequence, extremely difficult to be ascertained. This uncertainty will not appear surprising when it is considered that this sect started up suddenly in several countries at the same point of time, under leaders of different talents and different intentions, and at the very period when the first contests of the reformers with the Roman pontiffs drew the attention of the world, and employed the pens of the learned in such a manner as to render all other objects and incidents almost matters of indifference. The modern Mennonites (or Anabaptists) not only consider themselves as the descendants of the *Waldenses*, who were so grievously oppressed and persecuted by the despotic heads of the Romish Church, but pretend, moreover, to be the purest offspring of these respectable sufferers, being equally averse to all principles of rebellion on the one hand, and all suggestions of fanaticism on the other.

"It may be observed," continues Mosheim, "that the Mennonites (or Anabaptists) are not *entirely* in an error when they boast of their descent from the Waldenses, Petrobrussians, and other ancient sects who are usually considered as *witnesses of the truth* in times of general darkness and superstition. *Before the rise of Luther and Calvin*, there lay concealed in almost all the countries of Europe, particularly in Bohemia, Moravia, Switzerland, and Germany, *many persons* who adhered tenaciously to the following doctrine, which the Waldenses, Wickliffites, and Hussites had maintained, viz.: 'That the kingdom of Christ, or the visible church which he established on earth, was *an assembly of true and real saints,*' etc. This maxim is the true source of all the *peculiarities* that are to be found in the religious doctrine and discipline of the *Mennonites;* and it is most certain that the greatest part of these pecularities were approved by many of those who, *before the dawn of the Reformation,* entertained the notion already mentioned relating to the visible Church of Christ." (See *Mosheim's Church Hist.*, vol. 2, chap. 3, secs. 1 and 2, pp. 127, 128.)

"To the great Waldensian fraternity," says DR. T. G. JONES, "belonged the so-called German Anabaptists and the Mennonites or Dutch Baptists, to whose *high antiquity and apostolic origin*, testimony of the greatest weight by their opponents is borne. CARDINAL HOSIUS, president of the Council of Trent, who, as a Papist, certainly can not be charged with being too favorable to them, affirmed that the Baptists, or Anabaptists, as they were then called, had existed for *twelve hundred years.* ZUINGLIUS, a little earlier, says for *thirteen hundred years*—which would carry the Baptists up to the third century, when *immersion* was univerally practiced as baptism, save, perhaps, in a few cases of extreme illness," etc. And Dr. Jones adds:

"The writer of the article on the Baptists, in the Edinburgh Encyclopedia, says: 'It must have already occurred to our readers that the Baptists are the same sect of Christians which we formerly described under the appellation of *Anabaptists*. It is but justice to acknowledge that they *reject* the latter appellation with disdain, and maintain that, as none of the forms adopted by other churches are consonant to Scripture, the baptism of those churches is in reality *no baptism*. Hence, in their opinion, they do not *re*-baptize. Indeed, *this seems to have been their great leading principle* FROM THE TIME OF TERTULLIAN (A. D. 160–245) *to the present day.*'" (See *The Baptists*, pp. 86–88.)

Not only Mosheim, but Limborch, Neander, and a host of other Pedobaptist historians bear unwilling testimony to the *apostolic origin and succession* of the Baptists. Suffice it to say, that within the present century, the king of Holland appointed his chaplain, Dr. J. J. Dermont, and Dr. Upeig, Professor of Theology in the University of Groningen, both of the *Dutch Reformed Church*, to draw up a permanent history of the Dutch Baptists. In the authentic volume which they prepared and published at Breda, in

1819, they arrive at the following deliberate conclusion:

"We have now seen that the Baptists, who were formerly called Anabaptists, and in later times, Mennonites, were the *original Waldenses*, and who long in the history of the church, received the honor of that origin. *On this account the Baptists may be considered as the only Christian community which has stood since the days of the apostles, and as a Christian society which has preserved pure the doctrines of the Gospel through all ages.* The perfectly correct *external* and *internal* economy of the Baptist denomination tends to confirm the truth, disputed by the Romish Church, that the Reformation brought about in the sixteenth century, was in the highest degree necessary, and at the same time *goes to refute the erroneous notion of the Catholics that their communion is the most ancient.*" (See *Hist. Neth. Ref. Ch.*, as quoted in S. Bap. Rev., of April, 1859.)

Such is but a *specimen* of Pedobaptist testimony, all combining to prove that the Baptists are the *true representatives* and *real successors* of the Apostles; and as such, they "deliberately, and on principle" claim of *right* "whatever there is of sanctity and influence, in being in possession of a *true* ministry and of *valid* sacraments." In this sense, then, we do claim to be in possession of the *only* scriptural and valid baptism. But in another and important sense we do not claim the exclusive "*possession*" and *use* of "valid sacraments." To all our brethren of other denominations we affectionately say, abandon your errors on this subject, and heartily receive and practice the "*one baptism*," on a profession of the "*one faith*" in the "ONE LORD" (Eph. 4: 5), and the baptismal controversy will end forever. We claim no monopoly; neither sanctity nor sacraments belong exclusively to us; we only claim "whatever there is of sanctity and influence in being in possession of a *true* ministry and of *valid* sacraments." And, while we deny the *validity* even of Campbellite and Pedobaptist *immersions*, for the reasons already given, still we say to every true believer among them, come and welcome, and receive a baptism which *all practically admit* to be both scriptural and valid; and thus at once remove the *great barrier* to intercommunion at the Lord's Table. Where, then, is the "arrogance" of our claims, or the "exclusiveness" of our practice? And what becomes of the *bold assertions* of Albert Barnes, that "as a denomination they (the Baptists) are *but of yesterday?*" And he adds: "We go but a little way back in history till we come to a point when, if their theory is correct, there *was* no true church on earth. There is as little in *their* origin to be proud of as there is in the origin of *any* organization, civil or ecclesiastical, that has from a humble beginning worked its way into respectability." (See *Exclusivism*, p. 17.) Now, if such men as Albert Barnes display such a reckless disregard of the facts of history, what may we expect from the misguided and prejudiced multitudes who look to them for instruction? For the present, we must hand Mr. Barnes over to his more candid Pedobaptist brethren, who reluctantly admit that "THE BAPTISTS MAY BE CONSIDERED AS THE ONLY CHRISTIAN COMMUNITY WHICH HAS STOOD SINCE THE DAYS OF THE APOSTLES, AND AS A CHRISTIAN SOCIETY WHICH HAS PRESERVED PURE THE DOCTRINES OF THE GOSPEL IN ALL AGES." (See *Hist. Neth. Ref. Ch.* as above.) And in the language of the late DR. WAYLAND, we say: "Our *whole history* is in the highest degree honorable to us as a Christian sect. If any sect 'has occasion to glory, we more.' If any man among us does not feel a manly pride in the *sentiments* which have distinguished us, and in the *manner* in which we have maintained them, there must exist something peculiar, either in his head or his heart." (See *Principles and Practices of Baptists*, Note 21, pp. 121, 122.)

(2.) We are charged with *excluding* "*all others from a public recognition as having any claim to the title of* CHRISTIANS," merely "*on the ground of an external rite.*" (See *Barnes on Exclusivism*, p. 64.) This charge confounds *Christian* fellowship and *church* fellowship, as is usual with the advocates of mixed communion. As we have shown, the two things are entirely distinct, and the one may and often does exist in the absence of the other. This charge, therefore, is simply *false*, and is based upon an error of Dr. Barnes, held in common with all Mixed Communionists. We have Christian fellowship for all Christians so far as we know them, independent of baptism and church connections, just as we do for our own candidates for baptism; and we publicly recognize their " claim to the title of *Christians,*" by all those acts and exercises which pertain to the "communion of saints" *as such.* None are more liberal and unrestricted in *Christian* communion than the Baptists. But we can have church fellowship for those *only* with whom we sustain visible church relations, and, as no such relations exist between us and other denominations, we can not consistently and scripturally extend to them the appointed *tokens* of church fellowship. In a word, we hold *spiritual* communion with all those with whom we are spiritually united by faith in Christ, and *ceremonial* communion with those *only* with whom we ceremonially agree; and this is both reasonable and scriptural. Hence it is evident that our practice of *Church* Communion does not deny others " any claim to the title of *Christians,*" but merely denies them the *tokens* of visible church fellowship, which in fact does not and can not exist between Baptists and others.

(3.) The Baptists are charged with *classing* "*all others but themselves,* so far as their act can go, and so far as they can have any influence, *with aliens and apostates, Saracens and skeptics, Brahminists and Buddhists*—shut out from any *covenanted* mercy, and any *promise* of heaven," simply "by *re-baptizing* all who enter their communion," and " by *excluding* from their *communion* all who have not been *subjected* to the rite of *immersion.*" (See Barnes on *Exclusivism,* p. 66.)

Candor compels us to say that there is not one word of truth in this charge. And did we not know something of the strength of early education, the inveteracy of prejudice, the pride of position, and the almost invincible power of social and ecclesiastical connections, it would seem to us utterly unaccountable that a minister of the reputed intelligence and piety of Albert Barnes should have *deliberately written* such a charge against the Baptists in this age. Did he not *know* that we acknowledge "all others" who give satisfactory evidence of conversion, as our brethren in Christ, entitled to "covenant mercy" and the "promise of heaven" equally with ourselves, independent of external ordinances and visible church relations? Did he not *know* that the Baptists never immerse any person who does not profess a *previous* change of heart and remission of sins through faith in Christ; and that "by *re-baptizing* all who enter their communion" or fellowship they regard them as pious but *unbaptized?* Did he not *know* that Baptists practice Church Communion on the *same principles* upon which others practice mixed communion; and that "by *excluding* from their *communion* all who have not been *subjected* to the rite of *immersion,*" they do not unchristianize, but merely *unbaptize* them by that act? And did he not *know* that by making this charge against the Baptists he was misrepresenting and slandering a denomination of Christians, which he is *forced* to acknowledge, "*has reached a respectable, an honorable, and an influential position in the world, and is to be among the permanent arrangements for securing the spread of the Gospel on earth?*" (See *Barnes on Exclusivism*, p. 17.) Now if Albert Barnes knew not these facts when he wrote this charge, he was without excuse, for he *might* have known them; but if he did know them, then he is justly chargeable with *misrepresenting* and *slandering* "a respectable, an honorable, and an influential" denomination of acknowledged Christians.

(4.) The Baptists are charged with uniting with the Roman Catholic Church "in one of its *most offensive features*—in claiming to be the *only true church*, and in denying to every other church *all claim* to be regarded as *a part of the redeemed body of Christ*." (See *Barnes on Exclusivism*, p. 21.)

This charge is, in fact, the embodiment of all the other charges alleged against us by Dr. Barnes, and hence has been virtually answered, except as to our "claiming to be the *only true church*." It has been shown that our practice of *believer's* baptism and of *Church* Communion does not deny to any church the claim to be regarded as "a part of the redeemed body of Christ." Indeed, the Baptists maintain that *all true believers* constitute "a part of the redeemed body of Christ," and that none but believers are *fit subjects* for baptism.

They also maintain that *only* baptized believers are qualified for membership in a visible church of Christ, and that none but regular members of such a church have a scriptural right to the Lord's Table. On this point all practically agree with the Baptists. The Lord's Supper being a church ordinance, and valid baptism being essential to visible church membership, as all admit, our practice of *Church* Communion follows as a necessary consequence. It is on this very ground that Mixed Communionists debar their *own candidates for baptism* from the Lord's Table, though they regard them as "a part of the redeemed body of Christ;" just as the Baptists do their candidates for baptism. Hence it is plain that, by our practice of Church Communion, we simply deny "to every other church *all claim* to be regarded as" *baptized*, while we freely admit that the pious of all churches form "a part of the redeemed body of Christ."

But we are charged with "claiming to be the *only true Church*." This charge is based upon the Pedobaptist idea of a "*universal visible Church*," with the several Protestant churches as its "*branches*." (See Presbyterian *Confession of Faith*, chap. 25, sec. 2.) This may be true of those Protestant denominations which either directly or indirectly came out of the Church of Rome; such as the Church of England, and the Protestant Episcopal Church, the Presbyterian Church, the Methodist Episcopal Church, etc., of the United

States. But the New Testament knows nothing of a "universal visible church" with its various "branches." As we have shown, the word *church*, in its scriptural use, has but *two* significations, a figurative and a literal. It is used, (1.) *Figuratively* to denote *the spiritual body or Church of Christ*, embracing all the saved in heaven and on earth, and hence is *invisible*, as in Eph. 5: 25–27, and Heb. 12: 23; and (2.) It is used *literally* to denote *particular visible congregations of baptized believers*, each separate and independent, holding the doctrines and observing the ordinances of the Gospel, and worshiping together statedly in one place, with its pastor and deacons as its only scriptural officers; as for example, the *Church at Philippi* (chap. 1: 1), and the *churches of Macedonia* (2 Cor. 8: 1.) All true believers of all denominations and of no denomination belong to this spiritual body or Church of Christ, and are *fit subjects* for baptism and visible church membership. But none are, or can be, members of a visible church of Christ without immersion in water, into the name of the Trinity, on a personal profession of faith, with a proper design, by a scriptural administrator, and none have such baptism but the Baptists. In this sense, then, and in no other, do we claim to be the *only true churches* of Jesus Christ on earth, while we cheerfully admit that all the pious of other denominations are members of the *spiritual body or church of Christ*, and are religious societies, but not Gospel churches.

Hence, while we can and do, so far as they will permit, hold unrestricted *Christian* communion with the pious of all denominations, just as we do with our own candidates for baptism, we do not and can not hold *Church Communion* at the Lord's Table with any, except those with whom we are united in *church relations;* it would be *false* in symbol to do so.

Nor must the peculiarity of our views of the nature and constitution of a Gospel church be overlooked in considering the question of *Church* Communion. We have never acknowledged a visible and organized church *universal.* We have always contended that the people of God are, so far as they sustain outward church relations, comprised in *independent churches*, rather than in a *confederated church.* There are Baptist churches, and there is the Baptist denomination, but there is no such thing as *the Baptist Church,* embracing all our churches. In the language of a recent writer, we say: "It is not a *confederation* of Baptist churches, nor a continued *succession* of Baptist churches, that is the Baptist Church, but every local, independent body of baptized believers, holding the doctrines of the Gospel, and having the ordinances of the Gospel, that now exists, or has at any time or in any place existed, is and was *the Baptist Church* in the only sense in which there can be any such thing as the Baptist Church." (See *Inq. into Waldensian Origin of Dutch Baptists,* in So. Bap. Rev. for April, 1857.) And, in the language of Dr. Ripley, we add: "A church that came into existence yesterday, in strict conformity to the New Testament principles of membership, far away from any long-existing church or company of churches, and therefore unable to trace an outward lineal descent, is a true church of Christ—for Christianity is not a religion of circumstances, but of principles; while a church so called, not standing on the apostolic principles of faith and practice, and yet able to look back through a long line up to time immemorial, may have never belonged to that body of which Christ is the Head." (See *Intro. to Crowell's Ch. Manual*, p. 4.) Hence we see that the perfect *independency* of Baptist churches entirely frees us from the charge of *unchurching*, much less of *unchristianizing* other churches by our practice of Church Communion, whatever may be our views of those churches. Indeed, we deny the right of members of one Baptist church to communion in another Baptist church *as a right;* they can only partake by *invitation*. Nor is one Baptist church bound to invite to its communion the members of other Baptist churches; and yet we neither unchristianize nor unchurch each other.

It is manifest, therefore, that the Baptists can not, and ought not, to yield to the high *claims* and *demands* of modern Mixed Communionists, as set up by Albert Barnes, who says: "We *claim* and *demand* of the Baptists that they shall not merely recognize the *ministry* of other denominations, but their *membership also;* that while, if they prefer it, they may continue the practice of *immersion* in baptism as a part of their Christian liberty, they *shall* concede the same liberty to others, (*i. e.*, *to substitute adult and infant sprinkling and pouring* for believer's immersion;) and while they expect that *their* acts of baptism shall be recognized by others as valid, they *shall not* offer an affront to the Christian world by *rebaptizing* all who enter their communion, or by *excluding* from their *communion* all who have not been *subjected* to the rite of *immersion.* . . . . And—we *claim* and *demand* of the Baptist churches that they *shall recognize* the members of other churches *as* members of the Church of Christ. We do not ask this as a boon; we claim it *as a right.*" (See *Barnes on Exclusivism*, pp. 66 and 74.) Now, our forefathers of New England and Old Virginia were accustomed to such high claims and demands as these, but, thanks to a kind Providence, circumstances have changed. Yet this is the same spirit which led the Puritan fathers to banish Roger Williams, and to fine, imprison, and whip other Baptists for conscience' sake; and if DR. BARNES had the power, the spirit which prompted him to prefer such charges and to make such claims and demands of the Baptists, would, doubtless, prompt him to treat us *now* as the Puritans treated our forefathers. But the principles of civil and religious liberty, for which the Baptists contended and suffered then, have gloriously triumphed;

and we now enjoy the inalienable right to worship God according to the dictates of our own consciences, and, like our persecuted ancestors, we shall obey God rather than men, though it may subject us to similar persecutions.

Then Pedobaptists had the power, and, true to their principles, they not only *excluded* us from their communion tables as heretics, but also closed our meeting-houses, fined our church members, and imprisoned and whipped our ministers. But *now,* since our denomination, in the language of ALBERT BARNES, " *has* reached a respectable, an honorable, and an influential position in the world" (see *Exclusivism,* p. 17), they boldly "claim and demand, *as a right,*" that the Baptists shall not only recognize their *ministry,* but also indorse their *Pedobaptism,* and recognize their human organizations *as Gospel churches,* by admitting the *validity* of their baptism and receiving them to the Lord's Table. This, as conscientious Baptists, we can never do. While we cheerfully admit the piety and intelligence of their ministry and membership generally, and recognize them as brethren in Christ by all those Christian acts and exercises which belong to "the communion of saints," *as such,* still we do not, and can not, recognize the baptism and ordination of their ministers or the qualifications of their members for the Lord's Supper by receiving them to our communion.

We are not only charged with being "exclusive," but also "*illiberal*" in our practice of Church Communion. Now we boldly deny this charge, and claim to be even *more liberal* in our practice than Mixed Communionists themselves. We have seen that the Baptists and others agree in theory as to the *qualifications* for the Lord's Supper. They all maintain that the new birth, valid baptism, and regular church membership, are *indispensable prerequisites* to communion at the Lord's Table. This no honest and intelligent Pedobaptist or Campbellite will deny. Accordingly, they all withhold the communion from their *own candidates* for baptism, though they regard them converted; and Pedobaptists debar their *infant members* from their communion tables, though they regard them baptized; while the Baptists admit all their own members to the Lord's Table. In this we are more liberal than Mixed Communionists themselves.

The real issue, however, between the Baptists and others respects *baptism* rather than the Lord's Supper. This, as we have seen, many candid Mixed Communionists admit. In the language of Dr. Hibbard, "The only question, then, that here divides us, is: '*What is essential to valid baptism.*'" (See *Hibbard on Bap.*, part. 2, chap. 11, p. 174.) And even if it could be shown that the Baptists are in error upon the subject of baptism, they would not be chargeable with *illiberality* in their practice of Church Communion. In common with all others, we believe that none but the *baptized* are entitled to communion at the Lord's Table. And we believe that none are baptized, except such as have been *immersed in water into the name of the Trinity, upon a personal profession of faith, with a proper design, by a scriptural administrator.* Hence we can not, without gross inconsistency, as well as moral guilt, invite to the Lord's Table any, however exemplary and pious, who have not been thus immersed. Were we to do so, we would be unworthy of communion in any church, and we do not see how Mixed Communionists could consistently receive us to their communion tables.

But it has been shown that all denominations can and do *practically* admit the validity of *our* baptism, and hence could adopt it without any sacrifice of conscience, and with no more inconvenience than the Baptists esteem it a delightful privilege to encounter; while we can not adopt *their* baptisms without disobeying Christ and violating our consciences. It is manifestly *illiberal*, therefore, not to say unjust and unkind, in others even to *ask* or *invite*, much more to "claim and demand," intercommunion with the Baptists.

Now, if Mixed Communionists verily believe, as they say, that we are actuated by an "*exclusive*," "*illiberal*," and "*selfish*" spirit in our practice of *Church* Communion, it is certainly very *inconsistent* in them either to ask the privilege of communing with us at the Lord's Table, with *such a spirit*, or to invite us to partake with them.

But if they regard us honest and sincere in our faith and practice, then it is very *illiberal* and *unkind* in them to ask us to disobey Jesus Christ and to violate our own consciences merely to gratify them. This is admitted by some of their ablest and best men. For example, the late DR. DAVID MONFORT, while pastor of the First Presbyterian Church in Franklin, Indiana, in 1839, published a series of able "LETTERS"* on the subject of "INTERCOMMUNION," in the "*Presbyterian Protestant and Herald*," at Bardstown, Kentucky, edited by DR. N. L. RICE. In his *fourth letter*, Dr. Monfort gives the "REASONS" why he was opposed to giving a *free invitation* to members of *other churches*, and especially to the BAPTISTS. The following are his REASONS, viz.:

"1st. They do not belong to the *fellowship* (i. e., of the Presbyterian Church), and therefore they can not *consistently* receive the *tokens* of it. 2d. They profess to be *conscientious* in refusing the fellowship, and it is *uncharitable* and *unkind* to ask them to violate their consciences. 3d. Or were I uncharitable enough, *as some are*, to attribute their refusal to "*bigotry*," instead of conscience, I should deem them *unfit*, with *such temper*, to commune. Baptists say that we are *unbaptized*, and therefore they can not receive our (church) fellowship nor admit us to theirs. I conceive it

---

* Six of these letters were kindly furnished me by REV. WM. M. PRATT, D. D., who was laboring in Indiana when they were published.

therefore *unkind* to invite them, or to ask the privilege of them. 4th. To give an invitation, *faulty* in all these particulars, seems to me but to take occasion to vaunt our *superior catholicity* to the prejudice of these *honest Christians;* and such churches complain of such treatment on *our* part as *unkind*. Let an impartial sense of *justice* decide how correctly."

We most heartily concur with Dr. Monfort in the above statements, and so must every unprejudiced person who understands the *real ground* of our practice. It is obviously *illiberal*, as well as inconsistent and unkind, in others either to invite or to ask the privilege of intercommunion with Baptists. So far, then, from such heartless invitations and requests being evidences of "superior catholicity," they are real evidences of the *illiberality, inconsistency*, and *unkindness* of those who make them, whether so intended or not; and every Baptist should so regard and treat them. It is any thing else than Christian kindness and liberality in Mixed Communionists to claim and demand of the Baptists, that they shall sacrifice their conscientious principles and indorse what they believed to be error, by intercommunion with them at the Lord's Table. And instead of yielding to such illiberal and unjust claims and demands, we should stand fast in the liberty wherewith Christ has made us free, and keep the ordinances *as* they were first delivered to the churches by Christ and his Apostles.

The Baptists are not only charged with being "exclusive" and "illiberal," but also "*selfish*" in their practice of Church Communion. *Selfishness* is "the exclusive regard of a person to his own interest or happiness." (*Webster*.) Selfishness is *wrong*, whether found in an individual or in a society of individuals. But we deny that there is any thing selfish in our practice of *Church* Communion. On the contrary, it is the most *self-denying and self-sacrificing* part of our practice; and nothing but a consciousness of right and fidelity to Christ and his truth could sustain us under the accumulated misrepresentations and slanders which it brings upon us. It loses us thousands of valuable additions to our churches every year, and occasions multitudes of persons holding Baptist sentiments as far as they understand them, to unite with mixed communion churches and to give their influence and support to grave errors which they do not and can not believe and practice. Yet neccessity is laid upon us, and woe is unto us if we sacrifice *truth* to expediency, let it cost us what it may. This fact is verified in the history of those deluded Baptists who have tried the experiment of *free* communion both in England and this country. The number of such has grown "beautifully less," while *strict* communion Baptists have multiplied rapidly, notwithstanding their self-denying practice of Church Communion. These are facts which speak for themselves.

But while we deny that there is any thing selfish in our practice of communion, faithfulness compels us to charge our mixed communion brethren with *selfishness* in their practice. Do they not seek the interest and promotion of their own denominations with an exclusiveness unknown among the Baptists? Do they not use every possible means and put forth the utmost efforts to make proselytes and swell their numbers? Do they not boast of their "*open communion,*" and cry out against Baptist "*close communion,*" both privately and publicly, for the sole purpose of exciting prejudice in the minds of young converts and others *against* the Baptists and *in favor* of themselves? And having excited such prejudice against us, do they not urge and welcome to their churches many persons whom they *know* to be Baptists in sentiment, and opposed to their peculiar doctrines—such as baptismal remission, infant baptism, and many others? Do they, *like the Baptists*, rely upon fair dealing and God's Spirit and truth alone for success? Most assuredly they do not. These facts are known to others, whether Mixed Communionists will acknowledge them or not. And can we believe that they *really* wish the Baptists to abandon their *Church* Communion? Or if they do, is it for the truth's sake, or to secure our indorsement of their errors? Most unquestionably the latter.

Facts force us to the conclusion that the ostensible opposition to our practice of communion is really against our practice of *believer's immersion.* Deprive our opponents of their vaunted *open communion* and their popular outcry against "*Baptist close communion,*" and you rob them of their chief weapons of defense, and, like Samson, they would be shorn of their strength. How else, indeed, could they counteract and rebut our unanswered and unanswerable arguments in favor of "one Lord, one faith, and *one baptism?*" Hence it is that belligerent and opposing sects, the poles asunder in doctrine, suspend their mutual hostility for a time and unite together at an *occasional* communion season, professedly to show their love for each other, but really to oppose the Baptist doctrine of believer's immersion, under the guise of *close* communion. Such conduct is unworthy of political partisans, much more of professed Christians. Hence we see that Mixed Communionists are justly chargeable with the very *selfishness* which they allege against the Baptists.

8th OBJECTION: "*All Christians will commune together in heaven, and, therefore, all should commune together on earth.*"

After what has been said, it might be sufficient simply to ask the objectors why they do not commune with their *own candidates* for baptism, and with *pious Quakers,* since they acknowledge them to be *Christians,* and expect to commune with them *in heaven?* But as the above objection is often urged by sincere Christians, we will answer it seriously, though briefly.

This objection confounds *Christian* communion and *Church* Communion, which are entirely distinct, and differ essentially both as to their nature and design. *Christian communion* is spiritual intercourse between Christians *as such*. It is based upon similarity of moral character and substantial agreement in the fundamental doctrines of the Gospel, and it necessarily exists wherever mutual confidence in Christian character exists, independent of external ordinances and visible church relations; as, for instance, between a church and its candidates for baptism. As it is written: *"He that loveth is born of God; and every one that loveth him that begat, loveth him also that is begotten of him"* (1 John 4: 7, 21). This mutual love or fellowship is implanted in the hearts of penitent believers by the Holy Spirit in the work of regeneration, and it finds its appropriate exercise in Christian conversation, social prayer and praise, and mutual desires and efforts to do good unto all men, especially unto the household of faith. In such spiritual communion the Baptists most heartily unite with all Christians both *before* and *after* baptism; and every true Baptist can say with the pious psalmist, *"I am a companion of all them that fear God, and keep his commandments."* And we joyfully hope that erelong we shall unite with "the general assembly and church of the firstborn" in heaven, in all those acts of spiritual communion which belong to the heavenly state.

But *Church Communion* consists, in part, in a

joint participation of the Lord's Supper by the members of the same particular church *as such.* It is based upon the positive appointment of Jesus Christ, and is expressive, not of the Christian, but of the *church* fellowship subsisting between communicants at the same Table. The Lord's Supper, therefore, is specific and temporary in its nature and design, and when Christ shall come the second time, without sin unto salvation, *then* this sacred ordinance shall cease forever. In heaven there is no communion table, no bread and wine, and hence no *sacramental* communion there; symbols, will no longer be necessary, for we shall *see Jesus as he is and be like him.* But Christian communion will be renewed in that blissful world, and shall become increasingly delightful through endless ages. In the language of the sacred poet:

"There the saints of all ages in harmony meet,
Their Savior and brethren transported to greet;
While the anthems of pleasure unceasingly roll,
And the smile of the Lord is the feast of the soul."

Accordingly, Prof. Curtis remarks: "We are willing to commune with all those on earth with whom we expect to commune in heaven, and precisely in the same way, *i. e., spiritually.* We do not expect there to participate in the *outward symbols* of bread and wine. These were appointed to show forth the Lord's death *only* 'till he come.' All that can be said in regard to our practice is, that we decline to celebrate the symbols of a particular *Church* Communion with those between whom and ourselves there is no such relation existing as the symbols indicate." (See *Curtis on Communion*, pp. 127, etc.)

And the late Alexander Campbell, in answering a "*Catalogue of Queries*" on "Open Communion," says: "*Query* 11th. 'But do you not expect to sit down in heaven with all Christians of all sects, and why not sit down at the same Table with them on earth?' *Answer.* It will be time enough to behave as they do in heaven when we meet there. . . . I do expect to meet with some of 'all nations, tribes, and tongues' in the heavenly country; but while *on earth*, I must live and behave according to the *order* of things under which I am placed. If we are *now* to be governed by the manners and customs in heaven, why was any other than the heavenly order of society instituted on earth? There will be neither bread, wine, nor water in heaven." (See *Christ'n Bap.*, vol. 6, pp. 184, 185.)

Hence we see that this objection confounds Christian and Church Communion, and is based upon a false assumption. Many other objections might be noticed, but these are the most *plausible* and *popular*, and virtually embrace all others. We will pass on, then, to our next topic.

CHAPTER IV.

EVILS OF MIXED COMMUNION EXPOSED.

1. MIXED COMMUNION is *unscriptural*, and, as such, not binding upon the churches. 2. It perverts the design of the Lord's Supper, and hence *invalidates* the ordinance. 3. It tends to destroy the *effect* of church discipline, and compels a church to commune with its own excluded members. 4. It is *glaringly inconsistent* in the present divided state of the Christian world. 5. It compels its advocates to *indorse* and *fellowship* what they believe to be *error*. 6. It violates the *declared principles* of those who practice it. 7. It is not only bad policy, but *suicidal* to the Baptists.

1st. *Mixed communion is unscriptural, and, as such, not binding upon the churches.*

The New Testament furnishes no evidence that Christ and his Apostles either sanctioned or taught mixed communion. Nor is there any certain evidence that a member of one apostolic church ever communed out of his *own* particular church, even by *invitation*. This is admitted by some of the ablest advocates of mixed communion. For example, DR. HIBBARD says: "*The truth is, that the preponderance of Scripture evidence is against mixed communion.*" (*Hibbard on Bap.*, part 2, p. 186.)

When our Lord *instituted* the Holy Supper, he did not call together all his disciples in Jerusalem, but restricted his invitation to the "*twelve*," and administered the ordinance to them *alone* as the *founders and instructors* of his churches for all time to come. (See Matt. 26: 20-30, and Luke 22: 14-20.) This was emphatically "*restricted communion*," and it was the *divine pattern* given for our imitation. Yet no person ever supposed that, by thus restricting his invitation to the "twelve," our Savior intended thereby to "*unchristianize*" the "seventy other disciples" and his own *pious* mother Mary, or to deny them Christian fellowship.

The inspired Apostles delivered the Lord's Supper to the churches *as* they had received it from Christ. Accordingly, Paul said to the church at Corinth: "*I have received of the Lord that which I also delivered unto you,*" (1 Cor. 11: 23-26.) And it is recorded to the lasting praise of that church that it kept the ordinances of baptism and the Supper *as* the Apostle delivered them to it. Hence, Paul says: "I praise you, brethren, *that ye—keep the ordinances as I delivered them unto you.*" (1 Cor. 11: 2.) The teachings of all the Apostles on this subject was *uniform*, and the *order* established in one church was the order of all the churches: "*As I teach every-where in every church,*" adds Paul. (1 Cor. 4: 17.) Accordingly, all the apostolic churches, like the "*model*" church in Jerusalem, "continued steadfastly in the Apostles' doctrine and fellowship, *and in breaking of bread,* and in prayers." (Acts 2: 42.) This was apostolic order and practice.

Hence, we see that the Lord's Supper was instituted as a *church ordinance*, and was strictly observed *as such* by all the apostolic churches. Nor is there a plain and positive example in the New Testament of any person partaking of the ordinance with any other church, except the one of which he was a member, during the days of the Apostles. It has been supposed by some that Paul partook of the Lord's Supper with "the disciples," or church, at Troas, after preaching to them, when they came together on the first day of the week "*to break bread*," though this is doubtful. (See Acts 20: 7-11.) But if it were certain that the Apostle did partake of the ordinance with that church, this, of itself, would not be sufficient to establish the practice of intercommunion even among Baptists; for Paul was acting as one of the inspired founders and instructors of the churches, and might then have been a member of that particular church for aught we know. Besides, ministers sustain a different relation to the churches generally from what private members do, by virtue of their *ordination*. After all, it is possible that ALEXANDER CAMPBELL was correct in his interpretation of this passage when he said: "The *breaking of bread* spoken of *after* midnight (ver. 11), after the recovery of Eutychus, was most unquestionably a *private refreshment*. . . . . This refreshment was a natural and requisite one, preparatory to a journey," etc. (See *Christian Bap.*, vol. 6, p. 210.)

Intercommunion, however, between members of churches *similarly constituted*, and of the *same faith and practice*, as were all the apostolic churches, and as are all Baptist churches, differs essentially from *modern* mixed communion, which is based upon the unscriptural *assumption*, that all professed Christians of every name and order in good standing in their own churches have an *inalienable right* to the Lord's Supper in any and every church with which they may chance to meet; and that a refusal on the part of one church to invite all such persons to its communion table and to extend to them the *tokens* of church fellowship, is "*exclusive*," "*illiberal*," and "*selfish*," notwithstanding they do not and can not sustain visible church relations with that church. This makes the Lord's Supper, not a *church* ordinance, as all admit it is, but an *individual* ordinance. Such intercommunion is at war with the nature and design of the ordinance, and is both unreasonable and unscriptural.

But even if it were certainly true, as it is not, that the apostolic churches did practice intercommunion by *mutual invitation*, it would by no means follow that modern mixed communion is right and proper in the present divided and discordant state of the Christian world. For *then* there was but "*one Lord, one faith, one baptism*," and all the churches were *similarly constituted and governed;* but *now* there are *divers baptisms* (falsely so called), and no unity of government, faith, or practice;

and how can they walk together, except they be agreed? To give each other the *tokens* of church fellowship and unity, is to profess what does not and can not exist in the present state of things.

Hence it is clear that mixed communion is *unscriptural*, and therefore not binding upon the churches. It is a *human device of modern origin, based upon the false charity of the age*, and its advocates are justly chargeable with "*teaching for doctrines the commandments of men*" on this subject. Nor are we alone in this opinion. Some of the ablest Pedobaptists sustain this view of the subject. For example, the late DR. DAVID MONFORT, in his 6th *Letter* against *intercommunion* (published some years since in the "*Presbyterian Protestant and Herald*" of Ky.), says: "As to how far *catholic* or *open* communion has been practiced, I am not very accurately informed. The language of the divines of Westminster afford no evidence to me that it was sustained by them. It is very certain that *four* different denominations subscribing this *same confession of faith*, and adhering most tenaciously to it, *discountenance the practice altogether*. I am exceeding happy to be informed that in the SYNOD OF PITTSBURGH, where in our great struggle, Presbyterianism prevailed in its greatest purity, it is *not generally practiced*. The practice is of *recent date*. My own recollections and the testimony of older men, assure me that the practice of our forefathers was *exceedingly strict*. That it was rarely, *if at all*, the case with them for their *own members to commune out of the particular church to which they belonged.* That a *sojourner* was not admitted except on a *certificate* of his good standing in his own church. So far were our forefathers from the *present practice of laxness* in this day." These are facts, sustained by the best Presbyterian authority, and our Presbyterian brethren would do well to return to the practice of their *forefathers.*

The METHODIST DISCIPLINE, after its numerous changes and expurgations, is still "*close communion,*" (see pp. 215-220,) but it was even *more strict* fifteen years ago than it is now. The Discipline of 1850 (chap. 3, sec. 5, p. 76), in *Ans.* 2 to *Question* "Are there any *directions* to be given concerning the *administration of the Lord's Supper?*" says: "*Let no person that is not a member of our church be admitted to the communion without examination, and some token given by an elder or deacon.*" This and many other rules of the Discipline have been abolished by the General Conference without any mention of the fact in succeeding editions. Indeed no Methodist can know this year what his *superiors* will require him to believe and practice next year.

2d. *Mixed communion perverts the design of the Lord's Supper, and hence invalidates the ordinance.*

What is the design of the Lord's Supper? We have shown (chap. 1, pp. 35-42) that the Baptists and others agree that it is designed, (1), as a sacred *memorial* or *remembrancer* of Christ;

(2), as an *emblematic exhibition* of his *death;* and (3), as a *symbolic declaration* of our spiritual union and communion with Christ by faith. And ALBERT BARNES, in his "Notes" on the phrase "*In remembrance of me*" (1 Cor. 11 : 25), says: "This expresses the *whole design* of the ordinance. It is a simple *memorial* or *remembrancer,*" etc. So say the Baptists. Yet, strange as it may appear, the advocates of mixed communion, including Mr. Barnes, maintain that the Lord's Supper is *also* designed, (1), as *an efficacious means of salvation;* (2), as *an evidence and test of brotherly love;* and (3), as *a proof of our Christian liberality.* This is evident both from their teachings and practice. But we solemnly deny that the Lord's Supper ever was designed for any such purposes; it is a gross perversion of its design, and invalidates the ordinance.

(1.) Then we deny that the Lord's Supper is designed as "*an efficacious means of salvation.*"

The doctrine of the "*real presence*" of Christ in the Eucharist was among the *first radical errors* of the early Christian fathers, and it gave birth to the error that the Lord's Supper is "an *efficacious* means of salvation." Hence they administered not only baptism, but the Lord's Supper to *infants,* as well as to adults, as an efficacious means of salvation. The Christian fathers were led into this dangerous error partly by a *misapplication* of our Lord's words in John 6 : 53: "*Except ye eat the flesh of the Son of Man, and drink his blood, ye have no life in you;"* and partly by a *misinterpretation* of the language of the institution in Matt. 26 : 26–28. They understand our Savior *literally,* when he said of the bread, *"This is my body;"* and of the wine, *"This is my blood."* Thus they confounded the *sign* with the *thing* signified, and hence ascribed to the sign the *efficacy* which belongs alone to the thing signified. The same dangerous principle of giving a *literal* interpretation to *symbolic* language, gave rise also to the errors of baptismal regeneration, baptismal remission, infant baptism, transubstantiation, consubstantiation, masses for the dead, etc., as held to this day by the Roman Catholics, and others respectively. (In proof of this, see *Hinton's Hist. of Bap.*, pp. 323, 324; and *Howell on Com.*, pp. 208, etc.)

All those Protestant denominations who, either directly or indirectly, came out of the "MOTHER OF HARLOTS,"[1] employ language in their creeds and catechisms in regard to the *efficacy* of the Lord's Supper which the Baptists can by no means indorse; and it is certain that many of them do attach an unscriptural and dangerous efficacy to the ordinance, as they also do to baptism. Of all the great reformers of the sixteenth century, ZUINGLIUS was the only one who arrived at scriptural views of the Lord's Supper. He regarded the bread and wine as mere *symbols*, designed to *represent* the broken body and shed blood of Christ. While LUTHER rejected the Popish dogma of *transubstantiation*, he zealously contended for the "*real presence*" of Christ in the Eucharist, which he denominated *consubstantiation;* and hence he believed that communicants *actually eat the flesh and drink the blood of Christ* with the bread and wine, and thus *obtain* spiritual life. (See *Orm on the Lord's Supper*, p. 286.) And while CALVIN rejected both transubstantiation and consubstantiation, he maintained that, in partaking of the bread and wine, Christ, by the secret influence of the Holy Spirit, really *imparts* his body and blood to communicants. He says: "In his sacred supper, Christ commands me, under the symbols of bread and wine, to take, and eat, and drink, his body and blood. I doubt not that he truly presents, and that I receive them." (See *Institutes of Relig.*, vol. 2, bk. 4, chap. 17, par. 10 and 32.)

Accordingly, the EPISCOPALIANS teach that the Lord's Supper is "generally *necessary to salvation.*" When their candidates for confirmation are asked, "How many *sacraments* hath Christ ordained in his church?" they are required to answer, "Two only, as generally *necessary to salvation;* that is to say, baptism, and *the supper of the Lord.*" (See *Book of Common Prayer*, Catechism, p. 137.)

The PRESBYTERIANS teach that "the *sacraments*" of baptism and *the Lord's Supper* "become *effectual means of salvation*, only by the working of the Holy Spirit, and the blessing of Christ;" and that they were "instituted by Christ in his Church, to signify, *seal,* and exhibit unto those that are *within* the covenant of grace, the *benefits* of Christ's mediation." (See *Conf. of Faith, Larger Cat.,* Ans. *to* Ques. 161, 162.)

The METHODISTS agree substantially with the Episcopalians in regard to the *efficacy* of the Lord's Supper. It is well known, that their elders and ministers generally invite and urge "*seekers*" of religion to partake of the bread and wine as a *means of obtaining salvation;* and some of them relate instances of persons being converted in the *very act* of partaking, to encourage anxious sinners to come to the Lord's Table.

Accordingly, DR. ADAM CLARK, at the end of his Notes on 1 Cor., 11 chap. remark 3, says: "Every minister of Christ is bound to administer it (the Lord's Supper) *to every man who is seeking the salvation of his soul,* as well as to *believers.*" Now, what is this but to encourage sinners to eat and drink their *own condemnation?* Of course unbelievers can not *discern* the Lord's body, and yet, Paul declares that all those who partake of the ordinance, "not discerning" his body, "eat and drink damnation to their own souls." (See 1 Cor. 11 : 27 and 29.)

The CONGREGATIONALISTS agree with the Presbyterians on this subject. (See *Platforms,* Confession of Faith, chap. 30.) The LUTHERANS are divided, a majority holding with Luther to the "*real presence*" of Christ in the Eucharist, and a minority holding with other Pedobaptists that it is an "*efficacious* means of salvation." (See *Augsburgh Conf. of Faith*.)

This error, in slightly modified forms, is held by all Mixed Communionists, except the Free Communion Baptists and the Campbellites; and the Campbellites, to be *consistent*, ought to hold it. And if they believe their own confessions of faith and denominational catechisms, they are bound to attach an unscriptural and dangerous *efficacy* to the Lord's Supper, as also to baptism. Nor is it any abatement for individuals to plead that they do not believe this error. This may be true; yet they are responsible for it, so long as they continue to give their influence and support to denominations which hold and teach it.

Now we deny that our Lord had any reference to his Supper in John 6: 53, and we maintain that the bread and wine are only *symbols* of the broken body and shed blood of Christ. When Jesus said of the bread, "This *is* my body;" and of the wine, "This *is* my blood," he simply meant that the bread and wine *represent* his body and blood, using the *sign* for the thing signified—just as Moses said of the paschal lamb, "It *is* the Lord's passover" (Exod. 12: 11); that is, it *represented* the passover. The *saving efficacy* of Christ's broken body and shed blood can be received *only by faith*, and the bread and wine are the appointed *symbols* of his sacrificial death and of our participation in its saving benefits by faith. The Lord's Supper, then, was never designed as an "*efficacious means of salvation,*" and if there were no other reasons, the Baptists could not intercommune with those who administer and receive the ordinance for this purpose. It is a dangerous *perversion* of the Lord's Supper, and necessarily *invalidates* it as a *positive* ordinance.

(2.) Again, we deny that the Lord's Supper is designed as "*an evidence and test of brotherly love among Christians.*"

The advocates of mixed communion, without an exception, boldly maintain that the Lord's Supper is designed "*as an evidence and test of brotherly love among Christians as such,*" and hence they charge the Baptists with "*bigotry,*" "*exclusiveness,*" "*illiberality,*" "*selfishness,*" and "*want of charity,*" on account of their practice of *Church* Communion. We can only give a *specimen* of their faith and practice here.

For instance, the EPISCOPALIANS teach that "The Supper of the Lord is not only *a sign of the love that Christians ought to have among themselves one to another,*" etc. (See *Book of Common Prayer*, Art. of Relig., 28.) The METHODISTS teach the same thing, in the same language. (See DISCIPLINE, chap. 1, sec. 3, Art. of Relig., 18.)

The PRESBYTERIANS teach that the Lord's Supper is designed "To be *a bond and pledge of their communion* with Christ, and *with each other* as members of his mystical body; and they that communicate worthily — *testify and renew* their thankfulness and engagedness with God, and *their mutual love and fellowship each with the other as* members of the same mystical body." (See *Confession of Faith*, chap. 29, sec. 1, and *Larger Catechism*, Ans. to Q. 168.

The CONGREGATIONALISTS teach the same thing as the Presbyterians. (See *Platforms*, Conf. of Faith, chap. 30.)

So all other Pedobaptists hold and teach on this point. And so of the CAMPBELLITES, who advocate mixed communion on the same ground.

And the late ROBERT HALL, of England, the boasted leader of "Free Communion Baptists," declares, that the "Eucharist, in its secondary import, is intended as a solemn recognition of each other as members of Christ's body; and that as far as its social import is concerned, *it has no other object than to express that fraternal attachment which we actually feel*." (See *Hall's Works*, vol. 1, p. 324.)

Accordingly, mixed communion ministers invite and urge "*all Christians* in good standing in their own churches" to celebrate the Lord's Supper together, and thus, by this solemn "*bond and pledge, testify and renew their mutual love and fellowship for each other*, as members of the same mystical body." And hence they charge the Baptists with "denying to every other church *all claim* to be regarded as a part of the redeemed body of Christ" by their practice of *Church* Communion, and denounce us as "*exclusive*," "*illiberal*," and "*selfish*" for refusing to intercommune with them. (See *Barnes on Exclusivism*, pp. 21, etc.) Indeed,

Mixed Communionists harp so much upon the Lord's Supper as an "*evidence* and *test* of mutual Christian love," that not only the world, but even some uninstructed Baptists suppose that this is *really* a part of the scriptural design of the ordinance; and hence the "uneasiness and anguish" which they feel on our sacramental occasions, in seeing their friends and relatives of other denominations debarred from the Lord's Table.

Now, we freely admit that mutual Christian love is very becoming and desirable among communicants at the same table, as it is in all other branches of religious worship. But we most solemnly deny that the Lord's Supper ever was designed as an *evidence* or *test* of brotherly love among Christians, even of the same faith and order, much less of different denominations. Christ and his Apostles enjoin the duty of brotherly love and prescribe the various ways in which it should be manifested, but they nowhere intimate that this is any part of the design of the Lord's Supper.

The true evidence of mutual Christian love is not to be found in a joint participation of the Lord's Supper, but in visiting the sick, feeding the hungry, clothing the naked, comforting the distressed, etc. In proof of this fact, we have the authoritative and decisive testimony of our final JUDGE, who, at the last day, will say to all his saints,—"*Come, ye blessed of my Father, inherit the kingdom prepared for you from the foundation of the world,*" etc. (Matt. 25: 34-40.) But what are the *grounds* upon which they shall receive this distinguished blessing? Is it because some of them *occasionally* communed together at the Lord's Table? Emphatically, NO! The *reasons* assigned by our Lord are of a very different character: "*For I was an hungered, and ye gave me meat; I was thirsty, and ye gave me drink; I was a stranger, and ye took me in; naked, and ye clothed me; I was sick, and ye visited me; I was in prison, and ye came umto me.*" And in reply to the astonished inquiries of the righteous, the King shall answer: "*Verily, I say unto you, inasmuch as ye have done it unto one of the least of these my brethren, ye have done it unto me.*" (See verses 35–40.)

These are *real evidences* of brotherly love among Christians. They involve the exercise of tempers and the performance of duties, which require *self-denying* effort, without which, no matter how free may be our communion, or how loudly we may boast of our "superior catholicity," we are "as sounding brass or a tinkling cymbal." In giving such scriptural evidences of brotherly love, the Baptists are as *free* and *unrestricted* as any denomination in Christendom, if not more so. In the truthful language of Prof. Curtis, "We say therefore that the bread and the wine of the Lord's Supper were never designed to mark the *limits* of our spiritual fellowship, so that those not partaking at the same communion table should *therefore* be supposed not to have *true Christian* communion or fellowship with each other." (See

Curtis on Com., p. 87.) Hence it is manifest that the Lord's Supper never was designed as an *evidence* or *test* of brotherly love among communicants even of the same church, much less of different churches. And it is a gross perversion of the ordinance to administer or receive it for such a purpose.

(3.) And again, we deny that the Lord's Supper was ever designed as "*a proof of our Christian liberality.*"

The celebrated ROBERT HALL, of England, urged the "*impolicy of strict communion*" as an argument in favor of "*free communion;*" and adds, that "The first effect necessarily resulting from strict communion, is a *popular prejudice* against the party which adopts it." (See *Hall's Works*, vol. 2, p. 226.) Indeed, *policy* was at the bottom of all Mr. Hall's advocacy of free communion, as it is with the advocates of mixed communion generally. Now, it is painfully true, that a "*popular prejudice*" was excited by Mr. Hall and others against the *Strict* Communion Baptists of England, as well as against the *Church* Communion Baptists of America.

But the experience of half a century has demonstrated the "*impolicy*" of that great but misguided man, whose love of applause and natural timidity betrayed him into the unscriptural practice of mixed communion. Facts show, that, while his once flourishing churches at Bristol and Leicester, and many others in England, have waned under the pernicious influence of his boasted "*free communion,*" and some of them have long since become amalgamated with Pedobaptists and lost their denominational identity, *those Baptist churches* which faithfully adhered to the scriptural practice of *Church Communion,* have not only maintained their denominational existence, but have enjoyed internal peace and prosperity notwithstanding the "*popular prejudice*" with which they have had to contend; while sad experience has compelled many free communion churches and pastors in England to admit and deplore the *uncontrollable evils* of their practice.

And though all may not have the candor, like Robert Hall, to openly avow the fact, still it is unquestionably true that Mixed Communionists generally advocate the practice as a matter of *policy*, and celebrate the Lord's Supper to show the "*superior liberality*" of their churches over those of the Baptists, in thus gratifying the prejudices and wishes of friends and relatives belonging to different denominations. Hence they boast of their "*superior catholicity,*" and abuse and denounce the Baptists as "*bigoted*," "*exclusive*," "*illiberal*," and "*selfish*" on account of their practice of *Church* Communion. And as before stated, the hideous cry of "*close communion,*" alias immersion, every-where raised against us by time-serving ministers and their deluded people, is the most effective means now being employed by Mixed Communionists to prevent young converts and others from joining our churches, and to induce them to unite with their own. Of course those who will thus pervert and subsidize an ordinance of Jesus Christ to sectarian purposes, will deny the charge, and cry out misrepresentation and slander. Well, if their cause needs such helps, it would indeed be "*illiberal*" and "*uncharitable*" in Baptists to deny them. But if *our* cause can not succeed by fair dealing, with God's Spirit and truth, it must fail, for we had rather die in credit than live in shame.

By such unholy means many pious persons, entertaining Baptist sentiments, are filled with prejudice against us, and deluded into mixed communion churches, under the erroneous impression that they are "*more liberal*" than the Baptists, and with the vain hope of communing with their friends and relatives of other denominations. For example, Mr. B——, a worthy member of the First Presbyterian Church in Maysville, Ky., appeared unexpectedly in my congregation one Sabbath morning, and requested me to *immerse* him that day, saying:

"I believed in immersion as the only scriptural baptism when I first professed religion, and would have joined the Baptists then had it not been for their '*close communion*,' but my uncle, Dr. Green, prevailed on me to be sprinkled and to unite with the Presbyterians, where I could enjoy the privilege of communing with all my friends and relatives. As baptism was not essential to salvation, I consented to follow his advice, but have never felt satisfied with my baptism, and have refused to have my children sprinkled; although my brethren proposed to make me an elder of the church. Now, I wish you to immerse me, and let me join your church, with the understanding that I be allowed the privilege of communing with my Presbyterian brethren and friends."

I declined baptizing him then, stating that our *Church* Communion was the necessary result of our views of baptism, and that we were as certainly right in the one as in the other. I explained the nature and design of the Lord's Supper to him, and requested him to examine the New Testament on communion, as he had done on baptism, with the promise that he should be baptized as soon as he became satisfied with our practice of Church Communion. On his return home he named the subject to his wife, and, to his surprise, he found that she had come to the same conclusion from reading God's Word. They examined the subject of the Lord's Supper together, and after a few months, were both immersed by the Rev. George Hunt, and received into the Maysville Baptist Church, where they became useful members.

Other examples might be given, but I mention this case as a fair specimen of thousands who, through false teaching and prejudice, have been induced to give their influence and support to mixed communion churches, holding doctrines which they do not and can not believe, such as baptismal remission, infant sprinkling, sacramental salvation, etc. Now, while Mixed Communionists are guilty of thus prostituting the Lord's Supper to sectarian purposes, their deluded victims are no less guilty of *idolizing* friends and relatives, and of giving countenance and support to *radical errors*, merely to enjoy the unscriptural privilege of mixed communion, instead of following Jesus Christ in all his commands and ordinances blameless. Such erring and inconsistent brethren and sisters should consider the solemn declarations of our LORD and MASTER, who says: "*He that loveth father or mother more than Me, is not worthy of Me; and he that loveth son or daughter more than Me, is not worthy of Me. And he that taketh not his cross, and followeth after Me, is not worthy of Me.*" (Matt. 10: 37, 38.) "*And why call ye me Lord, Lord, and do not the things which I say?*" (Luke 6: 46.) "*Ye are my friends, if ye do whatsoever I command you.*" (John 15: 14.) Nor will they lose in the end by obeying Christ. "And Jesus answered and said, Verily, I say unto you, there is no man that hath left house, or brethren, or sisters, or father, or mother, or wife, or children, or lands, *for my sake and the Gospel's*, but he shall receive *a hundred-fold now in this time*, houses, and brethren, and sisters, and mothers, and children, and lands, *with persecutions;* and in the world to come *eternal life.*" (Mark 10: 29, 30.) Both duty and interest, then, require such deluded and inconsistent brethren and sisters to abandon their deceivers and to follow Christ in "all things *whatsoever* he has commanded."

Hence, we see that Mixed Communionists do administer and receive the Lord's Supper, not only as "an *efficacious* means of salvation," and as "an *evidence* and *test* of brotherly love," but also as "*a proof of their Christian liberality*," and *to gratify the wishes* of misguided friends and relatives belonging to different denominations. Yet the advocates of the practice admit that we have *no right* to administer or receive the ordinance for *any other design* than that which Christ has specified. As a *positive ordinance*, based upon *positive law*, it must be administered and received according to the *very letter* of the law, in the *exact manner*, and for the *specific design* prescribed by the Savior, or it is not the Lord's Supper. To alter or change a positive rite in any respect whatever, is to destroy its *validity* and *insult* the King in Zion. Now, we have shown that the Lord's Supper never was designed as an *efficacious* means of salvation, nor as an *evidence* or *test* of mutual Christian love, nor as a *proof of Christian liberality*, or to *gratify the wishes* of friends and relatives belonging to different denominations; and to administer or receive the ordinance for any such design is not only a *gross perversion* of it, but a *daring insult* to the Author of the institution. A *mixed communion table*, therefore, is not the *Lord's Table*.

3d. *Mixed communion tends to destroy the effect of church discipline, and compels a church to commune with its own excluded members.*

As we have shown, all denominations admit that the Lord's Supper is a *church* ordinance, and that each and every church is solemnly bound to protect the Lord's Table from the approach of unworthy persons by the exercise of a *restraining and watchful discipline*. And all agree that such discipline is essential to the safety of every church and to the purity of its communion. Now as each church is required to exercise such discipline over *all* its communicants, and to debar *all* unworthy persons from its communion table, and as one church possesses no disciplinary power or control over the members of other churches, it necessarily follows that communicants at the same table must be members of the *same church;* or, at least, members of the same denomination whose churches mutually respect and sustain each other's discipline. Accordingly, Prof. Curtis, speaking of the Lord's Supper, says: "It presupposes that watchfulness and discipline of holy love, by which improper persons are kept back from the number of the communicants. This all will admit, nor can any deny, that to the *churches of Christ as such*, and to them *alone*, has the power of discipline been confided. Admission to the Lord's Table, therefore, implies admission to it by *a particular church*, and this, in fact, settles the question that the Lord's Supper is a *church ordinance*.

For certainly no church in primitive times would have admitted any to its communion table whom it would have been *unwilling* to receive as a member of its own body. Each church was originally *independent*, with full power within itself to *receive* and to *exclude* from its communion table." (See *Curtis on Communion*, p. 136.)

Now it is unquestionably true that mixed communion necessarily tends to *paralyze* church discipline, and often compels a church to commune with its own *excluded* members. *For illustration*, suppose a Presbyterian church should exclude a member from its fellowship for reasons satisfactory to itself. That excluded brother can go and unite with an Episcopalian, Methodist, Campbellite, or any other mixed communion church, without repentance or restoration to the fellowship of the church which excluded him, and thus be again " in good standing in his own church," and, as such, included in the usual free communion invitation. At the very next communion season of that Presbyterian church, this restored brother can return to the sacramental table of his Presbyterian brethren who thus excluded him, under covert of their own invitation; and there and then both he and they are compelled to "*renew and testify*," by this solemn "*bond and pledge, their mutual Christian love and fellowship with each other,*" (see *Confession of Faith*, Larger Cat., Ans. to Ques. 168,) when, in fact, the church has neither Christian nor church fellowship for him. Yet there is no remedy for the evil; it is the legitimate and necessary consequence of mixed communion, and its advocates must bear it.

Thus, the effect of church discipline is paralyzed, and consequently the Lord's Supper exposed to the profanations of unworthy persons by the unscriptural practice of mixed communion. Nor is this a mere supposition. Hundreds of instances might be given, illustrative of this fact. For example,

"In a mixed communion church, not long since," says Rev. David E. Thomas, "there was a member who slandered the character of the pastor's wife. He was tried and expelled. In a few days he applied for membership in a church of another denomination, and, on account of his wealth and influence, he was received. He attended the communion season of the church from which he had been justly expelled, and the usual invitation was extended. When he saw his slandered victim advance to the table, he arose and accompanied her. She was paralyzed, and declined partaking of the sacred emblems. *He* partook with all boldness. The pastor was greatly embarrassed, and the whole church was thrown into a state of ebullition while one man exhibited the *legitimate fruits* of open communion." (See *Christian Manual*, pp. 349, 350.)

"In Wyoming, New York," says the late Judge Edmunds, "the Free-Will Baptist Church, after much discipline, excluded a prominent member for disorderly and immoral conduct. The Methodist Church was then holding a series of meetings, and he applied immediately for membership and was cordially received; and on the following Sabbath he attended the communion of the Free-Will Baptist Church, when the usual invitation was given to 'all Christians in good standing in their own churches.' Of course he had a right to consider himself invited, for he was in good standing in the Methodist Church. Accordingly, he partook of the elements in *token* of the mutual Christian love existing between them!"

Another "well authenticated fact" is given by PROF. HARVEY, in his recent essay on COMMUNION: "A devoted and conscientious deacon of a Congregational church commenced to labor with a member of the same church for unchristian-like conduct, but could obtain no satisfaction. He then took one or two brethren with him, and spread out all the circumstances before them; but the man still justified himself. The church was at last compelled to exclude the offender. He then went to a neighboring Methodist Church, represented himself as persecuted because he had honestly changed his sentiments, and was cordially received. The next communion season which this Congregational church enjoyed, (or would have enjoyed but for *mixed* communion,) he came forward, and with great care takes his seat by the side of the deacon who took up the labor with him, for the express purpose of aggravating his feelings. The good deacon says to a member of the Baptist church present, (with whom he was very intimate,) 'Brother, what shall I do? I do not feel as though I could commune with that man.' The Baptist replied: 'I pity you, deacon, from the bottom of my heart, but I can not relieve you; this is the effect of your wrong views of communion.' The church was thrown into such a state of perturbation as to disqualify them to receive so holy an ordinance with pleasure or profit." (See *The Baptist*, as quoted by Dr. T. G. Jones, pp. 161, 162.)

Many similar cases might be given did our limits allow. They are unavoidable consequences of the unscriptural practice, and there is no remedy but to return to the original practice of *Church* Communion. Mixed communion throws down the reins of church discipline, and opens the way for all excluded members to come to the communion of the churches from which they were expelled; and the only reason why such instances are not more common, is, because open communion exists rather in *name* than in reality. "Practically, open communion is a *nullity*. It is a mere *theory*. Pedobaptists, while extolling it, rarely practice it." A church of one denomination has no jurisdiction over the members of other denominations, and, therefore, mixed communion necessarily destroys the *effect* of church discipline, and compels a church to commune with its own *excluded* members. And this must continue to be the case until the pernicious practice is abandoned. Hence we see that it is both unscriptural and dangerous for any church to extend its invitation to partake of the Lord's Supper *beyond the limits* of its discipline; because it not only paralyzes church discipline, but compels a church to admit unworthy persons to its communion, over whom it has no disciplinary power whatever.

The case, however, is quite different in regard to churches of the same denomination. Between such churches there is a fraternal correspondence in ecclesiastical matters, and each respects and sustains the discipline of the others. Hence they may practice *intercommunion* among themselves without paralyzing their church discipline or exposing the Lord's Table to the unworthy. This is true of the churches of all denominations. For instance, a Presbyterian church may consistently and safely invite to its communion table the members of other Presbyterian churches, because they are of the same faith and order, and mutually respect and sustain each other's discipline. The same is true of the Methodists, Lutherans, Episcopalians, Congregationalists, Campbellites, and all other denominations. Such intercommunion may be consistently and safely practiced by the churches of each denomination; still, as we have shown, there is neither precept nor example for it in the New Testament, and it can do no real good, even among churches of the same faith and order.

But there is even more consistency and propriety in such intercommunion among *the Baptists*. Every Baptist church, like the apostolic churches, is an *independent* body, subject only to Christ as its Head and Lawgiver. Our associations, conventions, and councils are mere *advisory* and *coöperative* bodies, and possess no ecclesiastical or legislative authority whatever over the churches. With us, as with the first Christians, a church is the *highest* ecclesiastical authority upon earth; our ministers are the servants of the churches for Jesus' sake. Hence our advisory and coöperative bodies, *as such*, never celebrate the Lord's Supper, because they are not churches in any proper sense; and the Supper is confessedly a *church* ordinance belonging to each particular church *as such*. Were the million and a half of living Baptists now assembled together in convention, they would not dare to administer or receive the Lord's Supper, except *specially invited* by some particular church to partake with it, and even then they would not partake of it by right, but merely by courtesy.

Still there is no difficulty in the way of *intercommunion* between Baptists on all proper occasions. Each church can maintain its discipline and protect its communion table from unworthy persons while extending the *tokens* of its church fellowship to visiting members of other Baptist churches *known* to be in good standing. Among Baptists, occasional communion is *temporary membership* in the church thus celebrating the Lord's

Supper. The relation existing between regular Baptist churches is such as to give each a kind of *indirect* control over the members of the other churches; at least, so far as communion at the Lord's Table is concerned. *For instance*, if a member be excluded from one Baptist church, he can not unite with any other Baptist church until he is either restored on repentance to the fellowship of the church from which he was expelled, or is acquitted of blame and received into the fellowship of a sister church after a full and thorough examination of all the facts in the case for herself. Then, and not till then, has he a *right* to partake of the Lord's Supper in the church thus restoring him, or the *privilege* of partaking with any other Baptist church that may see fit to invite him. Much less can such excluded members unite with churches of other denominations with which we have no ecclesiastical connection, and then return and *force* themselves upon us at the Lord's Table, as in the case of mixed communion churches.

The mere fact, however, of being a member in good standing in one Baptist church, does not entitle an individual of *right* to partake of the Lord's Supper with any other Baptist church, no more than the mere fact of being a Jew entitled a person of right to enter the family of another Jew and partake of the Passover. The Lord's Supper is, as all admit, a *church* ordinance, as the Passover was a *family* ordinance. No Baptist, therefore, has any scriptural right to *claim* communion at the Lord's Table *out of his own particular church*. If another Baptist church think proper to invite him to its communion, then he may partake as an invited guest, and as a temporary member. But one Baptist church is not *bound* to invite the members of other Baptist churches to its communion table, any more than one Jewish family was bound to invite the members of other Jewish families to partake with it of the Paschal supper. Still it is the custom of *modern* Baptist churches to extend the *privilege* of intercommunion to visiting brethren and sisters *known* to be in good standing in their respective churches; and we can do so consistently and safely *on the ground* that such persons are of the same faith and practice and belong to churches similarly constituted and governed, which mutually respect and sustain each other's church discipline, and hence might be members with us permanently but for their inconvenience of location.

For the time being, therefore, such persons may properly be regarded and treated in this act *as if* they were members of the church thus inviting them. On this ground, and no other, and with this distinct understanding between the parties, can one Baptist church consistently and safely invite to its communion the members of other Baptist churches, *known* to be in good and regular standing in their own churches. But even then the church invites such members as *individuals*, and not as churches, and thus regards and treats them in this church act as *virtually members of its body* for the time being. And no Baptist, who understands the nature and design of the Lord's Supper, feels at liberty to partake of the ordinance with any other Baptist church, except his *own*, without a *special invitation;* nor has any Baptist a right to feel slighted if not so invited. Thus we see that, while Baptists churches may consistently and safely hold intercommunion with each other's members by mutual invitation, still it is a mere matter of *courtesy*, for which they can claim neither precept nor example in the New Testament; and, as such, ought to be abandoned in all our churches, except possibly in the case of *ordained* ministers, *known* to be in good standing, who sustain a peculiar relation to all the churches as the accredited officers of Christ's kingdom.

Such intercommunion among Baptists is not only without Scripture warrant, but does *much harm* and *no real good*. It often exposes the Lord's Table to unworthy persons professing to be Baptists, over whom we have no *direct* disciplinary control, and it necessitates an odious and useless discrimination on communion occasions, to the prejudice of our churches. The Lord's Supper being a church ordinance, as all admit, communion at the Lord's Table is a *church act;* and we have no scriptural right to extend our communion *beyond* the limits of our church discipline. And as one Baptist church has no absolute disciplinary power over the members of another Baptist church; and as every church is required to exercise a watchful and controlling discipline over all its communicants, it follows of necessity that no Baptist church has a *scriptural right* to invite to its communion the members of another Baptist church, though it may be done consistently and safely on the ground above explained. Nor has a member of one Baptist church any more right, *as a right*, to claim the privilege of communing in another church than he has to claim the privilege of *voting;* for both are equally *church acts and church privileges.* The practice, therefore, is unscriptural, and of evil tendency, and doubtless will be abandoned by all our churches as soon as they reflect properly upon the subject and can overcome the force of habit and prejudice. Baptists are a peculiar people, with no *authoritative* creed but the BIBLE; and they will not long maintain a practice for which they have neither precept nor example in the New Testament.

Hence we see that while churches of the same denomination may consistently and safely extend their communion to each other's members on the principles above explained, still there is *no scriptural authority* for such intercommunion—much less for *mixed* communion between churches of different denominations, which necessarily and unavoidably tends to destroy the *effect* of church discipline, and compels a church to commune with its own *excluded* members.

4th. *Mixed communion is glaringly inconsistent in the present divided state of the Christian world.*

How inconsistent is it for a church to invite to its communion and extend the *tokens* of church fellowship to persons whom it would be *unwilling* to receive into its permanent membership *just as they are*, without any change of faith or practice! This, indeed, is the ground upon which the Associate Reformed Presbyterians and others practice restricted communion. This is also one great reason why the Baptists restrict their communion to the members of their own churches. No true Baptist church will invite any person to its communion table whom it would be unwilling to receive into its membership *just as he is*, without the slightest change of faith or practice. And it is certain that no apostolic church would have admitted those to its communion whom it would not have been willing to receive as permanent members of its body *just as they were.*

But is this true of mixed communion churches? Would they be willing to receive into their church fellowship all those whom they invite and receive to their communion *just as they are*, without any change of faith or practice? Would the Campbellites, for instance, be willing to receive, as church members, the Pedobaptists whom they admit to their communion, with their adult and infant sprinkling for baptism? Or would the Pedobaptists be willing to admit the Campbellites to permanent church membership, with their baptismal remission and bold opposition to Pedobaptism? Would the Methodists, for instance, be willing to receive the Presbyterians as permanent members of their body, with their *hyper-Calvinism*, which John Wesley denounced as the doctrine of hell? Or would the Presbyterians be willing to admit the Methodists into church membership, with their *rank Arminianism*, which John Calvin denounced with equal severity? Most unquestionably they would not. Yet they are guilty of the glaring inconsistency of inviting and receiving each other to their respective communion tables and of thus mutually interchanging *tokens* of church fellowship, when they *would not* and *could not*, according to their standards, receive each other into permamanent church membership without a radical change of both faith and practice.

If it be said that the above remarks apply to "*permanent*" church fellowship, but not to "*occasional*" intercommunion, we answer, that the *same principles* must govern us in regard to "occasional" communion that govern us in regard to "permanent" communion. There can not be one class of principles to regulate occasional and another class to regulate habitual communion; for occasional communion is occasional or temporary *church membership* in the particular church celebrating the Lord's Supper. In the language of

Prof. Curtis, we say: "There is to us a most obvious inconsistency in admitting to our *occasional* communion those whom we would be unwilling to admit to our *church fellowship;* making an exception in favor of *irregularity.* It is as much as to say that those admitted are good enough for the *Lord's Table,* but not for *our church.*" (See *Curtis on Com.,* p. 108.)

Accordingly, the late Alexander Campbell, in answering a "*Catalogue of Queries*" on "Open Communion," says: "I object to making it a rule *in any case,* to receive *unimmersed* persons to church ordinances: 1st. Because it is nowhere *commanded.* 2d. Because it is nowhere *precedented* in the New Testament. 3d. Because it *necessarily corrupts* the simplicity and uniformity of the whole genius of the new institution. 4th. Because it not only deranges the *order* of the kingdom, but makes *void* one of the most important institutions ever given to man. It necessarily makes *immersion* of non-effect. For, with what consistency or propriety can a congregation hold up to the world either the *authority* or *utility* of an institution which they are in the *habit* of making as little of as any human opinions? 5th. Because, in making a canon to dispense with a divine institution of momentous import, they who do so assume the *very same dispensing power* which issued in the tremendous *apostasy* which we and all Christians are praying and laboring to destroy." (*Christian Baptist,* vol. 6, Ans. to Query 9, pp. 183, 184.)

Hence we see that mixed communion is *glaringly inconsistent* in the present divided state of the Christian world.

5th. *Mixed communion compels its advocates to indorse and fellowship what they believe to be error.*

Now, if the Lord's Supper be a church ordinance, and the appointed token of visible church relations, as all admit, then communion at the Lord's Table necessarily implies and involves *church fellowship* as existing between communicants at the same table. Hence, by the *very act* of intercommunion Mixed Communionists publicly indorse and recognize each other's churches and ordinances as *scriptural* and *valid*. This is the meaning of the act, and even the world so understand it. But are the advocates of the practice willing to admit what the act imports? If so, why the existence of separate denominations, and why the criminations and recriminations among them. *For instance*, the Old School Presbyterians regard the Campbellites, Congregationalists, Episcopalians, Lutherans, Methodists, and all others, as holding *errors* more or less fundamental. Indeed, it was on the charge of such errors that they excluded the New School Presbyterians from their fellowship, and still refuse to give them the tokens of church fellowship. So every other denomination regards all the others as holding errors so radical that it can not unite with them in permanent church relations. Hence, very few, if any of them, are willing to receive each other's members into their church fellowship without some change of faith and practice. These are facts which can not be denied. The creeds and standard writers of all denominations declare the same. For example, JOHN WESLEY, the founder of Methodism, in his sermon on "*Free Grace*," No. 55, pp. 293–295, speaking of *predestination*, as held by Presbyterians and others, says: "This doctrine not only tends to destroy Christian holiness, happiness, and good works, but hath also a direct and manifest tendency to *overthrow the whole Christian revelation*. . . . . It represents our blessed Lord—as a *hypocrite*, a *deceiver* of the people, a man *void* of common sincerity. . . . . It represents the most holy God as worse than the *devil;* as both more false, more cruel, and more unjust. . . . . This is the blasphemy for which I abhor the doctrine of predestination." On the other hand, JOHN CALVIN, the founder of Presbyterianism, on " *Secret Providence,*" speaking of the doctrine of *Arminianism*, as held by the Methodists and others, is scarcely less denunciatory and severe. And ALEXANDER CAMPBELL, the founder of Campbellism, speaking of all the sects, says: " *They are not churches of Jesus Christ, but the legitimate daughters of that Mother of Harlots, the Church of Rome.*" (See *Millennial Harb.*, vol. 3, p. 362.)

Nor are the followers of those great men more charitable toward each other's doctrines than were their founders. For instance, DR. ENGLES, editor of *the "Philadelphia Presbyterian,"* September 12, 1840, in showing *why* the Old School Presbyterians can not *consistently* intercommune with the New School and the Methodists, remarks: " As Presbyterians, we profess to receive our denominational distinction from the *symbols of faith* which we adopt; and we regard other denominations as having their distinctive belief and character, of which we judge by their public symbols. . . . . . It is presumed that a Presbyterian believes Presbyterian doctrine, or why is he a Presbyterian? And that a Methodist believes in the doctrines of his own church, or why is he not something else? The Methodists and Presbyterians alike believe that they have very good reasons for being as they are; nay, so potent are these reasons regarded to be, that neither imagines he could ever be induced to change his opinion. Now, all we have contended for is *consistency* in carrying this principle into practice."

" As our Methodist brethren," he adds, " have taken umbrage at our language, let us ask them if they are prepared to advise their people, on all favorable occasions, to go and *commune* with the Presbyterians? Do they wish them to think there is *no difference* between the denominations? Do they regard the differences as *so trivial* as to invite entire oblivion of them by their flocks when they stray into Presbyterian folds? We judge not. Why, then, should they be angry with us for following their example? Holding the faith we do, can we, or ought we to say to the sheep of our folds—yonder are pastures in which we believe there are *poisonous weeds* growing, but still there can be little danger in feeding *occasionally* there? In this matter we have never found our Methodist brethren a *particle more liberal* than ourselves. We have never found them backward in *decrying* Presbyterian doctrine; and we, on the other hand, candidly tell them, as we have *often* told them before, that we consider their system as VERY ERRONEOUS. For each of us thus to think is our right, in the exercise of Christian liberty, but is it *quite possible that we should forget this, and lay aside our strong feelings on the subject while we commune together?*" And in defending the Old School General Assembly against the charge of "*illiberality*," in refusing the fraternal invitation of the New School General Assembly to celebrate the Lord's Supper together, in 1845, in Philadelphia, Dr. Engles says: "*It is utterly inexpedient to hold communion with those churches.*" So all denominations regard and speak of each other's faith and practice.

Such is but a *specimen* of the oft-repeated and stereotyped views of the founders and leaders of mixed communion sects in regard to each other's doctrines and practices. Now if they believe their own statements, how can they *consistently* or *innocently* bid each other God-speed by giving and receiving the acknowledged *tokens* of church fellowship, and, as they all contend, the *evidences* and *tests* of Christian fellowship also? As it is written: "*If there come any unto you and bring not this doctrine (i. e., of Christ), receive him not into your house, neither bid him God-speed; for he that biddeth him God-speed, is partaker of his evil deeds,*" (2 John 9–11); and how could we more fully do this than by inviting them to our *communion,* and giving them the *tokens* of church fellowship? It is unquestionably true, then, that mixed communion compels its advocates to *indorse* and *fellowship* what they acknowledge and believe to be *error.*

But if this be true in regard to Mixed Communionists themselves, it is even more so in regard to them and the Baptists. No mixed communion church can *consistently* invite or receive a true Baptist to its communion table, *knowing,* as they must, that we regard them as *destitute* of some of the essential qualifications for the Lord's Supper. Yet, they not only invite and urge all Baptists to come to their communion, but abuse and denounce us in unmeasured terms for refusing the invitation. How inconsistent, not to say sinful, is this!

Accordingly, DR. DAVID MONFORT, a leading Presbyterian, in his fifth *letter* against "*Mixed Communion,*" remarks: "Members of other denominations, providentially placed within the bounds of a church of a denomination different from that of their preferment, may become members of that church if qualified. In this way two different denominations might extend the hand of protection to each other's members without disorder, confusion, or injury. And it does seem to me that this would be a much purer and vastly more consistent charity in all denominations, than that of throwing open the *doors* (to the ordinance of the Lord's Supper) to some *half dozen* of different sects, *hostile* to each other's peculiarities and *irresponsible* to each other. Some making a *profession* of piety and baptism a *condition*, and others *not*. Some enforcing infant baptism by *discipline* as other Christian duties, others not, or really *denying* the duty. *Against this, I do protest with heart and voice and lifted hands. I deny it to be Christian fellowship at all. It is handling, in the sight of God, angels, and men, the sacrament as emblems of what does not exist. It was never contemplated by the Westminster divines, and it has nothing, in my opinion, to support it but the false charity of the age."*

"I take the liberty again to say," he adds, "that in view of the actual state of the case, and on a question so plain, I can not suppress my *astonishment* that there should be *difference* of opinion and practice in any denomination." So say the Baptists. It can only be accounted for by the *necessities* of Pedobaptism. Thus we see that mixed communion compels its advocates to indorse and fellowship what they believe to be radical error.

6th. *Mixed communion violates the declared principles of those who practice it.*

This is evident from their respective creeds and

disciplines. For example, the EPISCOPALIANS maintain that their bishops are the *successors* of the Apostles, and that no minister of any denomination has a divine right to administer the "*sacraments*" of baptism and the Lord's Supper who has not received Episcopal ordination. They deny that any others have been scripturally inducted into the ministerial office, or are authorized to administer the ordinances. Hence the ministers of that denomination rarely, if ever, receive the elements of the Lord's Supper at the hands of other ministers, and if any of their people partake with others, they are bound to regard it as mere *lay*-communion. In fact, the rules of that church expressly deny the communion to all except their own members; and when, for prudential reasons, they condescend to admit others, they do it in known violation of their declared principles. As it is written: "*There shall none be admitted to the holy communion, until such time as he be confirmed, or ready and desirous to be confirmed.*" (See *Book of Common Prayer*, Art. Confirmation.) By this rule the members of all other churches, except the Roman Catholic, are *excluded* from the Episcopal communion, for not one of them has been *confirmed*, nor is any ready or desirous to be confirmed by an Episcopal bishop.

The PRESBYTERIANS, as we have shown, claim the *right* to declare the "*terms*" of admission into their communion, and to judge of the *fitness* of communicants at their Table (see *Confession of*

Faith, Form of Government, bk. 1, chap. 1); and accordingly their synods and standard writers have declared it *"inexpedient"* for Presbyterians to *"intercommune"* with those denominations holding *"Arminian sentiments;"* such as the Episcopalians, Methodists, and others. (See *Union and Evangelist, and Presbyterian Advocate* for 1820, vol. 2, pp. 96–99.) And the General Assembly of the Presbyterian Church, in 1839, fully sustained this position. Thus, all denominations, except the Baptists, and a few others, are debarred from the Presbyterian communion. This, indeed, is carrying *"close communion"* in theory quite beyond what the Baptists do. Yet notwithstanding these declared principles and express prohibitions, the Presbyterians are in the habit of inviting and urging all *Arminian* denominations to partake at their communion.

The METHODISTS can not practice mixed communion without violating their DISCIPLINE, which is the LAW of the church. *For instance*, the Discipline of 1868, chap. 5, sec. 1, p. 137, authoritatively declares, that *" No person shall be admitted to the Lord's Supper among us who is guilty of any practice for which we would exclude a member of our church."* Now, as this rule excludes *all* persons from the Methodist communion who are guilty of *" any practice"* for which a member or minister of the Methodist church would be excluded, let us briefly notice some of the *practices* punishable with exclusion.

1st. Practices for which *a member* would be expelled from the Methodist church: *Endeavoring to sow dissension in any of its societies by inveighing against either its doctrines or discipline.* It is required, that, " such person so offending shall be first reproved by the senior minister or preacher of his circuit; and if he persist in such pernicious practices, *he shall be expelled from the church.*" (See *Discipline*, chap. 4, sec. 4, p. 127.)

2d. Practices for which *a minister* would be expelled from the Methodist church: *Holding and disseminating, publicly or privately, doctrines which are contrary to its Articles of Religion.* "Against such offenders," says the Discipline, " let the same process be observed as in the case of *gross immorality*," i. e., exclusion from the church. (See *Discipline*, chap. 4, sec. 2, p. 115.) Other practices might be mentioned.

Such are a few of the many "*pernicious practices*" for which the Methodists are required to exclude their own members and ministers, viz.: (1.) *Inveighing against either their doctrines or discipline;* and (2), *Holding and disseminating, either privately or publicly, doctrines contrary to their Articles of Religion.* And, as before shown, they expressly declare that " *No person shall be admitted to the Lord's Supper among us who is guilty of any practice for which we would exclude a member of our church.*" The whole of this paragraph is printed in *italics* in the last edition of the Discipline, to show its importance in the estimation of the

"General Conference"—the *law-making power* of the Methodist Church, both North and South. This rule, then, is *authoritative*, and hence *binding* upon the *whole church*, and upon every member of it. This none can deny, for the Discipline is the SUPREME LAW of the church, by which it receives and excludes its members, and to which every member and every minister is required to pledge implicit obedience. *For instance,* when persons apply for membership in a Methodist church, they are required to give " *satisfactory assurances* " to "the preacher in charge," not only " of their desire to flee from the wrath to come and to be saved from their sins," and " of the genuineness of their faith," but *also* " *of their willingness to keep the rules of the church.*" (See *Discipline,* chap. 3, sec. 1, p. 90.) And every preacher on being received " into full connection at the Conference," is required to " give *satisfactory answers* to these questions," among others, viz.: " Do you know the *rules* of the Church? Do you *keep* them? Have you read the *form of Discipline?* Are you willing to *conform* to it? etc., with the solemn injunction by his "chief ministers:" "And do not mend our rules, but *keep* them; not for wrath, but *conscience' sake.*" . . "And remember! *a Methodist preacher is to mind every point, great and small, in the Methodist Discipline!*" (See *Discipline,* chap. 2, sec. 8, pp. 75–78.) And, in answer to "Quest. 1. What are *the duties of a presiding elder?*" the Discipline says: "Ans. 1. To travel through his appointed district. . . . . 6. To take care that *every part of the Discipline is enforced* in his district; and to report to the Annual Conference the names of all traveling preachers within his district who shall *neglect* to observe these rules," (see *Discipline*, chap. 2, sec. 6, pp. 65 and 66); one of which is, that "*No person shall be admitted to the Lord's Supper*" among Methodists who is guilty of "*any practice*" for which they would *exclude* a member from their church. (See *Discipline*, chap. 5, sec. 1.) And every presiding elder and every preacher at his ordination, solemnly promised, before God and his "chief ministers," that he would "*mind every point, great and small, in the Methodist Discipline!*" (See *Discipline*, chap. 6, sects. 1 and 2, pp. 178 and 194.)

Now, in view of all these facts, we boldly affirm that the Methodist Discipline is "CLOSE COMMUNION," even beyond any thing known among the Baptists; and that every presiding elder, and every preacher, is solemnly bound, "not only for wrath, but *conscience' sake*," to obey and enforce the rule requiring such communion. This rule necessarily *debars* the Baptists, Campbellites, Episcopalians, Presbyterians, and all others from the Lord's Supper in the Methodist Church; for they all "*persist*" in the "pernicious" practice of "*inveighing*" against both "the doctrines and discipline" of that church, and are confessedly guilty of "*holding* and *disseminating*," both privately and publicly, "doctrines *contrary* to its Articles of Religion." *For example,* the Baptists and Campbellites "persist" in "*inveighing*" against infant baptism and infant church membership, sprinkling and pouring for immersion, clerical domination, etc., and they "*hold* and *disseminate,*" both privately and publicly, many doctrines "*contrary*" to the Methodist Articles of Religion; while the Congregationalists, Presbyterians, and others *persistently inveigh* against the Methodist doctrines of Arminianism, "falling from grace," etc., and "*hold* and *disseminate*" the contrary doctrines, both privately and publicly.

But notwithstanding all this, Methodist presiding elders and preachers are in the habit not only of "admitting," but also of inviting and urging these opposing sects to come to their communion table, *knowing* at the same time that they are all guilty of the very same *practices* for which the discipline requires them to exclude their own members. And it is well known, that of all Mixed Communionists, none cry out more against Baptist "*close*" communion, or boast more of their "*open*" communion, than do the Methodists. Both ministers and people stigmatize the Baptists as "*bigoted,*" "*exclusive,*" "*illiberal,*" and "*selfish,*" both privately and publicly, on account of their *Church* Communion, and vaunt their "*superior catholicity and charity*" as an inducement to others to unite with their church. And by this means thousands of persons holding

Baptist sentiments are decoyed into the Methodist Church, and thus made to give their influence to infant baptism and other cardinal errors which they do not and never can believe. Thus, the *whole Methodist Church*, North and South, are guilty of violating their own DISCIPLINE by mixed communion for sectarian purposes. Both consistency and duty require that they should either abandon the unscriptural practice, or abolish their Discipline.

The CAMPBELLITES also violate their declared principles by mixed communion. As a body, they hold and teach that "*faith, repentance, and immersion* are the three conditions of pardon, and *all equally necessary* to salvation;" and that all these conditions must be complied with, in order to entitle any person to church membership and to communion at the Lord's Table. This, no Campbellite who understands his own distinctive doctrines will deny. Indeed, if Campbellism be true, there are no Christians on earth, except those *pure* Campbellites who have been immersed by Campbellite preachers for the *actual* remission of sins—all those deluded Baptists and others among them who professed conversion through faith in Christ *previous* to baptism, being yet in their sins.

Still the Campbellites generally boast of their "*open communion*," and permit all Pedobaptists who will to "*break the loaf with them;*" notwithstanding they *know* that some of these Pedobaptists were sprinkled in infancy, and others after they professed conversion. According to *our* views, we can regard all who believe in Christ as *Christians*, while we regard them as *unbaptized*, and, as such, *unfit* for communion at the Lord's Table. But according to Campbellism, no *unbaptized* person can be a Christian. It is fatal to Campbellism to admit that Pedobaptists, or even Baptists, are Christians; for none of them have been baptized in order to *obtain* the remission of their sins; and if "faith, repentance, *and immersion*" be the three conditions of pardon, and all "*equally necessary to salvation,*" as all true Campbellites hold and teach, then it is impossible that any except those who have complied with *all* these conditions can be Christians. It is vain to say that God will take the *will* for the *deed* in baptism, any more than he will in faith and repentance, if all are "*equally necessary;*" for our final Judge has declared, that "He that believeth not, *shall* be damned;" and "except ye repent ye *shall* all likewise perish." And if baptism be a con*d*ition of pardon, like faith and repentance and "*equally necessary,*" then we must be *baptized* or perish. According to Campbellism, there is no alternative but *immersion* or *perdition*. If I believed this doctrine, I would be immersed for the *actual* remission of sins before I slept.

Now, if the Campbellites really believe their own doctrines, they are bound to regard all Pedobaptists, if not all Baptists, as *unconverted*, much less baptized, and, as such, unfit for the Lord's Supper. Yet it is a notorious fact, that they not only intercommune with such persons, but boast of their "*free*" communion and denounce our *Church* Communion, both privately and publicly, as a means of prejudicing others against us, and of inducing them to join their churches! Thus, many uninstructed Baptists and Pedobaptists, and others who were converted under our preaching, have been drawn into Campbellite churches. Such persons are deluded, and both consistency and duty require them to come out of Campbellite churches, and unite with churches holding doctrines which they believe.

Hence we see that mixed communion violates the declared principles of the Campbellites. The same is true of the Congregationalists, Lutherans, New School Presbyterians, Cumberland Presbyterians, and all others who practice such communion. It necessarily violates the declared principles of its advocates.

7th. *Mixed communion is not only bad policy, but it is suicidal to the Baptists.*

We have shown (see *Evil* 1st) that mixed communion, even where valid baptism is held as prerequisite, is unscriptual and of evil tendency. But "*free communion*," as held and practiced by English Baptists generally and by a few American Baptists, is not only unscriptural, but subversive of Gospel baptism and destructive of Gospel churches. The very *origin* of "free communion" is enough to condemn it with Baptists. It originated in Poland after the middle of the *sixteenth* century with FAUSTUS SOCINUS—*an arch-heretic*—from whom the Socinians derive their name. He denied the Trinity, the Divinity of Christ, total depravity, vicarious atonement, spiritual influence, etc.; and in 1580, he wrote a work on "*Water Baptism,*" in which he denies its binding force. Accordingly, he refused to submit to the ordinance himself, and admitted all *unbaptized* believers to the communion in his churches. He was the first man known to history, who ever denied that baptism was *prerequisite* to the Lord's Supper. This he acknowledges in the *Preface* to his "Discussion on Water Baptism." In the language of the late ABRAHAM BOOTH, of London, "It never was disputed prior to the *sixteenth* century, that *unbaptized* believers should be debarred from the Lord's Table." (See *Apology*, p. 34.) Says DR. WALL: "Among all the absurdities that ever were held, none ever maintained that any person should be admitted to the Lord's Table *before* he was *baptized.*" And ROBINSON, in his *Hist. of Bap.*, pp. 461, 462, says: "All the early churches of the Baptists were *strict* in their terms of fellowship," or communion. In his *Hist. of Inf. Bap.*, vol. 2, p. 298, speaking of the Baptists of the 16th century, DR. WALL adds, that "the Baptists do hold it necessary to renounce communion with all Christians that are not *immersed*, and this prejudice is deeply rooted in them." For additional FACTS on this point, see "ORCHARD'S HISTORY OF OPEN COMMUNION;" "HISTORY OF FREE COMMUNION," given in the *English edition* of "Howell on Communion," published "*under the superintendence of the Committee of the Baptist Tract Society, London, in* 1847;" and "WALL'S HISTORY OF INFANT BAPTISM."

"About the middle of the sixteenth century," says MOSHEIM, "the zeal, vigilance, and severity of Catholics, Lutherans, and Calvinists were *united* against the Arians, Moravians, and Baptists; and these three communions, forgetting their dissensions, joined their most vigorous counsels and endeavors. To avoid the unhappy consequences of such a formidable opposition, *great numbers of them retired into Poland*," etc. (See *Ch. Hist.*, 16th cen., part 2, chap. 4, p. 8.) "In this oppressed situation," says ORCHARD, "the inflexible and stringent features of these primitive creeds and their indomitable tempers became pliant toward others of opposite views, from suffering, mutual intercourse, and sympathy in affliction." (*Hist. of Open Com.*, p. 32.) And Wm. NORTON, of Dalston, Middlesex, England, in his "*History of Free Communion*," states, that "Baptist churches were formed at Cracow, Lublin, Pinczow, Luck, Smila, and in several other parts of Poland. That the church at *Cracow*, where Faustus Socinus settled on his arrival in Poland, in 1579, was formed in 1569, and received only *immersed believers* to its communion. He endeavored to join it, but not being himself baptized, was for some time refused admission. He succeeded, however, after a time in inducing them to receive the *unbaptized*, to tolerate *infant baptism*, and to adopt a more *liberal discipline*. . . . . Their previous discipline was not suited, it appears, to the character of the *Palatine nobles*, of whom there were many among the Lutherans, but whose fierce and barbarous bravery and similar characteristics were scarcely compatible even with the *strict morality* previously required by those churches." (*Robinson's Res.*, pp. 602-605; and *Mosheim*, as above.)

Socinus plead, just as did Robert Hall, that "it did not seem possible" that his denial of baptism, as *prerequisite* to communion, "could do *any harm*, whether received or not; but that if received, it would *certainly lead to much good*, by producing *concord, peace, and union* among those who otherwise already acknowledged one another as true brethren and disciples of Christ." "The result proves," says Mr. Norton, "how fallacious were his expectations; they are, however, in perfect agreement with the oft-repeated assurances of the advocates of mixed communion in the present day." (See *English edition* of Howell on Com., chap. 11; "*Hist. of Free Com.*," pp. 223-233.)

Mr. Norton adds: "Socinus advocated communion with *unbaptized* believers on the ground that *baptism has ceased to be binding*. As to the *nature* of baptism his views were correct; he held that it neither *confers* nor *confirms* grace, but is the giving up of ourselves publicly to Christ by being immersed in his name, and that 'he who wishes to be rightly baptized, must believe with his whole heart on him.'" (See *Life and Works of Socinus*, chap. 5.) He denied, however, that baptism was intended to be either *permanent* or *universal*," etc. (See p. 229, as above.) "It appears singular," says Mr. Norton, "that although the Lord's Supper rests on the *very same authority* as baptism, the former should be said by him to "agree with the law of Christ" (chap. 5); and that he should admit that there is '*no cause* which will allow *any Christian to abstain from it.*' " (See *Life and Works*, chap. 14, p. 732.)

Such was the *origin* of mixed commmunion, especially among the Baptists. It commenced with the abandonment of our *distinctive principles*, and the indorsement of *fundamental errors*, and the result was that Baptists and Pedobaptists, Arians and Socinians, all united together in one discordant mass, and Baptist identity was destroyed by the introduction of *free* communion.

"The principle of free communion," says Mr. Norton, "is found *in association with Arianism and Socinianism in the old connection of the General or Arminian Baptists, of England.* The name of *Anabaptists* was familiar in England long before the churches were formed from which the present English Baptist churches trace their spiritual descent. Walter Lollard brought the sentiments of the Waldenses to England, between 1315 and

1320, and they are said to have prevailed all over the kingdom." (See *Allex, Gilly, Collier*, etc., "*Hist. of Free Com.*," p. 240.) And says ABRAHAM BOOTH: "The ingenious author of the Pilgrim's Progress was among the first, if not the *very first* man in England, to assert that *no baptism* was necessary to communion at the Lord's Table, and who acted accordingly." John Bunyan commenced preaching in 1656, and died in 1688. Free communion, then, commenced in Great Britain in the latter part of the *seventeenth* century; but it made but little progress until Robert Hall published his treatise on the "TERMS OF COMMUNION," in 1815— just *fifty-four* years since.

Now the inquiry naturally arises, "What have been the EFFECTS of free communion upon the Baptists of England?" Our limits will not allow us to answer this question in detail. Suffice it to give the "GENERAL RESULTS" of free communion among the Baptists in England, as summed up by MR. NORTON, an eye-witness of its *evil effects*. Says Mr. Norton: "Among the GENERAL RESULTS of free communion among the particular Baptists of England, may be mentioned—

1st. *The habit it has introduced among them, of uniting with Pedobaptist churches*, on slight and often most unjustifiable grounds—such as that of trifling inconvenience, the respectability of the congregation, or the talent of the minister; thus giving their full sanction and nearly all their support to *Pedobaptist objects;* while the

Baptists in general experience at best only their *occasional* aid, and the *strict Baptists* their most rooted opposition. So much has this practice prevailed of late, that Mr. Knibb, of Jamaica, himself a Free Communion Baptist, when in London, in 1842, in a speech which will ever be remembered by those who heard it, *spoke of this as one grand cause of the comparative weakness of the Baptist body,*" etc.

"2d. Another of the results of mixed communion is *the general omission of baptism from the ordinary ministrations of the pulpit.* Mr. I. T. Hinton, of America (late of England), in his *History of Baptism*, p. 84, says: 'Clearly, the whole counsel of God has not been preached, however fervently repentance and faith may have been urged, if the sinner is left uninformed of his *immediate duty* so soon as he does truly believe; and it is time that the *primitive practice* of preaching baptism as *constantly* and *as simply as repentance and faith* was revived among all who know the truth.' . . . The practice of mixed communion has tended to make it a part of *good taste* and *right feeling* not to mention the subject too often," etc.

"3d. Another result of mixed communion is, that by representing some errors and acts of disobedience as *fundamentals*, and others as *non-essentials*, it has established a distinction between them similar to that made between *mortal* and *venial* sins by the Church of Rome; and tended to establish it as a received opinion that there are some *errors* and *inconsistencies* which, whatever the state of the heart respecting them, can not affect its eternal state."

"4th. Another of the evils of free communion is, that it deprives the churches of their *executive functions*, by assigning them to their *pastors*, or, as it is in some cases, by leading the pastors to assume a right to act in violation of their *acknowledged rules*. It is the pastor, or pastor and deacons, of a mixed church, who have generally to decide, in the room of the church itself, who are, or are not to be admitted to church fellowship in the Lord's Supper. Some of the pastors also of *strict* churches have assumed such authority over them as to claim the right to administer the Lord's Supper *contrary* to their established rule; as at *Bristol*, and also at *Leicester*, after Mr. Hall had failed to introduce the practice of mixed communion there." (See *Hall's Works*, vol. 1, p. 121.) For other instances, see *Prim. Ch. Mag.*, etc.

"5th. The introduction of mixed communion has been *injurious to the cultivation of kind feelings between Baptists and Pedobaptists*. Some regarding the practice as a stroke of *policy* to draw away their members from them, have, notwithstanding their general praises, *stood aloof* whenever they have thought their churches in danger; and some have expressed *cordial dislike* of the system. Others, expecting from the practice the *cessation* of controversy on the subject of baptism, seem to have regarded its revival as a kind of *breach* of the tacit pledge which they understood to be given for its discontinuance. It seems, in short, to be admitted on all hands that the Independents have displayed *considerably more hostility to the Baptists since the prevalence of mixed communion* than they did previously. . . . . . Besides this, the practice of mixed communion has enabled Pedobaptists to *remove attention from baptism*, by fixing it on what they are sanctioned even by Baptists themselves, in calling the *bigotry* and *illiberality* of 'close communion!' By this means prejudice has been excited, both against baptism and the apostolic constitution of the church," etc.

"6th. A much more painful result, however, of the introduction of mixed communion into our churches, is the *division of sentiment, feeling, and action it has produced among Baptists themselves.* Many Free Communionists are *so alienated* from their brethren that they will give little or nothing to either churches or societies maintaining the practice of *strict* communion, notwithstanding their admission of its *apostolic origin*. . . . *Mixed communion is at present subverting every one of our institutions from its original end; it is aiming to destroy the apostolic constitution of every one of our churches, and to subvert the recognized sentiments of the whole denomination.* It already possesses the *means* by which these ends may be effected, and is applying them with the utmost diligence to the attainment of its object. As *strict* communionists, we are being rapidly *excluded* from our own churches. .... It is, in fact, a struggle for *life* or *death* as to all our denominational institutions, and it is *impossible*, therefore, that any thing but tumult and intestine strife should be promoted by the course which our Free Communion brethren have adopted. .... The time, however, has evidently arrived when the *forbearance* which has led some of our churches hitherto to occupy in hope a position *inconsistent* with their principles can with safety be exercised no longer. *The strict Baptist churches must, as churches, act upon their principles or surrender them.* They must wait on the Lord and keep his way, or see the spiritual temples he has reared become moldering ruins before the desert blast. How sad to think that all this is the result of a system which speaks of *union* and of *love!*"

"What, then," asks Mr. Norton, "is the *conclusion* to which this ample induction of evidence, comprising the individual history of most of the leading Free Communion churches in the kingdom, and the general statistics of no small portion of the whole of them, conducts us? What but that THE PRACTICE IS RUINOUS TO THE DENOMINATION, AND FATAL TO THE INTERESTS OF TRUTH?" (See *English edition* of Howell on Communion. "*Hist. of Free Communion*," chap. 11, pp. 310–316.)

Such are a few of the many EVILS of mixed communion, as developed in the last half century among our churches in England, all going to prove that the practice is *suicidal* to the Baptists.

Hence we see that the *whole history* of free communion among Baptists shows that it not only does no good, but is *disastrous* to our churches and tends to *destroy* our denominational existence, while it builds up and promotes Pedobaptism. *For instance*, John Bunyan, the father of Free Communion Baptists, first admitted Pedobaptists to the Lord's Supper in his church at Bedford, and having granted them this church privilege, consistency compelled him to admit them to permanent church membership. Soon the Pedobaptists gained the ascendency, and after his death they overruled the Baptists and elected a Pedobaptist pastor; and from that time until the present they have controlled the church. The same is true of many other Baptist churches in Great Britain.

Accordingly, the Rev. G. H. Orchard, of Nottingham, England, in his "*History of Open Communion*," says: "Many an old Baptist meeting-house in London, and in the provinces, are now occupied by Socinians, Arians, and Pedobaptists. Look to the neighborhood of Bedford where Bunyan set the example and defended disobedience to Jesus. *Bedford, Cotton End, Malden, etc.,* Baptist meeting-houses, are now in the possession of Pedobaptists, with independent ministers. Property to a considerable extent is connected with the old Baptist meeting-house at Bedford. Any one or more candidates offering themselves for baptism is accepted quietly, and at an early hour—say *six o'clock* on a summer morning—the ordinance is appointed. Some upland Baptist, a time-serving man, is requested to immerse the candidates at this early period. The dry-shod brother may read a portion of the Scriptures, but he is to make *no comment* or *speak* on the ordinance of believer's immersion. There are Baptist ministers, *proto pudor!* who are guilty of this dereliction of duty. The subject is not heard from the pulpit, and, if any are immersed, the obedience springs from force of an honest, unaided conviction. Several of these bastard churches act over this pantomime, and brethren called Baptist ministers fully sanction these murky immersions. These eclipsed baptisms the writer is personally acquainted with. . . . The consequence of this line of proceedings is *now* obvious to the churches, though the *open* advocates are reluctant to yield. In the first instance, a serious state of things is before the eyes of all. Coldness or the chilly hand of spiritual death is allowed to depress our churches, and a general indifference to the Bible and the truth is ostensible. *One truth*, baptism, was not worth contending for, and now the BIBLE ITSELF is in danger of neglect. . . . . . Virtually, the Bible, as an inspired perfect law, is abandoned, and to be consistent, should be repudiated altogether.' (See *History of Open Com.*, pp. 76–79.)

And REV. MR. WHEELOCK, in a letter from England, published in the *Christian Watchman*, dated December, 1847, states: "While in London,

I casually learned that the ordinance of baptism was to be administered in one of the largest and most popular Baptist churches of the city. At the hour appointed, about *twilight*, on Thursday evening, I went to the chapel to witness the baptism. The church contained, rising eight hundred members. On entering, I perceived the lamps were lit, but few in attendance, and the pastor addressing the people. Eleven were baptized, and after changing their raiment, they retired into the chapel, and received the right hand of fellowship. I asked the administrator why the baptism was on a week-day evening, and at an hour when so few could attend. He answered, that about *one-half* of the church were Pedobaptists; and for the peace of the church, they were careful to select an evening and hour when there was no other appointment, not even for a committee meeting, or meeting of Sabbath school teachers, or Bible class, or any thing else, lest the peace of the church might be disturbed by the Pedobaptists members, thinking they had been entrapped to secure their presence at the baptism. For the same reason, he told me, the right hand of fellowship was given at the baptism, instead of the communion on the following Sabbath, that nothing might be said then that might endanger the harmony of the church. In some mixed churches, the Baptist members have been *disciplined* and *excluded*, because they propagated among the people *Baptist sentiments*."

Many similar facts might be given, but these are sufficient to show that "free communion" among Baptists is not only inconsistent, but necessarily tends to destroy our denominational existence and to build up Pedobaptists wherever it has been fairly tested. This is conceded by some of its ablest advocates. For example, a Baptist minister, formerly of London, but now of Virginia, himself an advocate of the practice, candidly admitted, says Dr. Howell: "That so well convinced are many of the churches in the metropolis and other parts of Britain, that *free* communion is *bad policy*, that on this ground alone they have abandoned it." And Dr. Howell adds: "The church in Leicester, of which Robert Hall was pastor, and afterward that in Bristol to which he removed, notwithstanding their '*free communion*,' and the unrivaled eloquence, amazing learning, unaffected piety, and unprecedented popularity of their minister, who wrote on the subject the most elaborate works which have ever been published, were *no more* numerous or flourishing than many other churches of fewer advantages, and who practiced '*close communion.*' I have the best authority for the remark—that of a clerical eye-witness, the REV. JONATHAN DAVIS, author of the History of the Welsh Baptists— *that in Mr. Hall's church not a single Pedobaptist habitually communed*, nor was it to have been expected, unless, as in the case of Bunyan, they were assured they could take possession of the church and succeed its Baptist pastor with a minister of their own." (See *Howell on Communion*, pp. 222 and 224.)

Hence it is manifest that *mixed* communion is *suicidal* to the Baptists. Accordingly, the *Christian Era* says: "We question whether the leading Baptist churches of England have a *right* to be called Baptist. They are a *conglomeration* of Baptists, Pedobaptists, and all sorts. Mr. Brock's church is so made up. So is the church of Mr. Lewis." And the editors of the *Religious Herald* add: "So *open communion* tends to make an *end* of the Baptist denomination." This, indeed, Robert Hall expressly concedes. "Were that practice universally to prevail," says he, "the mixture of Baptists and Pedobaptists in Christian societies would probably ere long be such, that the appellation *Baptist* might be found not so properly applicable to churches as to individuals." (See *Hall's Works*, vol. 2, p. 228.)

If we may judge the practice by the *comparative increase* of our denomination for the last fifty years in Great Britain, where *mixed* communion generally prevails—and in this country where *Church* Communion is almost universal—we shall find that the Baptists in the United States have increased in a ratio of more than *seven to one* in Great Britain. Says Prof. Curtis: "The rise of the Baptist denomination in England and in this country, was at about the same time, under circumstances even more favorable to their progress in the old than in the new country." And he adds: "That where the results of mixed communion and our practice are capable of being fairly compared, the result shows, as clearly as statistics on a large scale can show any thing, that the plan of mixed communion palsies the strength and prevents the growth of our denomination, and even retards, as in Great Britain, the spread of our principles." (See *Curtis on Com.*, pp. 214 and 222.)

And, says DR. HOWELL: "Of the great Baptist family in the United States, some small fractions, the Free-Will churches for example, practice *unrestricted* communion. They are pious, intelligent, and zealous, but are they more popular, prosperous, or happy than we are? It will not be considered invidious, every one knows it to be true, if I reply *they are not*. The opposite, indeed, is the fact. Little churches have sprung up in several States, at different times, upon the '*free* communion' principle. They have had talented and laborious ministers, and pious and efficient members. But they have invariably dwindled, and in a few years ceased to exist. Such has been, and such I apprehend ever will be, the history of churches conducted upon this principle. (See *Howell on Communion*, pp. 225, 226.)

Accordingly, the "SOUTHERN PRESBYTERIAN," speaking of the proposition entertained by certain English Baptists for ecclesiastical union with Pedobaptists, says: "It is a result, doubtless, of the principle of '*open communion,*' which the best Baptists of England have long held and reduced to practice; a principle *wholly inconsistent*, as they now perceive, with that dogma of '*one baptism,*' which logically operates to the *unchurching* of all who believe in pouring or sprinkling as a scriptural mode. There are *many American Baptists** who also believe that they ought to admit Chris-

---

* It is not true, as Pedobaptists vauntingly assert, that "*many*" American Baptists believe in *open* communion. "The wish is father to the thought." Yet one would suppose from their papers that the entire Baptist family were upon the eve of going into open communion. But not so; there is really no more truth, and no more prospect of this, than that Baptist churches are ready to abandon *immersion* and adopt *sprinkling* as baptism. The adoption of the one would be followed by the other, and no Baptist church is prepared for this yet—*never will be*. "There are yet 14,000 churches, and 9,000 ministers, and more than one million members, who have not bowed the knee to Baal—*never will*." (See *Baptist Visitor* for November, 1868.

The imprudence of a few erratic ministers who aspire to become the Halls and Spurgeons of America, has given occasion for all this Pedobaptist gossip; such, for example, as REV. CHAS. H. MALCOM, of Newport, R. I., and REV. CRAMMOND KENNEDY, of Brooklyn, N. Y., who figured recently in the "Heavenly Communion," in the latter city. By such pseudo-charity, a few brethren may and do place the whole denomination in a false attitude before the religious public, and wound the Savior in the house of his friends. Mr. Kennedy, late of Scotland, known as "the preacher boy," never was regarded as a sound Baptist, and now stands excluded from his church on the ground of heterodoxy. His little book, styled "CLOSE OR OPEN COMMUNION," is a *weak dilution* of Robert Hall, equally at war with Baptists and Pedobaptists, and retians of other denominations to their communion boards, and who thus choose to be *nobly inconsistent* with their doctrine, that no one is in the church who has not been in the water. But by thus departing from this doctrine for the sake of showing themselves a part of the common fold of believers, *they certainly are preparing themselves more or less unconsciously for joining hands with us*

futes itself. Any one who would be influenced by such a book, had better be something else than a Baptist.

In speaking of Dr. Lincoln's RESOLUTIONS, offered in the "*Warren Association*" last fall (1868), and referred to a Committee to report the next year, the "BAPTIST VISITOR," of Dover, Del., remarks: "These resolutions were offered by Rev. Heman Lincoln, D. D., with a view of re-affirming the principles of our Baptist faith, because of the *open communion* position of the Second Baptist Church of Newport, *Rev. Charles H. Malcom*, pastor. The history of Brother Malcom is known to most of our readers. It is not known by all, however, that the church of which he is pastor is not a *regular* Baptist church, but a body of "SIX PRINCIPLE BAPTISTS," holding immersion in common with the regular Baptists, but differing from them in other respects." "These resolutions were adopted by the '*Boston Association*,' North, a few days after, without a dissenting vote." And the "*Old Philadelphia Association*, comprising sixty-seven churches and over seventeen thousand members," recently adopted still stronger resolutions "*with hearty unanimity.*" Such erratic and inconsistent brethren are "*not of us*," and ought to be required to go "*out from us.*"

Even the Pedobaptists, while enjoying "heavenly communion" with Mr. C. H. Malcom, think him *too liberal*, inasmuch as he exchanges pulpits with UNITARIANS. The *Missouri Presbyterian* says: "Such excessive courtesy is a high-handed insult to a *Divine* Savior." (See *Religious Herald*, of Feb. 11, 1869 *heretics altogether.*" In the language of the editors of the *Religious Herald,* "We call the special attention of Baptists to this double concession: That *open* communion is '*wholly inconsistent*' with the belief that the immersion of believers is the *only* scriptural baptism; and that *open* communion ' certainly *prepares* the way ' for the *abolition* of Baptist churches altogether !"

Hence it is evident that "Free Communion Baptists," are not only very inconsistent, but *practically surrender* their denominational principles, and *virtually indorse* the errors of Campbellites and Pedobaptists, by the *very act* of intercommunion with them. In view of all these facts, the great Baptist brotherhood can but deplore the sad and ruinous consequences that must and will follow the unscriptural practice in England, backed as it is by the growing influence of REV. C. H. SPURGEON. In the midst of the almost super-human labors of that remarkable man, it is to be supposed that he has never found time to investigate the communion question thoroughly in the light of Scripture and history. With his candor and independence of mind, we are forced to believe that such an investigation would lead Mr. Spurgeon to adopt *Church* Communion. Nothing could afford his American brethren more pleasure than to know that the weight of his influence was in favor of this scriptural practice. A most fearful responsibility, in the providence of God, rests upon that brother on this subject, and the adoption of Church Communion by him would constitute a *glorious era* in the history and progress of English Baptists. In the meantime, we tender to our *strict* communion brethren of England, our heartfelt sympathy, and bid them God-speed in "keeping the ordinances" *as* they were delivered to the primitive churches. "Truth is mighty and will prevail." And each may confidently say, "*The Lord is my helper, and I will not fear what man shall do unto me.*" (Heb. 13: 6.)

Hence it is manifest that Mixed Communion is not only bad policy, but absolutely *suicidal* to the Baptists. In the language of REV. G. H. ORCHARD, we add: "The practice has divided brethren and professing communities, who otherwise hold the same doctrines and practice. Our pecuniary resources are, we think, weakened, when *open* churches can divert a portion of its collections to Pedobaptist funds. A feeling of chilly indifference exists among a portion of the ministers who differ on the *terms* of communion, and some *strict* brethren have felt the sneer of contempt. The advocates of an '*unbounded love,*' are found exceedingly deficient *in charity* toward those who differ from them on this question, and those who cheerfully contributed to our funds in years past feel themselves justified in *denying aid*, if the table is not open to them. It is not in my power," says he, "to record the full extent of *evils* resulting from this licentious course." (See *Hist. of Open Com.*, p. 76.) The whole tendency of the practice, therefore, is *evil and only evil* continually. What conscientious Baptist, in view of these facts, can give his influence to the pernicious practice?

In view of these undeniable facts, let American Baptists take warning, and check the *very beginnings* of mixed communion in our churches, and especially among our ministers. Not only the New Testament, but the law of *self-protection* requires that we should shun the very appearance of the evil. The few uninformed but well-meaning members in our churches, whose feelings incline them to the practice, only need instruction and kindness to establish them in the truth. But those ambitious and time-serving ministers among us, who know better, and yet are vaunting themselves at the expense of the whole denomination and God's truth, justly merit exclusion from the body. If they really love other denominations so much better than they do the Baptists, they ought to be with them; and the sooner we get rid of all such erratic and inconsistent brethren the better for the cause of Christ. We can well afford to spare such brethren. They are doing what they can to destroy the denomination, whether they intend it or not.

Such are a few of the many EVILS of mixed communion: 1st, It is unscriptural, and, as such, not binding upon the churches; 2d, It perverts the design of the Lord's Supper, and hence invalidates the ordinance; 3d, It tends to destroy the effect of church discipline, and compels a church to commune with its own excluded members; 4th, It is glaringly inconsistent in the present divided state of the Christian world; 5th, It compels its advocates to indorse and fellowship what they believe to be radical error; 6th, It violates the declared principles of those who practice it; and 7th, Mixed communion is not only bad policy, but it is *suicidal* to the Baptists.

CHAPTER V.

FACTS DEDUCED FROM THE SUBJECT.

1. Church Communion, as practiced by the Baptists, is both consistent and scriptural. 2. Mixed communion is not only unscriptural and inconsistent, but *a great evil.* 3. It is not "close communion" in fact, but *close baptism* that separates the Baptists and others at the Lord's Table. 4. Mixed Communionists, by their unholy opposition to *Church* Communion, do great injustice to the Baptists, and great injury to the cause of Christ and the souls of men. 5. Free Communion Baptists are very inconsistent, and *practically* surrender their denominational principles. 6. The Campbellites are the most inconsistent of all others in their professions of mixed communion. 7. There is not, in fact, any such thing as "*open communion*" in existence. 8. The duty of all Christians, and especially of the Baptists, in regard to the Lord's Supper.

From the whole subject we learn the following important FACTS:

1st. *That Church Communion, as practiced by the Baptists, is both consistent and scriptural.*

Now we have already shown the POINTS OF AGREEMENT between the Baptists and others in regard to the *nature, design,* and *qualifications* for the Lord's Supper, and that the Baptists practice *Church* Communion on principles *held in common* with Mixed Communionists. The distinctive difference, therefore, between them and ourselves on this subject is, that we *carry out* our principles *in practice*, while they, professing the same principles, *violate* them in their practice of *mixed* communion. We have also proved that *Church* Communion, as held and practiced by the Baptists, is *scriptural*, that *mixed* communion was unknown in the apostolic churches! and is a recent invention of men, based upon the false charity of the age.

Accordingly, PROF. CURTIS says: "The ground which we take in regard to the Lord's Supper practically harmonizes with that of Christians of all ages and climes. It is *simple, charitable,* and *consistent* with itself. We have a *full* and *perfect* fellowship or communion *as Christians*, with all the followers of Christ so far as we know them. With those who agree with us *ceremonially*, we ceremonially commune. Where we agree as to *ordinances*, we celebrate ordinances together; where otherwise, we do not. We differ from many as to what baptism is, and we feel sure that we are right. All denominations most fully coincide with us, that those *only* who agree as to ordinances— *i. e.*, who regard as *valid* each other's baptism— should partake together of the Lord's Supper. But with all Christians *as such* we commune most heartily and truly. We commune in prayer, which was the great ancient test; in *preaching*,* in sing-

---

* As to what is termed "*Pulpit communion,*" it is a mere matter of *expediency* with us, and hence to be governed wholly by circumstances. As has been shown, there is nothing in our

ing, in experience, in many Christian efforts—in every thing, except that in which they do not agree with us, viz., *Church ordinances.* Can any thing be more just, truthful, and proper?" (See *Curtis on Communion,* p. 126.)

And Dr. HIBBARD, with a candor and magnanimity which very few Methodist writers evince, truthfully remarks: "The Baptists, according to their views of baptism, certainly are *consistent* in

---

views, rightly understood, to prevent such communion, on all proper occasions, with those ministers of other denominations who give satisfactory evidence of piety and a divine call, and who hold and preach the fundamental doctrines of the Gospel, notwithstanding we regard them destitute of *valid* baptism and ordination, and hence can not consistently and scripturally recognize their *official acts* as valid, or admit them to our communion table. We can and do rejoice in the success of all ministers who hold truth enough to save souls, though they be unbaptized, and in error on many points. The great obstacle, however, to "pulpit communion" between the Baptists and others is *mixed communion;* and until mixed communion preachers learn to do us justice in regard to our *Church* Communion, they can not reasonably expect Baptist ministers to hold pulpit communion with them. So long as they continue to subsidize the Lord's Supper to sectarian purposes, and to say, as they do, that "the Baptists will let us *work* for them, but refuse to let us *eat* with them," when they *know* that we practice Church Communion on principles held *in common* with themselves, and refuse the communion to them simply because we regard them *unbaptized,* it is certainly *inexpedient* for us to furnish them with *clubs* with which to beat our own heads. Let them stop their misrepresentations of our Church Communion; *then,* and not till then, can we consistently and safely hold **pulpit communion** with them. Will they do it?

restricting thus their communion;" *i. e.*, to the members of their own churches. (See *Hibbard on Baptism*, part 2, p. 174.) As we have seen, Drs. Griffin, Monfort, and other Presbyterians admit the consistency of our practice. So do the most intelligent and pious of all denominations. Indeed, no one who understands the grounds of our practice can view it otherwise.

Hence we see that *Church* Communion, as practiced by the Baptists, is both *consistent* and *scriptural*.

We learn from this subject—

2d. *That mixed communion is not only unscriptural and inconsistent, but a great evil.*

That it is *unscriptural*, we have before shown. There is neither precept nor precedent for it in the New Testament, and we challenge its advocates to produce one. "The truth is," says Dr. Hibbard, "the *preponderance* of Scripture evidence is *against* mixed communion." And Dr. Monfort boldly affirms that it is of "*recent date*," and is based upon the "*false charity of the age.*" In the language of Abraham Booth, "The ingenious author of the Pilgrim's Progress was the first to advocate it in England;" and he denied that any baptism was necessary to communion—a position opposed by all Mixed Communionists, except the Free Communion Baptists.

Mixed communion is not only unscriptural, but also *inconsistent* in the present divided state of Christendom. This has been clearly shown, and those who practice it are inconsistent with themselves. *For illustration,* suppose two pious Pedobaptists attend a Campbellite church on Lord's day, and one should embrace the "ancient order of things," make the "good confession," and be received for baptism, and the other should not. That church would debar the former from her communion table *until* he had been immersed for the remission of his sins, but permit the latter to unite with her in "*breaking the loaf,*" notwithstanding she regards him as *unbaptized,* if not unconverted, and, as such, *disqualified* for the Lord's Supper. How inconsistent is this! Yet it is even so.

Moreover, a large proportion of Pedobaptist churches consists of *infants,* whom they regard as *church members.* On this point the Presbyterian Confession of Faith (chap. 25, Form of Gov., bk. 2 of Discipline, chap. 1) expresses the sentiments of all Pedobaptists viz., "The *visible* church consists of all those throughout the world that *profess* the true religion, *together with their children;*" and "all baptized persons are *members of the church,* are under its care, and are subject to its government and discipline." Yet no mixed communion Pedobaptist church in this country or in England will now permit its *infant members* to partake of the Lord's Supper. Thus quite *one-half* of the acknowledged members of Pedobaptist churches are at once excluded from this privilege of church membership. Anciently this was not so. In the

FACTS DEDUCED FROM THE SUBJECT. 249

language of DR. HOWELL: "Their fathers did not act thus inconsistently. Infant baptism was originated in the third century. From that time onward, during more than eight hundred years, they scrupulously took all their baptized children with them to the Lord's Table, rightly judging that they had the same title to the one that they had to the other of these ordinances. They declared that they administered them both to their infants upon the authority of *tradition* from the Apostles. . . . . 'When Pedobaptists,' says Dr. Hinton, 'give their children both ordinances, they will be consistent; but while *they* withhold the Lord's Supper from their children, let them not complain of others withholding baptism.'" (See *Howell on Com.*, p. 243.)

And DR. PRIESTLY, a distinguished Pedobaptist, says: "No objection can be made to the custom of giving the Lord's Supper to *infants*, but what may, with equal force, be made to the custom of baptizing infants." And he adds: "*Infant communion* is, to this day, the practice of the Greek Church, of the Russians, the Armenians, the Maronites, the Copts, the Assyrians, and, probably, all other oriental churches." (See *Address to Protestant Dissenters*, pp. 28, 31.)

"It is at this point," says Prof. Curtis, "that all denominations of Christians, except the Baptists, exhibit such a singular and inconsistent restriction of their communion. Regarding, as they all do, baptism as the door of their several churches, they, on the one hand, baptize children into church membership, and, on the other, *refuse them the Lord's Supper*, thereby excluding half or three-quarters of their own members from the symbols of church fellowship. What makes this inconsistency more remarkable, is its contrariety to all those ancient church customs to which our Pedobaptist brethren appeal as their chief evidence in favor of infant baptism. It is notorious that the proofs from church history of infant participation in the Lord's Supper are as clear, as early, and as universal as those of infant baptism, so that they must stand or fall together. That our Pedobaptist brethren are substantially right in not considering infants proper persons to participate in the Eucharist, we do not deny. It is one of those happy inconsistencies that results from their being so far ' *Baptists in theory*,' as Dr. Bushnell declares that they are. But a most strange and serious *inconsistency* there certainly is, in first declaring them *members* by baptism, and then refusing them the *tokens* of membership." (See *Curtis on Com.*, pp. 93, 94.)

Hence we see that the Baptists are far more *consistent* and *liberal* in their practice of *Church Communion* than are the advocates of mixed communion. We admit *all* our own members to the Lord's Table, and give them the *tokens* of church membership; while Pedobaptists debar more than *one-half* of theirs from their communion, and deny them the *rights* of church members. In the language of Dr. Howell: "We receive all. None are debarred. Ours, therefore, is by far the most free and liberal communion of any denomination existing." (See *Howell on Com.*, p. 244.)

We learn from this subject—

3d. *That it is not "close communion" in fact, but close baptism that separates the Baptists and others at the Lord's Table.*

We have seen that all denominations, except the Quakers and Free Communion Baptists, hold and teach that *valid* baptism is essential to *visible* church membership, and that both valid baptism and visible church membership are *indispensable* prerequisites to communion at the Lord's Table. On this point there is perfect agreement between the Baptists and others, how much soever they may differ as to the action, subjects, design, and administrator of baptism. The great question, then, that here divides us, is: WHAT IS SCRIPTURAL AND VALID BAPTISM? Here is the *real issue* between us, and here the battle must and should be fought. And with "*the sword of the Spirit which is the Word of God*" in our hands, and the records of church history in our favor, we have no fears of the final result. *Believer's immersion*, as instituted by Christ, and as held and practiced by the Baptists, has survived the fires of persecution, and triumphed over the combined powers of earth and hell, and come down pure to the present generation.

Now we have shown that the Baptists can not remove this *great barrier* to intercommunion without the sacrifice of conscience and truth, and the indorsement of error and irregularity, while Mixed Communionists *can* remove it without any such sacrifice or indorsement. They all admit the *validity* of our baptism, and the *regularity* of our churches, and hence can adopt *our* baptism and church polity without any real sacrifice, but we do not and can not admit either the validity of their baptisms or the regularity of their churches, and hence can never adopt or indorse them. The obligation, therefore, to remove these and all other barriers to intercommunion rests solely upon the advocates of mixed communion, and they are solemnly bound to either remove them or hold their peace in regard to our *church* communion. If intercommunion between them and ourselves be as important as they seem to suppose, surely they will remove the barriers without delay. Until they commune with us in *believer's immersion and church government*, we can not consistently and scripturally commune with them at the Lord's Table; and, as has been shown, it is both unkind and uncharitable in them to ask it. Hence we see that the charge of "*close communion*" is no more applicable to the Baptists than to others. It is not close communion in fact, but *close baptism* that separates us and others at the Lord's Table. This is admitted by the ablest advocates of mixed communion. For example, Dr. Griffin, as before quoted, says: "We *ought not* to commune with those who are *not baptized*, and of course, are *not church members*, even if we regard them as CHRISTIANS."

And, DR. HIBBARD, with singular candor and truthfulness on this subject, says: "It is but just to remark, that, in *one principle*, the Baptist and Pedobaptist churches agree. They both agree *in rejecting* from communion at the Table of the Lord, and *in denying* the rights of church-fellowship to *all who have not been baptized*. Valid baptism they (the Baptists) consider as *essential* to constitute visible church membership. This also we (Pedobaptists) hold. The only question, then, that here divides us, is: " *What is essential to valid baptism?*" The Baptists, in passing the sweeping sentence of disfranchisement upon all other Christian churches, have *only* acted upon a principle *held in common* with all other Christian churches, viz., *that baptism is essential to church membership.* They have denied our baptism, and, as *unbaptized persons*, we have been excluded from their Table. That they err greatly in their views of Christian baptism, we, of course, believe. But, according to their views of baptism, they *certainly are consistent in restricting thus their communion*. We would not be understood as passing a judgment of approval upon their course; but we say their views of baptism *force* them upon the ground of *strict* communion, and herein they act upon the *same principles* as other churches, *i. e.*, they admit *only those whom they deem baptized persons* to the communion table. Of course, they must be their *own judges* as to what baptism is. It is evident, that, according to *our* views of baptism, we can admit them to our communion; but with *their* views of baptism, it is equally evident they can never reciprocate the courtesy. And the charge of *close communion* (italics his) is no more applicable to the Baptists than to us, inasmuch as the question of *church fellowship* with them is determined by as *liberal principles* as it is with any other Protestant churches, so far, I mean, as the present subject is concerned; *i. e.*, it is determined by *valid baptism.*" (See *Hibbard on Baptism*, part 2, chap. 11, pp. 174, 175.) The real issue between the Baptists and others on this subject is here presented fairly and truly by Dr. Hibbard. It is *close baptism*, and not close communion.

"It is admitted," says the *Episcopal Methodist*, of Raleigh, "that baptism must *precede* the Supper." *That's* the doctrine of " *close-*communion " in a single sentence.

Accordingly, the "INDEPENDENT," an able Congregational organ, remarks: "For our own part, we have never been disposed to charge the Baptist churches with any special narrowness or bigotry in their rule of admission to the Lord's Table. Indeed, we have never been able to see satisfactorily how *their principle* differs from *ours*. We can see how it differs from Robert Hall's principles, and how it differs from that imputed to Mr. Beecher, of Brooklyn, and the Plymouth Church, but we do not see how it differs from that commonly admitted and established in the Presbyterian and Congregational churches. The principle is, *that only members of churches are admitted or invited to the Lord's Table, that only baptized persons can be members of churches, and that in all disputed cases the church that gives the invitation is to judge what is baptism.* When Congregationalists give up this principle, perhaps the Baptists will be constrained to do likewise. Meanwhile, it can hardly be expected that the Baptists will be argued out of it—much less that they will be *driven* out of it by taunts and reproaches on their 'close communion.' The closeness of their communion, as compared with ours, lies simply in their definition of *what is essential to baptism*—a definition too narrow, indeed, but held by them in all good conscience, and in exemplary deference to what they regard as the testimony of Scripture." (As quoted by the "*New York Examiner*," for April 28, 1859.) This is candid and just, as all must admit.

Hence, we see that it is not "close communion," in fact, but *close baptism* that separates the Baptists and others at the Lord's Table. As all admit the *validity* of our baptism, and as we can not admit theirs, it is unreasonable in them to demand it of us. Mixed Communionists, by adopting adult and infant *sprinkling* for believer's immersion, and other errors, have erected the *barriers* to intercommunion between us, and they alone can remove them. As the Baptists stand upon scriptural ground in their baptism, others must come to them.

We learn from this subject—

4th. *That Mixed Communionists, by their unholy opposition to Church Communion, do great injustice to the Baptists, and great injury to the cause of Christ and the souls of men.*

That the Baptists are unjustly blamed for their practice of Church Communion, has been fully shown. How unjust is it to charge "a respectable, an honorable, and an influential" denomination of acknowledged Christians with "*bigotry*," "*exclusiveness*," "*illiberality*," and "*selfishness*," and thus create "*a popular prejudice*" against them, simply and solely because they conscientiously carry out *in practice* principles held *in common* with all other denominations. Yet this is constantly done, both privately and publicly, by Mixed Communionists. They employ every means and improve every opportunity to embarrass and place the Baptists in a false attitude before the world. *For instance,* ALBERT BARNES, of Philadelphia, a few years since in a *union prayer-meeting*, proposed and urged the celebration of the Lord's Supper, when he *knew* that the Baptists could not participate without the sacrifice of their principles and the violation of their consciences; and when his *own confession of faith* expressly declares that the Lord's Supper was instituted by Jesus Christ, "to be observed *in His Church* unto the end of the world." DR. DAVID MONFORT, an able and influential Presbyterian, in condemning such treatment of the Baptists by his brethren, justly remarks: "It seems to me but to take occasion to vaunt our *superior catholicity* to the prejudice of these *honest Christians;* and such churches complain of such treatment on *our* part as *unkind*. Let an impartial sense of *justice* decide how correctly." (See *fourth letter* against "*Mixed* Communion.")

Mixed Communionists thus not only do great injustice to the Baptists, but also great *injury* to the cause of Christ and the souls of men. By their denunciations and misrepresentations of our *Church* Communion, "*a popular prejudice*" is excited against us, and the ears of many are closed against the truth as it is in Jesus. Thus, not only Christians, but many sinners are so blinded by prejudice, that it is out of our power to benefit and save them. Eternity alone can fully develop the injury thus done to the cause of Christ and the souls of men by Mixed Communionists. If it be true, that "*one sinner destroys much good,*" as Solomon declares, then a fearful account awaits the opposers of Church Communion, as held and practiced by the Baptists.

We learn from this subject—

5th. *That Free Communion Baptists are very inconsistent, and practically surrender their denominational principles.*

The great Baptist family have abundant reason to be thankful that *so few* of their brethren, especially in America, are guilty of such glaring inconsistency and faithless surrender of their distinctive principles. As honest Christians, Free Communion Baptists are bound to admit that the *immersion in water into the name of the Trinity of a penitent believer, with a proper design, by a scriptural administrator,* is the only *valid* baptism; and hence, in order to practice intercommunion with Campbellites and Pedobaptists, they are driven to the singular necessity of denying that *any baptism* is necessary to communion at the Lord's Table. In this view of the subject, however, they stand *alone;* for all other Mixed Communionists maintain as strongly as we do that scriptural and valid baptism is an *indispensable prerequisite* to the Lord's Supper. Accordingly, JOHN BUNYAN, the originator, and ROBERT HALL, the defender, of free communion among English Baptists, were *forced* to deny that baptism is a *necessary* prerequisite to communion at the Lord's Table; and hence they invited all Christians, *as such,* to their communion tables, regardless of baptism. For, says Mr. Hall, "Let it be admitted that baptism is, under all circumstances, a *necessary* condition of church fellowship, and it is IMPOSSIBLE for the Baptists to act otherwise (than to *restrict* their communion to members of their own churches). They both (Baptists and Pedobaptists) concur in *a common principle,*" namely, that *valid* baptism is essential to *church membership,* and that church membership is *essential* to communion at the Lord's Ta-

FACTS DEDUCED FROM THE SUBJECT. 259

ble—"from which the practice (of *strict* communion) deemed so offensive is the *necessary* result." (See *Hall's Works*, vol. 2, pp. 212, 213.)

Hence we see that the advocates of mixed communion can never call in Robert Hall as a witness against *Church* Communion Baptists, for he differs more widely from them on this subject than he does from us, and denies the *validity* of their baptism as boldly as we do. He says: "We are compelled to look upon the mass of our fellow Christians as *unbaptized.*" And he adds: "The Apostles admitted the *weak* and *erroneous*, providing their errors were not subversive of Christianity. *We do precisely the same.*" (See *Hall's Works*, vol. 1, pp. 212, 216). Are the advocates of mixed communion willing to acknowledge themselves "*unbaptized, weak, and erroneous?*" Will they practice intercommunion with Baptists on such terms? We presume not. Yet these were the *only terms* upon which even Robert Hall could admit them; and these are the only terms upon which any Free Communion Baptist church can admit them. These terms are even more offensive than those of *strict* communion Baptists; and this may account for the fact which Mr. Hall complained of so bitterly, that "*very few persons* of other denominations ever partook of the Lord's Supper in his church." Thus we see that Free Communion Baptists, in order to carry out their unscriptural practice, are compelled to deny that *any baptism* is prerequisite to communion, and to admit Pedobaptists and others as "*unbaptized, weak,* and *erring* brethren."

This is indeed a remarkable stretch of Christian charity! With what mingled emotions of pity and contempt must all intelligent Pedobaptists look upon such inconsistent Baptists! Such pseudo-Baptists can neither expect the blessing of God nor the respect of other Mixed Communionists.

Moreover, Free Communion Baptists, by the *very act* of intercommunion with Pedobaptists, not only give up their baptism, but also surrender their *denominational principles.* For instance, they practically relinquish the *constitution* and *government* of their churches, and indorse that of Pedobaptists. All true Baptists maintain that the apostolic churches were constituted of *immersed believers,* and of such *only,* and that every such church was an *independent executive democracy* in the visible kingdom of Christ, *i. e.,* the *supreme power* was vested in the membership of each church, just as it is in all Baptist churches. Nor can this power be *delegated* to a minister, session, presbytery, conference, or council. Every true Gospel church is an *independent judicial and executive body* for itself in the visible kingdom of Christ, to which the laws and ordinances of that kingdom are committed, subject only to Christ as its Head and Lawgiver. Such a church has full power to administer the ordinances and execute the laws of Christ, but no power to alter, amend, or repeal those laws and ordinances.

FACTS DEDUCED FROM THE SUBJECT. 261

Now we believe that Pedobaptists have radically changed both the *constitution* and *government* of Christ's churches. We maintain that all Pedobaptists have changed the *divine constitution* of the churches by admitting *infants* to church membership, and by substituting *effusion* for believer's immersion; and that all except the Congregationalists, have changed the *government* of Christ's churches by depriving the people of supreme judicial and executive power, and subordinating them to diocesan bishops, presiding elders, church sessions, presbyteries, and higher judicatories, claiming and exercising both *legislative* and *executive* power over the churches. Now, while we gladly recognize the intelligence and piety of our Pedobaptist brethren generally, still we do not, nor can we, recognize their churches thus constituted and governed, as *Gospel churches*, any more than we can recognize their infant sprinkling as Gospel baptism. Yet by intercommunion with such churches, Baptists necessarily indorse and fellowship them as true and regular Gospel churches; for the Lord's Supper is, as all admit, a *church ordinance*, and as such, involves and expresses *church fellowship* as subsisting between communicants at the same table. And as the advocates of mixed communion hold that baptism is *prerequisite* to the Lord's Supper, Free Communion Baptists are justly regarded by them as *indorsing* their baptism as *valid* by the *very act* of intercommunion. How inconsistent, not to say sinful, is this in Baptists!

And this indeed underlies the *whole policy* of Mixed Communionists, as some of their ablest men admit. For example, MR. THORN, of Winchester, England, author of "*Modern Immersion not Christian Baptism,*" says of the Baptists: "By adopting the plan of *open communion*, they practically concede the *validity* of our baptism, as it respects both the *mode* and *subjects*; as they profess to act only from plain examples or apostolic precepts." And a celebrated Pedobaptist author and preacher said to Mr. Newman, of England: "Open the door of your churches, and we do not fear the result." (See *Orchard's History of Open Communion*, p. 73.) As we have stated before, the advocates of mixed communion cry out against our *church* communion, and boast of their *open* communion as a means of *swelling their numbers*; "and," says an able English writer, "as an *expedient* to accommodate worldly men and the undecided with the privileges of the Gospel." Hence they urge Baptists to intercommune with them, not because they really desire such communion, but for sectarian purposes; knowing that the *very act* is a practical abandonment of our denominational principles, and a virtual indorsement of their peculiarities. Thus, in effect, Free Communion Baptists cease to be Baptists and become Pedobaptists and Campbellites.

We learn from this subject—

FACTS DEDUCED FROM THE SUBJECT. 263

6th. *That the Campbellites are the most inconsistent of all others in their practice of mixed communion.*

The Baptists *could* practice mixed communion with far more consistency than the Campbellites. We believe and maintain that a person must experience *a change of heart and the pardon of sins* before he is scripturally qualified for baptism. Hence we can and do regard our Pedobaptist brethren generally as "*the children of God by faith in Christ Jesus*" (Gal. 3: 26), and, as such, needing only immersion in water on a profession of their faith, with a proper design, by a scriptural administrator, and union with Gospel churches, to fit them for communion at the Lord's Table. With many of them, particularly the Congregationalists, Methodists, and Presbyterians, we substantially agree on *experimental religion*, including a change of heart, justification, pardon, and adoption through faith in Christ and by the agency of the Holy Spirit, and which fit an individual for baptism; and hence we can consistently hold *Christian* Communion with all such—just as we do with our candidates for baptism—notwithstanding we do not and can not hold *sacramental* communion with them, because not scripturally baptized, and consequently not regular church members.

But the Campbellites not only believe—as do Mixed Communionists generally—that *valid* baptism is an *indispensable* prerequisite to the Lord's Supper, and that *believer's immersion* is the only valid baptism—as do all Baptists—but they also hold and teach that baptism, in connection with faith and repentance, is in order to *obtain* the remission of sins, and that there is *no promise* of salvation without compliance with all three of these supposed conditions of salvation. In other words, they boldly maintain that it is in the *very act* and at the *very instant* of immersion, and *not before*, that a believer has the promise, and *actually receives* the remission of his sins, and is adopted into the divine family. That this is a fair and true statement of their views on this subject, is evident from the voluminous writings of ALEXANDER CAMPBELL, the founder of the sect, and from the preaching and teaching of his leading *ministers* and *writers*. Our limits will allow but a few plain and pointed extracts.

For instance, Mr. Campbell remarks: "I proceed to show that we have the most explicit proof that God forgives sins for the name's sake of his Son, or *when* the name of Jesus Christ is *named upon us* in immersion; that *in and by the act of immersion*, so soon as our bodies are put under water, at *that very instant* our former, or old sins, are all washed away: provided only that we are true believers. . . . . . Peter, to whom was committed the keys, opened the kingdom of heaven in this manner, and made *repentance*, or reformation, *and immersion equally necessary to forgiveness*. . . . . . When a person is immersed *for* the remission of sins, it is just the same as if expressed, **in order** *to obtain* the remission of sins. . . . . .

I am bold, therefore, to affirm that every one of them who, in the belief of what the Apostle spoke, was immersed, *did, in the very instant in which he was put under water, receive the forgiveness of his sins, and the gift of the Holy Spirit.* If so, then, who will not concur with me in saying that *Christian immersion is the Gospel in water?*" (See *Christian Baptist*, revised, pp. 416 and 417.) And on page 520, he adds: "*I assert*"—and truly it is but an assertion—"that there is but *one action* ordained or commanded in the New Testament to which God has *promised* or *testified* that he will forgive our sins. This action is *Christian immersion.*"

Again, Mr. Campbell, in his last book on baptism, says: "*In our baptism, we are born into the divine family, enrolled in heaven. We receive justification or pardon; we are separated or sanctified to God, and glorified by the inspiration of his own Spirit.*" (See *Campbell on Baptism,* p. 276.) All this, mark you, "IN OUR BAPTISM!" Hence we see that with Mr. Campbell, baptism was a *sine qua non*, not only to communion at the Lord's Table, but also to *salvation itself.* And if there is any one thing in which the whole "current reformation" agree, it is in the doctrine of *baptism for the actual remission of sins.* It is found in every book, in every tract, and in every periodical, and it constitutes the burden of almost every sermon. With Campbellites, "*Christian immersion is the Gospel in water!*" A popular proclaimer and graduate of

Bethany College, in addressing a large assembly in my hearing a few years since, said: "*We not only believe, but we know that immersion is the only baptism; and no man can be saved without baptism.*" This is *pure* Campbellism.

Accordingly, ELDER MOSES E. LARD, Mr. Campbell's chosen and indorsed champion to review Dr. Jeter's "*Campbellism Examined,*" speaking of Acts 2: 38, says: "Now, we affirm that this passage teaches that baptism, with repentance, is *for* —that is, *necessary to*—remission of sins; that it makes remission depend on *baptism* in precisely the *same sense* in which it makes it depend on *repentance;* and that a connection is thus established between them of a nature so permanent that remission is *in all cases* (previous exceptions of *infants* and *idiots* aside) *consequent* on baptism and never precedes it. (See *Review of Campbellism Examined*, p. 193.)

Now, if these views of Mr. Campbell and his representatives be correct (which every Baptist most emphatically denies), then it necessarily follows that our Pedobaptist brethren are not only *unbaptized*, but they are *yet in their sins;* for many of them have never been immersed, and none of them were even *sprinkled* in order to *obtain* the remission of their sins. Hence, Mr. Campbell says: "Infants, idiots, deaf and dumb persons, innocent Pagans, wherever they can be found, with *all the pious Pedobaptists*, we commend to the mercy of God." (See *Christian System*, p. 233.) This, indeed, is all he could do with them, for there is no other hope for such "*pious Pedobaptists*" according to Campbellism. How inconsistent is it, therefore, in Campbellites to *intercommune* with such pious sinners! and how inconsistent in Pedobaptists to reciprocate the courtesy! Yet it is a notorious fact, that American Campbellite churches and evangelists generally are guilty of this glaring inconsistency almost every Lord's day, under the plea of not inviting these "pious Pedobaptists;" while they boast of their "*superior catholicity*" for sectarian purposes, and abuse and stigmatize the Baptists both privately and publicly as "*bigoted,*" "*exclusive*" "*illiberal,*" and "*selfish,*" on account of their *Church* Communion. By this unholy use of the Holy Supper, great injustice is done to us and to the cause of Christ, and many honest inquirers after truth, holding Baptist sentiments, are inveigled into the ranks of the "current reformation," who do not and can not believe Campbellism.

It is not strange, therefore, that the representatives of the Campbellite churches in Great Britain, at their last annual meeting, adopted the following RESOLUTION: "That we learn with *deep regret* that some *evangelists* in America commune at the Lord's Table with *unbaptized persons*, who, without formal invitation, and, it is alleged, on their own responsibility, partake; and we hereby decline to sanction evangelic coöperation with *any brother,* whether from America or elsewhere, who knowingly communes with unbaptized persons, or who, in *any way,* advocates such communion." (*Religious Herald.*) Hence the *Journal and Messenger* asks: "How is it possible for the Disciples to be so widely different in views and practice in England and America? How are they so unanimous for *close* communion there and for *open* communion here? The answer is obvious enough. The animus of the whole matter is *antagonism to the Baptists.* The Baptists of Great Britain are chiefly *open communion* in their views; hence the Disciples there are *intensely close.* In this country, the predominant sentiment among the Baptists is for *close communion;* hence the Disciples of this country are *earnestly for open!*"

Well, if Campbellites will act thus inconsistently to make proselytes to their party, we can only commend them to the mercy of God. "Sink or swim, survive or perish," *we* will not "handle the Word of God deceitfully," nor make merchandise of the ordinances of Christ. "*Whatsoever things are true, whatsoever things are honest, whatsoever things are just, whatsoever things are pure, whatsoever things are lovely, whatsoever things are of good report*" (Phil. 4: 8), we will approve and practice, and nothing else. We believe in fair and honest dealing, and we had rather be *right* than popular, if we can not be both. We feel sure that in our practice of *Church* Communion we are consistent with truth and duty, and hence we "have a conscience void of offense both to-

FACTS DEDUCED FROM THE SUBJECT. 269

ward God and men." We feel it to be our solemn duty to "*keep the ordinances*" as they were delivered by Christ and his Apostles to the first churches; and not only to preach and practice the *whole truth*, but also to bear our united testimony against *all error;* and hence we affectionately, but faithfully, testify against the errors in faith and practice of our brethren of other denominations, though it costs us bitter persecution. The records of history show that such unflinching fidelity to truth and duty has cost many Baptists their heads, and it has subjected the whole denomination to ceaseless misrepresentation and slander. But none of these things move us, neither count we our lives dear unto ourselves, that we may finish our course with joy. God helping us, we will continue to do our whole duty whether men praise or blame.

But, after all, is it true that the more intelligent Campbellites *really believe* in mixed communion? Do they believe that Pedobaptists possess the *scriptural qualifications* for communion at the Lord's Table? We answer, *they do not.* Why, then, do they not, as honest men, frankly tell them so, both by word and action? How can they innocently neglect it? And how is it possible to reconcile their *principles* and *practice* on this subject? When Dr. N. L. Rice pressed this point in the Lexington debate, Alexander Campbell replied: "*We, indeed, receive to our communion persons of other denominations*"—of course *unbaptized,* if not unconverted, persons—"*who will take upon them the responsibility of partaking with us.*" Yet, to Rev. Wm. Jones, of London, who inquired, "*Do any of your churches admit unbaptized persons to the communion?*" Mr. Campbell replied: "*Not one, so far as known to me;* there is neither *law, precedent,* nor *license* for it." (See *Camp. Exam.*, p. 290.) And just before his death, in a controversy with Dr. D. R. Campbell, late president of Georgetown College, which was published both in the *Millennial Harbinger* and the *Western Recorder*, Alexander Campbell emphatically denied that *either he or his people ever had held mixed communion* as practiced by others. Indeed, no intelligent Campbellite can believe in mixed communion. I have conversed freely on this subject with many leading Campbellite preachers, who have frankly acknowledged that they did not regard the Pedobaptists as qualified for communion at the Lord's Table; among whom was *Elder Jacob Creath* and others.

But whether the Campbellites really believe in mixed communion or not, one thing is certain, they generally practice it in this country, and boast of the fact, notwithstanding it is in direct violation of their declared principles. And thousands of persons, entertaining Baptist sentiments, have thus been deluded into Campbellite churches. Now, if the Campbellites do not believe that the Pedobaptists are scripturally qualified for the Lord's Supper, they are solemnly bound to declare the fact both by word and action. If they believe them to be in error, on this subject, then consistency and fidelity require that they should warn them of their error, and endeavor both by precept and example to reform them. They are under obligations not only to declare the scriptural *terms* of communion, but also to *debar* from the Lord's Table in their churches all those who have not complied with these terms. On this subject there is room for *a reformation* among Campbellites worthy of the name.

If it be said, "It is the *Lord's Table*, and therefore we have no right to invite or refuse any one," we answer, Then we have no right to debar any person; and hence the fornicator, the covetous, the idolater, the railer, the drunkard, and the extortioner may all partake of the sacred ordinance, though the Scriptures forbid it. (See 1 Cor. 5: 11.) As we have shown, the Lord Jesus Christ has established his Table *in each particular church*, and requires every church to exercise a watchful discipline over all its communicants and to debar unworthy persons from its communion. This all admit. Yet it is a melancholy fact, that Campbellite churches generally are in the habit of *admitting* Pedobaptists to their communion tables, and their bishops and deacons freely offer the bread and wine to all professed Christians present, when they *know* that many of them have never been immersed, and therefore have no divine right to partake of the elements. Thus they *neu-*

tralize their own testimony in favor of believer's immersion, and confirm the Pedobaptists in their neglect of the ordinance.

Accordingly, ALEXANDER CAMPBELL, in answering a "*catalogue of queries*" on OPEN COMMUNION, says: "I am opposed, *in any case,* to admitting *unimmersed* persons to church ordinances; because it is nowhere *commanded* in the Scriptures; because it is nowhere *precedented;* and because it not only deranges the *order* of the kingdom, but makes *void* one of the most important institutions ever given to man. It necessarily makes *immersion* of non-effect. For with what consistency or propriety can a congregation hold up to the world either the *authority* or *utility* of an institution which they are in the habit of making as little of as any human opinion?" (See *Chr. Bap.*, vol. 6, p. 184.)

And PROF. CURTIS remarks: "It is *action* that produces action. To tell a person that he is in error, but that it is of no importance, will rarely incite investigation, but never rouse the sluggish conscience to *action*, which is what is here chiefly requisite. *Pure self-denying example* is all important.". (See *Curtis on Com.*, p. 261.)

Hence we see that the Campbellites are the *most inconsistent,* not to say sinful, of all others in their professions of mixed communion. They not only violate their own principles, but stultify their testimony for believer's immersion, and indorse adult and infant sprinkling as baptism by the *very act* of such intercommunion.

FACTS DEDUCED FROM THE SUBJECT. 273

We learn from this subject—

7th. *That there is not, in fact, any such thing as "open communion in existence."*

Communion, to be *open*, must embrace *all professed Christians* in good standing in their own churches. The advocates of mixed communion admit this in *theory*, but contradict it in practice. They boldly maintain that we have no right to judge of the *fitness* of others for communion at the Lord's Table, but that every communicant must judge of his *own fitness*, and so partake. Accordingly, they charitably invite to their respective tables "*all Christians* (*i. e.*, all who *claim* to be Christians) *in good standing in their own churches.*" This is an *open* invitation, we must admit. But it necessarily embraces not only the Baptists, Campbellites, Congregationalists, Episcopalians, Lutherans, Methodists, and Presbyterians, but also Arians, Roman Catholics, Latter-day Saints, Quakers, Swedenborgians, Universalists, Unitarians, and all others who profess to be Christians, and who are in good standing in their respective churches; for they are clearly included in the invitation, and all have a right to come. Such would, indeed, be an *open table*, and nothing short of this is such. It is evident, therefore, that if the advocates of open communion *practiced* according to their *professions* (and consistency requires it), such would be the *heterogeneous mass* of good and bad that would surround the Lord's Table in their churches. If they debar *one sect*, then it is no longer open, but *restricted* communion—the very thing which they condemn in the Baptists as "*bigoted,*" "*exclusive,*" "*illiberal,*" and "*selfish;*" yet they not only assume the right to judge and debar one, but *many sects* of professing Christians; for of the fifty different denominations in the United States, only some *eight* will intercommune with each other. Thus we see that these open advocates are guilty of the *great sin* for which they abuse and denounce the Baptists in such measured terms!

But the truth is, there is no such thing in existence as *open communion*. It is the religious HUMBUG of the age, and ought to be exposed. We boldly affirm, without the fear of successful contradiction, that there is not a church or denomination in Christendom that practices *unrestricted* communion—NOT ONE. As we have already proved from their own creeds and disciplines, the advocates of mixed communion can not practice it without violating their own *declared principles*. And their discriminating and restricted practice justifies us in believing that they do not invite each other *in good faith* to their respective communion tables.

The deluded masses no doubt are sincere in believing in mixed communion, but how is it possible for their *preachers* to believe and practice it, when they are *solemnly pledged* to obey and enforce their respective creeds and disciplines, which forbid the practice? We can not believe that

FACTS DEDUCED FROM THE SUBJECT. 275

they mean what they say when they invite "*all Christians in good standing in their own churches*" to their communion, nor can they reasonably expect us to believe it while their *practice* contradicts their *profession*. *For instance*, the Presbyterians generally do not regard the Campbellites as fit participants of the Lord's Supper; and hence they do not *intentionally* invite them to their communion, nor will they "*break the loaf*" with them, unless forced by circumstances to do so. *For example*, not long since a Presbyterian doctor of divinity in Southern Kentucky, visited a neighboring town, and, after preaching, administered the Lord's Supper. The reverend gentleman charitably extended the usual "*open* communion" invitation to all, and piously berated the Baptists on account of their "*close* communion." A few Methodists came to the first table with the Presbyterians. Next came other Methodists and a few Campbellites, among whom was Colonel E——, a prominent lawyer, whose own brother witnessed the scene and gave me the facts. The liberal doctor covered his face in *holy horror* with his hymn book until the solemn farce was ended, and then dismissed the assembly. Soon after this, the Campbellite lawyer received a long letter, in which the Presbyterian doctor assured him of his high personal regards, and his readiness to unite with him in the advocacy of temperance, but stated that he wished it distinctly understood, that when he invited *evangelical* Christians to the

Lord's Table he did not include the CAMPBELL-ITES. Accordingly, DR. N. L. RICE, a true exponent of Presbyterian views, (in his recent tract on "*Campbellism*," p. 39, published by the Presbyterian Board of Publication,) says: "*Certainly evangelical Christians and churches can not acknowledge such a body*" (as the Campbellites) "*as a Church of Jesus Christ;*" which they would necessarily do by holding *intercommunion* with them; for the Lord's Supper is confessedly a *church* ordinance, and, as such, involves and expresses *church fellowship* as subsisting between communicants at the same table.

The same is equally true of Congregationalists, Episcopalians, Methodists, and all other Pedobaptists. They do not and can not intercommune at the Lord's Table, without the grossest inconsistency and the most palpable violation of their own creeds and disciplines. In the language of Dr. Jones: "Not only do Pedobaptists exclude Quakers from their communion, they often exclude each other. A few years since, the members of the Old School Presbyterian General Assembly refused a request for *intercommunion*, formally preferred by the members of the New School General Assembly, then in session in the same place. The Episcopalian, in his own church, will commune with the Presbyterian, but he will not reciprocate the compliment, by receiving the sacred elements in the Presbyterian church from what he regards as '*unconsecrated hands.*'" The

FACTS DEDUCED FROM THE SUBJECT. 277

several Scotch Presbyterian churches, the Associate, the Associate Reformed, the Reformed Presbyterian or Covenanters, and the United Presbyterian, refuse to commune with any sect." (See *Dr. Jones on the Baptists*, pp. 152, 153.) And it is well known that the sage advocates of apostolic succession and divine rights do not recognize these Calvinistic and Wesleyan usurpers as authorized ministers of Jesus Christ, but merely *endure* them because public sentiment compels them to do so. Hence it is that they seldom, if ever, intercommune with others. Thus Episcopalians are consistent in their *practice*, but most inconsistent in their *professions* of open communion; while the Methodists, Presbyterians, and others are consistent in their *principles* on this subject, but strangely inconsistent in their *practice*.

Accordingly, the CHURCH INTELLIGENCER, an Episcopal organ, argues that, under the LAW of the church, " no habitual coming to the communion should be allowed where the purpose to be *confirmed* is denied;" and professes that it can not understand how any clergyman can "justify so plain a violation of so plain a law" as an invitation to those who are not of their communion.

The Campbellites, also, generally claim to be *open* in their communion, and occasionally partake with the Pedobaptists, but the favor is very rarely reciprocated by any; because the advocates of open communion, particularly the Methodists and Presbyterians, do not generally regard them as *true* and *orthodox* churches of Christ, and hence they can not consistently extend to them the appointed *tokens* of church fellowship. *True,* the Methodists will occasionally intercommune with Campbellites, as a matter of policy, in order to make them a *cat's-paw* with which to claw the Baptists, and *vice versa,* but these are exceptional cases.

Thus we see that, while all these denominations *profess* open communion, not one of them practice it. They not only refuse the communion to many persons—as, for example, to the *Quakers,* whom they acknowledge to be Christians—but many of them deny the sacred elements to *more than one-half* of their own members. They sprinkle infants and declare them *church members,* subject to church discipline, and then deny them the *tokens* of church membership. In the language of their own creeds and disciplines, they "bring them *within* the covenant" by baptism; make them "*members of the church*—engraft them into Christ;" and then deny them the *rights* and *privileges* of church members. This is not only inconsistent, but unjust to these unoffending "*little ones.*" Thus largely upwards of *one-half* of the acknowledged members of all Pedobaptist churches are debarred from their own communion. In the language of Prof. Curtis, we say: "*The Baptists have no such close communion as this.*" We freely admit *all* our own members to the Lord's Table; and in this we are far more *open* than the advocates of open communion themselves.

What, then, is the *real difference* between the Baptists and others in regard to the Lord's Supper? It is simply this: We hold *Church* Communion, and practice accordingly; *i. e.*, we admit to our communion *all* and *only* the members of our *own churches* with whom we sustain church relations, and over whom we can and do exercise church discipline; while they profess *open* communion, and accordingly invite "*all Christians*" in good standing in their respective churches to partake with them, but, *in fact*, restrict their communion to some *half dozen* different sects whom *they* are pleased to regard as *evangelical*, with whom they do not and can not sustain church relations, and over whom they can exercise no church discipline whatever, and, at the same time, they debar *full one-half* of their own members from the Lord's Table. Hence it is evident that the advocates of open communion really practice *restricted* communion, and herein they act on the *very same principle* that we do; *i. e.*, they admit to their communion only those whom *they* deem qualified for the Lord's Supper. Now this principle is right and proper, but what we complain of is this: they openly *profess* one thing and habitually *practice* another, and then abuse and denounce us in unmeasured terms because we practice what we profess.

Hence it is manifest that there is not, *in fact*,

any such thing in existence as *open* communion; it is *a deception* palmed upon the unsuspecting masses for sectarian purposes, and deserves to be exposed and reprobated by all good and honest men. Accordingly, Dr. T. G. Jones remarks: "Thus we see that there is no such thing as the much vaunted *open* communion among Pedobaptist denominations. They are as *close* as Baptists—though with not half their consistency. Nay, they are *closer* than Baptists. To crown their closeness and inconsistency, all these denominations refuse the communion to a large portion of their own membership. They will administer the rite of *baptism*—taking, as they suppose, the place of circumcision to *infants*—but they will not administer *the Lord's Supper*—taking the place, as they equally believe, of the passover—to these *same infants*. In the preceding section, we saw that it was considered exceeding narrow in the Baptists to refuse baptism to children. Is it less so in Pedobaptists, after baptizing them, to deny them the Lord's Supper?" (See *The Baptists*, p. 153.)

Practically, then, *open* communion is a *nonentity*. It exists only in *theory*. Its advocates, while extolling it, never practice it. Indeed, very few ever practice even their "much-vaunted open communion" in its *restricted* form; and many of its most noisy advocates never practice it at all. For example, a grave Presbyterian elder in a city where the writer was laboring some years since, **was berating the Baptists on account of** "*close* *communion,"* when a Baptist deacon asked him how often he had communed *out of his church.* The elder, with some hesitation, answered, "I have never availed myself of the privilege of communing with others." What a privilege must that be which they seldom or never wish to enjoy!

CONCLUDING REMARKS.

1. Recapitulation. 2. The duty of Mixed Communionists.
3. The duty and interest of Baptists. 4. The special duty
of Baptist ministers. 5. All boasting and severity disclaimed.
6. Desire and prayer of the Author.

1st. *Recapitulation of the main arguments.*

We have shown the *distinction* between Christian, Church, and Denominational fellowship, with their respective tokens; and that the Lord's Supper is ever the *token*, not of Christian nor of denominational, but of the *church fellowship* subsisting between communicants at the same Table.

We have also given the POINTS OF AGREEMENT between the Baptists and others, as to the *nature*, *design*, and *qualifications* for the Lord's Supper; showing that all agree *in principle* on these points, however much they may differ in practice.

We have briefly explained and defended CHURCH COMMUNION as held by the Baptists; proving that it is *scriptural*, and that we practice *church* communion on principles *held in common* with the advocates of mixed communion; and that we can not remove the *barriers* to intercommunion without the sacrifice of these admitted principles, while others can remove them without any such sacrifice; and hence they ought to do it.

We have also answered the most plausible OBJECTIONS to Church Communion as held by the Baptists, showing that no valid objection can be urged against the practice; that the opposition to *Church* Communion arises from mistaken views of the nature and design of the Lord's Supper, and from a misunderstanding of the grounds of our practice; and that correct views of the subject would entirely relieve the minds of Baptists and others.

We have exposed the EVILS of mixed communion, especially as held by English Baptists, proving that it is unscriptural and inconsistent; that it not only does no good, but much evil; and that it *necessarily tends* to a compromise of principle, to laxity of discipline, latitudinarianism of doctrine, and to a consequent lowering of the standard of individual piety, and of the character and efficiency of the churches, while it is absolutely *suicidal* to the Baptists as such.

From the whole subject we deduced some important FACTS, evincing that *Church* Communion is both consistent and scriptural, while *mixed* communion is not only unscriptural and inconsistent, but *a great evil;* that it is not "close communion" in fact, but *close baptism* that separates the Baptists and others at the Lord's Table; and that there is not, in fact, any such thing as *open* communion in existence, but that it is a mere *theory,* based upon the false charity of the age, and advocated for sectarian purposes, and not for its own sake.

2d. *The duty of Mixed Communionists.*

As we have seen, the advocates of mixed communion agree with the Baptists *in principle* as to the Lord's Supper, though they differ widely in practice. And as has been shown, they can remove the *barriers* to intercommunion without any sacrifice of conscience or principle, while the Baptists can not do it without the sacrifice of both. It is clearly the duty, therefore, of Mixed Communionists either to remove these barriers, or to cease their abuse and misrepresentations of the Baptists on account of their practice of Church Communion. This every reasonable person will admit. Especially is it the duty of mixed communion PREACHERS to take the lead in this work of *reform* among their people, as they have hitherto done in waging the unjust warfare against us. To his ancient people God said, "*O my people, they who lead thee cause thee to err*" (Isa. 3 : 12); and shall this continue to be true of the *leaders* of mixed communion? Will they not rather instruct their congregations on the subject of our Church Communion, and, instead of exciting their prejudices and inflaming their passions against us, labor in good faith to remove the barriers to intercommunion? Both consistency and duty require that they should either do this or hold their peace in regard to "close communion."

The Baptists are not responsible for "close

communion," as it is falsely termed. The advocates of mixed communion have "*fenced*" the Lord's Table against us, by substituting adult and infant *effusion* for believer's immersion, and by subordinating the churches to " higher judicatories," and they *alone* can remove these barriers to intercommunion between us. And we take it for granted, that if they really desire such intercommunion for its own sake, they will do it. In the truthful language of the " BAPTIST VISITOR" of Dover, Del., we say : "All who practice sprinkling *shut us away* from their communion table by such practice. Then they try to throw all the *blame* on the Baptists, and say *we* erected the ' barriers.' These ' *barriers*,' erected by those who ' teach for doctrines the commandments of men,' are surely to be swept away by the mighty tide of *believer's immersion*."

Never in the history of the world was such gross injustice done to any denomination of acknowledged Christians as has been done to the Baptists in regard to their practice of *Church Communion*; and this fact will be conceded by all candid and unprejudiced persons when our principles are correctly understood. And God helping us, we intend that our views on this subject shall be understood by all who are willing to know the truth.

But notwithstanding the combined opposition of Mixed Communionists, the *progress* of Baptists and Baptist principles for the last hundred years has been unprecedented in the history of any denomination of Christians; and doubtless it would have been much greater if all Baptists had been true to their principles. Strong in our apparent weakness, but "mighty through God," our final success is certain, *provided* we advocate and practice the truth and oppose error in *faithfulness and love*. The Baptists are a POWER in the land. The *Church Union*, which has no love for us, says: "The Baptist denomination are the most *aggressive* and *positive* power in Christendom." (See *Baptist Visitor* for Nov., 1868.) And in the language of the great NEANDER, we say: "There is a *future* for the Baptists." Only let our rising ministry be properly educated and trained, and, by the Divine blessing, Baptist principles and practices will universally prevail at no distant day.

All we ask of our mixed communion brethren is, to lay aside their prejudice against our practice, and examine our views of Church Communion in the light of Scripture and facts. Let them candidly hear and read our views, and then oppose whatever they find to be unscriptural. We court investigation, and invite a candid hearing. If our opponents find us wrong, then let them oppose our views and practice in a Christian spirit; but if they find us right and scriptural, let them beware how they fight against God and his truth. Common as it is, it is sinful to misrepresent and slander even the Baptists.

3d. *The duty and interest of the Baptists.*

As has been shown, we can consistently hold *Christian* communion with all saints, irrespective of external ordinances and visible church relations, and it is both our duty and privilege to do so in all proper ways, such as prayer, praise, religious conversation, etc. In such communion we are perfectly *free* and *open*, except so far as others *restrict* us by confounding Christian and Church Communion. A closer union and fellowship among Christians, *as Christians*, is the great want of the age, and it is both our duty and interest to cultivate and seek it with all saints. We are bound to feel and act toward others *as they ought to feel and act toward us*, whether they reciprocate it or not. If they *will not* commune with us *as Christians*, because we *can not* commune with them *as churches*, then our obligation ceases, and the sin rests upon their heads.

But while it is our duty and privilege to hold unrestricted communion with all Christians, *as such*, still we are solemnly bound to *keep the ordinances as they were delivered to the first churches*, and to *restrict* our communion at the Lord's Table to the members of our own particular churches. We can not intercommune with others at the Lord's Table without indorsing their errors and sacrificing our conscientious principles by the very act. Both Mixed Communionists and the world so understand the act. Every Baptist, therefore, who partakes at a mixed communion table, and every Baptist church which admits to the Lord's Table the members of other denominations is practically guilty of such indorsement of error and such abandonment of principle. With what surprise, not to say contempt, must intelligent Mixed Communionists look upon such pseudo-Baptists!

It is a notorious fact that our views and practice of Church Communion are generally misunderstood, and hence every-where misrepresented. In consequence of this, multitudes of persons holding Baptist sentiments have been driven into Campbellite and Pedobaptist churches. And Baptists have been criminally delinquent on this subject. We have been satisfied to act merely on the *defensive*, and have not used the necessary effort and means to impart information and to correct misrepresentation and slander. Hence many of our own members, particularly the young, are troubled on the subject of Church Communion, and do not understand the reasons for it. It is not enough to be satisfied ourselves, we should instruct others and endeavor to satisfy them; and this is especially important, since our views and practice are constantly being misrepresented.

We are as certainly right in our practice of *Church Communion* as we are in our practice of *believer's immersion*, and they must stand or fall together, for the one is the necessary result of the other. The New Testament knows nothing of any other baptism or communion. And if we explain and defend our views of communion in a *Christian spirit,* all honest inquirers after truth will see the *correctness* of our practice; and even the most prejudiced advocates of mixed communion will hold their peace in regard to our *communion,* as they are more than willing to do in regard to our baptism. We have every thing to gain and nothing to lose by this course. To say nothing of duty, it is *bad policy* to be silent on the subject. The better others understand our views of communion, the better they will feel toward us, and the more cordial and unrestricted will be our Christian communion with them. This, at least, is the result of my own experience and observation for a quarter of a century in the ministry. I have always preached believer's immersion and Church Communion, as a matter of course, and as necessary parts of the Gospel, and my hearers expect it and receive it kindly. It is important to *accustom* our congregations to hearing the whole counsel of God; and if we preach the truth and oppose error *faithfully* and *kindly,* no right-minded person will take offense. At the close of a sermon on communion, not long since, an intelligent stranger came forward and handed me five dollars, saying, "I am not a professor of religion, but I have believed for years that the Baptists were right in every thing except *close communion,* and you will please accept this small sum for relieving my mind on the subject. I now believe that you are right in your views and practice of communion, as well as of baptism."

Hence we see that it is both the duty and interest of Baptists to inform themselves on the subject of communion, and to explain and defend our practice on all proper occasions. They should supply themselves with suitable *books* and *tracts* on this subject, and urge their children and neighbors to read them. Mixed Communionists do this continually, and it behooves us to exert a counteracting influence. Indeed, we can not innocently neglect this duty. As it is written: "*To him that knoweth to do good and doeth it not, to him it is sin.*" As honest men and women, we believe that we are right, and we ought to desire and seek to bring all others right. If we do not respect and sustain our own views and practice, we can not expect the confidence and respect of others.

Yet many timid and some time-serving Baptists have acted the part of Saul of Tarsus at the martyrdom of Stephen. They have stood by and held the clothes of our opponents, while they were stoning the truth on this subject. And some, through false charity, complain of their pastors for preaching on the subject, and thus give their influence against the truth and in favor of error. Such conduct is unworthy of our noble origin and sacred principles. Let every Baptist awake to righteousness, and sin no more.

4. A peculiar obligation rests upon Baptist minis-

ters to explain, defend, and enforce the truth. It is not only their duty to preach the whole truth, but also to expose all error, in the spirit of the Gospel. To evangelists and pastors chiefly must the people look for instruction in righteousness. And while we should not give undue prominence to any one doctrine or ordinance, but present all in their relative proportions, still we should give special attention to those subjects which are misunderstood and perverted, as is the case with *Church* Communion.

Baptist ministers, therefore, should *preach* frequently on this subject, explaining and defending our practice, and exposing the opposite practice. There is no *substitute* for preaching; it is God's own appointment, and a necessary provision for man. As it is written: "*How shall they hear without a preacher?*" This instrumentality, then, must be employed; all others are mere *helps*. Still suitable BOOKS and TRACTS are valuable *auxiliaries* to the ministry, and, by the divine blessing, do good in the absence of the minister. And if on examination, my brethren, you think that this little treatise, with all its defects, is calculated to be useful among your people, will you not order twenty, fifty, or a hundred copies each, and distribute them in your respective congregations? In this way you may do good, with profit to yourselves. The work is offered *one-third* under present prices, with liberal deductions to purchasers. (See *Prices and Terms*, p. 2.)

Thus other denominations disseminate their views among the people. *For instance*, every Methodist preacher is a BOOK AGENT in his own field, to circulate Methodist books and tracts, and the *profits* often exceed his salary for preaching. Reports are made to the Annual Conferences, and *premiums* awarded publicly to those who have sold the largest number of books and tracts. The press thus employed is the *strong arm* of Methodism. The same is true of the Presbyterians, Campbellites, and others. And shall not *Baptists* imitate their example? Will not our *ministers* take the lead in this great work? Others beside Baptists will purchase our books and tracts, and will profit by reading them. Thus *good books*, containing the truth as it is in Jesus, would take the place of erroneous works and corrupting novels, and our own people, at least, would become established in the truth. Especially should our *theological students* engage in this work; each one may clear *one hundred dollars per month*.

5th. *All boasting and severity disclaimed.*

To those ignorant of our principles, our claims may seem arrogant. But we disclaim all intentional boasting. As Baptists, we do claim to hold *the truth*, unmixed with error, and to keep the ordinances in their *original purity*. Nor is this claim arrogant. All denominations *practically* admit it, and many standard historians declare that " *The Baptists may be considered as the only religious community which has continued from the days of the Apostles, and as a Christian society which has kept pure, through all ages, the evangelical doctrines of religion.*" (See *Hist. of Neth. Refd. Church*, as before quoted.) Accordingly, all acknowledge the *orthodoxy* of our churches and the *validity* of our ordinances. They admit that we are right and scriptural *as far as we go*, and only object to what we *do not* believe and practice. But we claim to go as far as the New Testament goes, and we have no right to exercise our charity at the expense of God's truth.

In answering the ill-founded objections to our practice, and in repelling the base slanders heaped upon us, we have used great plainness of speech, but even in this we have spoken the truth in love. We speak the truth and lie not when we say that we love all who love our Lord Jesus Christ in sincerity, and we can and do hold *spiritual* communion with all such of our acquaintance, though we can not hold *ceremonial* communion with any except those with whom we ceremonially agree. And we joyfully hope to spend a blissful eternity with all the saved in heaven, where Christian communion is perfect and perpetual, and where sacramental communion is no longer necessary. In the language of Dr. T. G. Jones, "We have endeavored to speak the truth; and much more in defense of our brethren than in aggression upon others. And we should deeply regret if, while zealously striving to vindicate the Baptists from unjust charges, we should seem to be unjust even to their most prejudiced and inveterate opponents." (See *The Baptists*, p. 227.)

6th. Finally, we commend these pages to the divine blessing with the earnest desire that they may be a means of promoting truth and righteousness, and of suppressing error and prejudice among God's people; and that they may tend to unite Christians in faith and practice, and to bring all back to the primitive custom of CHURCH COMMUNION. "Now, the God of peace that brought again from the dead our Lord Jesus, that great Shepherd of the sheep, through the blood of the everlasting covenant, make you perfect in every good work to do his will, working in you that which is well-pleasing in his sight, through Jesus Christ, to whom be glory forever and ever, Amen!"

THE END.

A
Biographical Sketch
of
William W. Gardner
(1818-1894)

by
John Franklin Jones

A Biographical Sketch of William W. Gardner (1818-1894)

William W. Gardner was born October 1, 1818, at Barren County, Kentucky, the eldest son of Richand and Jane Gardner (*ESB*).

He began the study of medicine at age eighteen (Cathcart). William was converted at age twenty and joined Mt. Gilead Baptist Church, Todd County (*ESB*) in 1838 (Cathcart). He was licensed to preach in 1839 and entered Georgetown College in the Spring of 1839 (*ESB*), graduating in 1843 (Cathcart).

He was ordained to preach in 1844 and called to pastor the Shelbyville Church (*ESB*). He became pastor at Maysville in 1847. He became an agent of the Baptist General Association of Kentucky in 1851 and assumed the pastorate of Mayslick Church at the end of the same year, He was pastor of church at Russellville 1857-1869 and theology professor at Bethel College (*ESB*).

He left the church to devote his duties singularly to the professorship in 1869. The theological departments at Bethel and Georgetown Colleges were abolished when the Southern Baptist Theological Seminary relocated from Greenville, South Carolina to Louisville, Kentucky. Upon that dissolution, Gardner returned to the pastoral office at Glasgow, Kentucky (Cathcart). He died December 1, 1894 near Elk Creek, Kentucky.

JOHN FRANKLIN JONES

Gardner's published works include *Bible Inspiration* (1886); *Church Communion, As Practiced by the Baptists Explained and Defended* (1869); *Historical Sketch of Elk Creek Baptist Church for 100 Years, 1994-1894*; *Missiles of Truth* (1874); and *Modern Dancing: in the Light of Scripture and Facts* (1893) (*ESB*).

BIBLIOGRAPHY

Cathcart, William, ed. *The Baptist Encyclopaedia: A Dictionary of the Doctrines, Ordinances, Usages, Confessions of Faith, Sufferings, Labors, and Successes, and of the General History of the Baptist Denomination in All Lands, with Numerous Biographical Sketches of Distinguished American and Foreign Baptist, and a Supplement*. Philadelphia, Louis H. Everts, 1881; reprint, Paris, AR: Baptist Standard Bearer, 1988. S.v. "Gardner, William W., D.D."

Encyclopedia of Southern Baptists. S.v. "Gardner, William W." by Leo T. Crismon.

BY JOHN FRANKLIN JONES
CORDOVA, TENNESSEE
JUNE 17, 2006

THE BAPTIST STANDARD BEARER, INC.

a non-profit, tax-exempt corporation
committed to the Publication & Preservation
of the Baptist Heritage.

CURRENT TITLES AVAILABLE IN
THE BAPTIST *DISTINCTIVES* SERIES

KIFFIN, WILLIAM — A Sober Discourse of Right to Church-Communion. Wherein is proved by Scripture, the Example of the Primitive Times, and the Practice of All that have Professed the Christian Religion: That no Unbaptized person may be Regularly admitted to the Lord's Supper. (London: George Larkin, 1681).

KINGHORN, JOSEPH — Baptism, A Term of Communion. (Norwich: Bacon, Kinnebrook, and Co., 1816)

KINGHORN, JOSEPH — A Defense of "Baptism, A Term of Communion". In Answer To Robert Hall's Reply. (Norwich: Wilkin and Youngman, 1820).

GILL, JOHN — Gospel Baptism. A Collection of Sermons, Tracts, etc., on Scriptural Authority, the Nature of the New Testament Church and the Ordinance of Baptism by John Gill. (Paris, AR: The Baptist Standard Bearer, Inc., 2006).

CARSON, ALEXANDER	Ecclesiastical Polity of the New Testament. (Dublin: William Carson, 1856).
BOOTH, ABRAHAM	A Defense of the Baptists. A Declaration and Vindication of Three Historically Distinctive Baptist Principles. Compiled and Set Forth in the Republication of Three Books. Revised edition. (Paris, AR: The Baptist Standard Bearer, Inc., 2006).
BOOTH, ABRAHAM	Paedobaptism Examined on the Principles, Concessions, and Reasonings of the Most Learned Paedobaptists. With Replies to the Arguments and Objections of Dr. Williams and Mr. Peter Edwards. 3 volumes. (London: Ebenezer Palmer, 1829).
CARROLL, B. H.	*Ecclesia* - The Church. With an Appendix. (Louisville: Baptist Book Concern, 1903).
CHRISTIAN, JOHN T.	Immersion, The Act of Christian Baptism. (Louisville: Baptist Book Concern, 1891).
FROST, J. M.	Pedobaptism: Is It From Heaven Or Of Men? (Philadelphia: American Baptist Publication Society, 1875).
FULLER, RICHARD	Baptism, and the Terms of Communion; An Argument. (Charleston, SC: Southern Baptist Publication Society, 1854).
GRAVES, J. R.	Tri-Lemma: or, Death By Three Horns. The Presbyterian General Assembly Not Able To Decide This Question: "Is Baptism In The Romish Church Valid?" 1st Edition.

	(Nashville: Southwestern Publishing House, 1861).
MELL, P.H.	Baptism In Its Mode and Subjects. (Charleston, SC: Southern Baptist Publications Society, 1853).
JETER, JEREMIAH B.	Baptist Principles Reset. Consisting of Articles on Distinctive Baptist Principles by Various Authors. With an Appendix. (Richmond: The Religious Herald Co., 1902).
PENDLETON, J.M.	Distinctive Principles of Baptists. (Philadelphia: American Baptist Publication Society, 1882).
THOMAS, JESSE B.	The Church and the Kingdom. A New Testament Study. (Louisville: Baptist Book Concern, 1914).
WALLER, JOHN L.	Open Communion Shown to be Unscriptural & Deleterious. With an introductory essay by Dr. D. R. Campbell and an Appendix. (Louisville: Baptist Book Concern, 1859).

For a complete list of current authors/titles, visit our internet site at:
www.standardbearer.org
or write us at:

he Baptist Standard Bearer, Inc.

NUMBER ONE IRON OAKS DRIVE • PARIS, ARKANSAS 72855

TEL # 479-963-3831   *FAX # 479-963-8083*
EMAIL: Baptist@centurytel.net   *http://www.standardbearer.org*

Thou hast given a standard to them that fear thee; that it may be displayed because of the truth. — Psalm 60:4

www.ingramcontent.com/pod-product-compliance
Lightning Source LLC
Chambersburg PA
CBHW032002220426
43664CB00005B/107